American Spirit

Profiles in Resilience, Courage, and Faith

Taya Kyle
and Jim DeFelice

HARPER LUXE

An Imprint of HarperCollinsPublishers

HarperCollins books may be purchased for educational, business, or sales promotional use. For information, please e-mail the Special Markets Department at SPsales@harpercollins.com.

FIRST HARPERLUXE EDITION

ISBN: 978-0-06-291236-7

HarperLuxe™ is a trademark of HarperCollins Publishers.

Library of Congress Cataloging-in-Publication Data is available upon request.

19 20 21 22 23   ID/LSC   10 9 8 7 6 5 4 3 2 1

American Spirit

ALSO BY TAYA KYLE AND JIM DeFELICE

American Wife

Dedicated to our children,
and to all people who use their lives, liberty, and
freedom to love their neighbors and lift others up.
You make this country a place we love living in.

Contents

American Spirit

INTRODUCTION
Hoping

The Pioneer Spirit Lives On

The pioneer spirit built America. The first European settlers forged new trails in the hills, swamps, and forests of the East, then onward into the mountains, across the plains, through the desert and high passes, to the West Coast. They plowed virgin earth, hardscrabble as well as fertile, raised crops, and learned to live with sometimes helpful, sometimes hostile neighbors. They did not always do it with grace, and there is much we regret in retrospect—the treatment of natives and people from Africa, most especially—yet the communities and nation they created were, in the end, one of history's great achievements.

The pioneers sacrificed and endured incredible hardship, not so much for themselves but for the next generations—for others far more than for themselves.

It is tempting today to say that spirit—the American Spirit, if you will—has passed on. Many people complain about the present state of our country. They cite social conflict, economic hardship, and stagnant opportunity as examples of how far we have fallen. Political discord, religious intolerance, prejudice, hypocrisy—the list of failures, barriers, and even evils seems endless.

There is much to that. Sometimes I, too, feel our country and the world at large are a nest of chaos and that the laws of physics dictate it can only get worse. Entropy and indeed disaster are inevitable.

And yet . . .

On a day when I am at my absolute lowest, a random person in a checkout line smiles at me and offers to let me go ahead of them in a long line. I hear a story about a friend's child who gave a year's worth of her allowance to a homeless shelter. A friend returns from a mission trip to Africa, brimming with stories about digging a well that brought fresh running water to a village whose inhabitants once walked five miles to a polluted stream each morning.

Maybe I am just a die-hard optimist—guilty, surely—but I didn't start that way. I came to this outlook out of necessity to combat the pain of the world. These stories fill me with hope and inspiration. So, too, do tales of heroism, not just on the battlefield, where it's expected, but in big cities and small towns: neighbors rushing past flames to retrieve sleeping babies, ten-year-olds standing up to bullies picking on newcomers in class. Random acts of everyday kindness: a young man shoveling an elderly neighbor's driveway after a snowstorm, a retired gentleman cutting the lawn for the pregnant wife of a deployed serviceman—all of these things fill me with hope.

I see them as signs of community. Minor sacrifices, maybe, yet affirmations that the same core values and the same selfless impulses that helped build this country are not gone or even dormant.

We are bombarded with negative stories because, frankly, they sell. Maybe it's part of a survival mechanism to see the worst, so we can prepare for it and learn to avoid it in our own lives.

That's not me. I hate other people's pain. I find my day inevitably brightened when I hear about such things on a grand scale—the husband and wife who, after losing a daughter, began a foundation to help children with the same disease. I feel a tingle, and even a sense of satisfaction, when I read a story about someone famous and busy who, for altruistic reasons, gave her time to visit with wounded soldiers or went out of her way to make sure an elderly stranger had a warm meal that day.

Am I wrong to think that these things are a sign of hope for the future? Should I suppress the sense of joy that comes when I see a ripple effect of everyday kindness: the town that got involved after a single child raised money for a food pantry, the national organization that was inspired by a local businessman's pledge to help his neighborhood?

I don't think so.

I have had the privilege of traveling across America and meeting many people in the years since my husband, Chris, was cruelly murdered by a man he was trying to help. So many people have offered me comfort—and, more than that, they have told me stories about the *good* things their neighbors are doing, accounts of how they were helped or inspired by others. Each has a different perspective: Some point to God's hand in our daily lives; others talk about innate human kindness. Some talk of miracles. Others see a complicated logic of cause and effect.

All, I think, are testimony of the best America has to offer: her American Spirit. It's still alive. We may not see it on television or read about it on the internet. But that's our individual shortcoming, not the failure of God, or Nature, or mankind. Chaos surely is present— but if the same fearful laws of physics tell us that for every action there is an opposite and equal reaction, surely there are opposing forces fighting to establish a better balance and a better future.

I acknowledge the propensity of man for evil. I believe it is the only way to truly appreciate the good. I believe we can fight evil with goodness in order to prevent chaos from consuming us. I think there is good in everyone, literally everyone, but it is up to them to access it.

Shining a light in the darkness produces more light. It ripples, and in so doing, it multiplies its effect through our communities, our nation, and the world in general.

It doesn't happen on its own, but it doesn't require much to start a ripple. We simply need to pay attention and take action. As the ripple grows, there will be small and large sacrifices. There also must be thought, planning, and spontaneity as well. It takes leadership, even if those who are called to be leaders don't realize that's the role they've taken on.

Focusing on the beauty rather than the ashes in life warrants celebration, a highlighting of the efforts to brighten a sometimes very dark world.

That's why my friend and collaborator Jim DeFelice and I are writing this book. Over our time traveling and just living, we, both of us reformed skeptics and cynics, have spent more than a year meeting and talking to different people who have shined a light in the darkness. Many of these people have overcome tremendous handicaps or suffered great losses. Many have been blessed with an uncomplicated, rich life. Some have lucked into success; others have had worldly success denied in the harshest ways. But all have drawn on the best of themselves and in turn encouraged the American Spirit in others.

The people and organizations you'll meet in this book are, we hope, a cross section of America. A few are famous, a few are very young, many are wise, but they don't share one particular quality other than heart and a desire to do good in order to help their fellow man and, in turn, mankind.

The people and organizations you'll meet in the pages that follow are each doing their own part to bring order to chaos and to show up for other people. I believe they improve the lives of all of us every day just by tipping the scales in favor of good rather than evil. Each one represents a different way of either overcoming adversity, helping others, or both. Each one, in his or her own way, represents the pebble that lands in the middle of the pond, generating ripples of help and hope outward.

Their actions are an example for the rest of us. If a "notorious" bad-ass like Jesse James can help the homeless, if a preteen from Middle America can raise money for cancer victims with a lemonade stand, if a few socks can brighten a shut-in's day—what can we do to make a difference? And what—perhaps less noteworthy— actions do we take that imprint on the next generation in ways we may never know, simply because we lived a good life caring about others. What tips will they pick up? How will the pebbles of our actions create ripples? It isn't ours to know; it is only ours to do right, live well, and help others. The beauty about ripples is that they take care of themselves.

I don't mean to preach, but it occurs to Jim and me that there's something here for everyone in these stories we've compiled. We are from opposite coasts with a wide range of experiences and friendships between us. There isn't anyone we know who can't appreciate some highlighting of good in the world. My hope is to combat the influx of negativity with some positivity to benefit your soul as it has mine. My desire is for you to know that every action, big or small, has the potential to spark someone else's movement. My fondest wish is that someone reading our book will see themselves in one of the stories and go out and do something similar. Or better.

I've learned many things while working on this book: lessons about resilience, about courage, about generosity. Lessons about God and religion, lessons about human nature. But what I've taken away most importantly is this:

Despite what the haters, the politicians, and the antagonists say, the beauty in the American Spirit is still very much alive. It hasn't died; it's not even on life support. It does have to be nurtured—but that's always been true, from the very first settlements in Florida, Massachusetts, and Virginia. It was true on the frontier, in 1860, 1890, 1941. It's true now.

It's good to look back to the pioneers for examples; it's important to celebrate the achievements of the Greatest Generation. And it's critical to look at what others are doing today, to look at our lives, and to say, *What have I done to build on the promises their achievements made? What else can I do tomorrow?*

I hope our book will provide a few hints to what the answers might be.

ONE

Growing a Future

Our Kids as the Future

It's a cliché—our kids are our future.

But clichés are often clichés precisely because they are true, and this one is no exception; it's baked into our DNA. Our progress as communities and a country, and our collective and even in many cases our individual futures, literally depend on them. Our survival as a species depends on them.

That's one reason so many pioneer families moved from other countries to the U.S., and why so many others—and, in many cases, the same ones—moved westward to the frontier. They were willing to sacrifice their own comfort, even their own lives, for their children.

We see that same spirit today—mothers and fathers working two and even three jobs to provide for their kids, to send them to school or simply pay the bills.

But at the same time, negative undercurrents about the "next generation" are a separate cliché. I'm sure you've heard the comments:

Today's kids don't know the value of hard work.

When I was young, we had respect for teachers . . . pastors . . . police . . . adults . . .

What is this generation coming to?

Now, I can't deny that yes, our society has its share of problem children. And no sane mother can say with a straight face that everyone under voting age, or even the age of reason, is an angel. Even the best kids can be a trial and burden at times, and I doubt there is a mom or dad on Earth that hasn't come close to despair at some point when raising their children—or at least when observing the antics of some of their children's friends.

But those moments and bad apples don't negate the reality that, on the whole and at heart, children are capable of great things, not just in the future, but now. Children can be a source of hope and even strength. They can inspire us with their kindness; they can make us see beauty where we noticed only the mundane. They can make us stop and think; they can push us to do better.

My own kids were an important part of my recovery from despair.

Not only were they my reason to push through, but their ability to understand what was happening in a way far beyond their years motivated me. It made me see how wise they are and how hopeful we can be about the future. And not just my kids but others' as well.

The year after Chris died, I carried through with a commitment to coach my daughter's soccer team. Those girls were an inspiration—and a workout! I'm sure at first they must have thought I was crazy, as we ran around the field to warm up boot-camp style. But they found they were more capable than they ever imagined. I believe grit is an innate quality and an opportunity we waste when we don't encourage it in the young. Why wait to show children they are stronger than they think and more capable of making a difference than they can ever imagine?

Determination and generosity are best when they go hand in hand. I've been so privileged to meet strong, generous young people who are helping others in their community in big and small ways. I respect not only them but their parents; they've caught the ripple of good works and magnified it.

Trick, Treat, Triumph
Nick Blair

Take Nickolas Blair, an eleven-year-old in Independence, Missouri.

Independence, which sits next to Kansas City and borders the Missouri River, was the starting point for many pioneers during the Westward Expansion of the nineteenth century; settlers would gather in town to form wagon trains before heading out on the California, Oregon, and Santa Fe Trails. It's also Harry Truman's hometown, the place where our thirty-third president learned exactly where the buck stops when you're in charge.

Nick is one of four kids in his family, and he was a sixth-grader at Bridger Middle School when he came home and told his parents that he wanted to do something a little different for Halloween. He'd been hearing some stories of people who didn't have enough to eat, and on a trip through town, he saw several people sitting in the streets begging for money so they could buy food. Rather than just feeling sad about them, he'd come up with a way to help them.

Rather than trick-or-treating for candy, why not trick-or-treat for canned goods and other items that could be donated to the local food pantry?

If an adult had come up with that idea, undoubtedly he or she would have focused on the questions and roadblocks—how do you get the food to the pantry, how do you figure out who gets it, how-do-you-how-do-you-how-do-you?

But when you're eleven, the questions all have a simple answer and the roadblocks just disappear.

Not by magic, of course. Nick's parents thought the idea was great, and after a little research on Facebook, his mom, Natalie, found Hands and Feet of Jesus, a local church organization that helps the homeless get back on their feet. The group was enthusiastic, but their response was nothing like the local community's or that of Nick's schoolmates. As Nick told friends and neighbors about his idea, it suddenly went viral—not only did everyone think it was a great cause, but they wanted to do it, too. A journalist heard about it, wrote a story . . . the local television station came around . . . within a few days, everyone in town was talking about it. Who knew collecting food for the homeless could be a big deal?

But it was. It seemed as though the whole city was in on it by the time Halloween came around. Not only did kids want to help, but adults wanted in as well, stockpiling nonperishable food to donate. The local Kmart's management and employees stepped up to act as a collection point for people outside of Nick's neighborhood.

Now, this being Halloween, Nick and his clan couldn't just go around in suits and ties to ask for donations. Mom and Dad fixed him up with a costume based on one of his favorite video-game characters: Sonic the Hedgehog. They decorated a toy wagon to take with them for the "loot," and off they went.

Good thing they brought the wagon. Nick and his family and friends collected nearly three thousand cans in their neighborhood, along with copious amounts of dried goods such as mac and cheese. The family car was enlisted to bring some of the goods to the pantry, but bigger guns had to be called in—a truck and trailer were enlisted to pick up the donations.

Was Hands and Feet of Jesus happy to get the food?

"Their eyes lit up like diamonds when they saw what Nick brought in," says Nick's dad, Matthew.

Just so you don't get the wrong idea, Nick did not give up on candy completely; he only *suggested* that people give him food instead. If they still wanted to give candy—or, even better, both—that was fine with him. He'd have his treats and eat them, too.

Just as important as the food Nick and his friends picked up was the community spirit they ignited. There is already talk of starting this as a local tradition, with other kids and families doing the collecting. A motorcycle club has already signed on to help.

This young man has a bright future ahead of him, even if his present dreams—becoming a veterinarian or a video-game designer—get changed along the way. Most important, he's planted a seed that surely will grow in the future.

When Life Gave Him Cancer, He Made Lemonade

Ulises

Kids can be amazingly generous, but what really amazes me is how resilient and brave they can be at the same time.

Imagine undergoing brain surgery at age eight.

Brain surgery is an ordeal under any circumstance, but in the case of Ulises and his family, logistics seemed to conspire to make everything even more difficult. And yet somehow the young man not only got through it but turned his recovery into a springboard to help others.

Ulises—his name is a variation on the spelling of the Greek hero Homer wrote about—was born with cavernoma hemangioma. Those ominous-sounding Latin words can be translated, roughly, as a bunch of messed-up blood vessels getting tangled in your brain.

I hope that's not too technical.

It's a strange sort of condition, and one that isn't always obvious at birth. But I'll leave the complicated explanations and data to the doctors and just say that in many cases there are no symptoms, at least for a while.

That was the case for Ulises, who was like any other active, outgoing young boy until he was around six years old. It was then that his mom noticed that he was walking funny and that he didn't seem to have the full use of his left hand.

It took a while for the doctors to figure out what Mom knew instinctively: something was seriously wrong. Finally, an MRI revealed that he had a benign tumor caused by errant blood vessels in his brain. The tumor was pressing on the cells around it in a such a way that it hindered their proper functioning; that in turn was affecting his walking and his use of his hand.

That wasn't the worst of it. The doctors were worried that if one of the blood vessels began to bleed, the result could be catastrophic. Ulises needed surgery to remove the tumor.

Brain surgery is a tricky specialty, and the nearest doctor who could perform the operation worked in Wichita, several hours from their home. Mom and Dad arranged their schedules so they could be with him through the operation and then through the several weeks it took for him to recuperate. They often found themselves sleeping in his hospital room or even in the car just so they could gain a few extra hours with their son.

Recovering from brain surgery is not like getting over a cold; you have to retrain your body and your brain to work together as a unit again. Ulises reprogrammed himself with the help of rehab specialists at Madonna Rehabilitation Hospital in Lincoln, Nebraska.

Madonna is a superb institution. Taking patients from all across the country, it helps them recover from strokes, spinal cord injuries, traumatic brain injuries, and, yes, brain surgery. The hospital's programs take a multidisciplinary approach and aim to involve the whole family in the recovery as much as possible. There's a special team that works with pediatric patients.

Ulises stayed in rehab at Madonna for seven weeks. The better he got, the more he wanted to do something for the staff that was working so hard to help him.

He wasn't sure what that would be, until his younger sister came up with an idea—why not open a lemonade stand? Everyone loves lemonade.

He'd thank the staff with free lemonade—and maybe earn a little money on the side from others.

The powers that be at another hospital might have shot down that idea pretty quickly. But Madonna is known for its innovative approach to rehabilitation, and the staff took Ulises's idea and ran with it.

Actually, it was more like a walk—they encouraged Ulises to set up his "stand" on a cart and wheel it through the wards, offering his wares to staff and patients and anyone who needed a drink.

Technically, he wasn't charging for the lemonade. But donations were gladly accepted—and wouldn't you know, recipients chipped in to the tune of some forty dollars, most of which he opted to promptly donate back to the hospital to buy presents for other children.

This wasn't the only time Ulises's native generosity came out. His father still marvels at the boy's decision to turn over more than a hundred dollars he had saved from birthdays and other occasions to his elementary school in order to help needy families.

One of the inspirations for his generosity was the kindness of the teachers and staff at his school, who had raised money for him and his family to help them with the surgery and recovery. Kindness encouraged more kindness; help inspired more help. And of course his parents and other family members had taught him about the importance of helping others all along.

We talked to him nearly eight months after his surgery. He still had a limp and was not quite back to full strength or mobility. But the tumor had not affected his memory or brain functions, and it certainly didn't dampen his spirit—or his ambitions.

"I would like to be a doctor when I grow up," Ulises told Jim when they spoke by phone.

Why?

"I can help a lot of people."

Here's hoping that his dream comes true.

Toward a Sweetish Cure

Alex's Lemonade Stand

Kids and lemonade seem to go together. And the most famous lemonade stand in the world—Alex's Lemonade Stand—is all about doing good.

Spoiler alert: Alex's is not a physical lemonade stand, per se. It's more like a lot of lemonade stands, all across America, doing good in as many ways as there are kids.

It started with one girl—Alexandra "Alex" Scott. Born in 1996, Alex was a typical toddler, sweet and energetic, when shortly before her first birthday, she was diagnosed with neuroblastoma, a relatively rare form of cancer that affects the sympathetic nervous system.

That's the part of our nervous system controlling things we aren't directly conscious of. Let's say you get a sudden fright. In the milliseconds before you can run away or otherwise react, your body increases your blood flow, dilates your eyes, and primes your sweat glands. All of that is done without your conscious decision making, courtesy of the sympathetic nervous system.

Neuroblastomas act in a wide number of ways; in some cases, they seem to simply stop growing on their own. However, the disease can be extremely aggressive and difficult to treat. A child's prognosis depends on a wide range of factors, including her or his age and the location of the cancer.

On Alex's first birthday, her doctors provided an update that wasn't very welcome. Not only was her prognosis very poor, but they predicted that even if she did beat the disease, she would never walk.

They obviously didn't know Alex or her parents, Jay and Liz Scott. By the time she was two, Alex was walking with the help of leg braces. Even better, her body was fighting the cancer and she was gaining strength. Among the different treatments that helped was a type of radiation therapy known as MIBG Therapy. Radioactive iodine was injected into her bloodstream; the radioactive chemicals attached themselves to the cancer cells and killed them.

But all these therapies could not succeed in completely eliminating the cancer, and things took a turn for the worst around the time she was four. As the tumors grew, Alex went to the hospital to get a stem cell transplant in 2000.

Stem cell transplants definitely save lives, but they are difficult for patients, and they were especially hard in the early years of the therapy when Alex was a patient. Not the least of it was the long hospital stay it required. (Now, some transplants are done on an out-patient basis, but considerable care is still needed.)

Plus, there were then and there are now no guarantees that the procedure will successfully eliminate the cancer or meaningfully prolong life.

Alex really showed her spirit when she went into the hospital. She told her parents that when she got out, she was going to open a lemonade stand. Not because she was thirsty—she wanted to raise money to help doctors help other children just like her.

She underwent the operation and recovered. When she was well enough to go home, she kept her promise with the help of her older brother. The family set up the stand after the operation.

Alex had a unique, quirky story—fighting cancer with a lemonade stand. The local media heard about it, and suddenly it went viral. Even so, her parents had no idea that she would be so successful.

"We teased her," says Jay. "'You're going to get five or ten dollars.'"

She got two thousand.

Other people heard her story and rallied to the cause as she and her family continued running lemonade stands as a way of supporting the hospital and the fight against cancer.

Alex raised about twelve thousand dollars from her second stand.

As phenomenal as that was, the third time was the charm. People came from miles away in the pouring rain to buy some lemonade and make a donation. Alex collected $18,000.

"People traveled from all over the East Coast all day," remembers her dad. "Our yard was ruined from so many people standing there."

After that, Alex started getting letters from strangers every day.

We heard about you on the news. We had our own stand. Here's the money.

As Alex's fund-raising continued, she asked her mom what the money was being used for.

You know already. Neuroblastoma research.

"That's selfish," said Alex. "Other kids want their cancers to go away, too."

And so the family began spreading the money around. As the lemonade stands and publicity continued—*viral* is hardly the word for it—Alex told a reporter that she would raise a million dollars.

"Last year I raised a hundred thousand," she said. "This year, it'll be over a million with the help of others."

"You can't tell a reporter you're going to raise a million dollars," said Alex's mom when she hung up.

"If people continue to help me, I think I can do it."

The reporter's story attracted a lot of attention—including calls from TV producers for programs like *Oprah Winfrey* and the *Today* show. Alex accepted many of the invitations. Her fund-raising idea had gone national.

Alex's parents tried to talk her out of going on Oprah's show. By that point, her health was in serious decline. She was undergoing treatment and bleeding internally from one of the cancer-fighting treatments. But Alex insisted; finally, a compromise was suggested—if her doctor gave her the OK, her parents said they would relent.

Her doctor gave his OK. Alex flew to Chicago, doing the show and returning in a single day.

The story just kept getting bigger and bigger. Helping spread the word was an incredible book called *Alex and the Amazing Lemonade Stand,* written by Alex's parents and illustrated by her aunt Pam Howard. Then a supermarket chain in the Midwest—Hy-Vee Supermarkets—hosted a Midwest Lemonade Days in Kansas City, Missouri. Alex's idea was rippling out.

The million-dollar goal was achieved only a few months after she announced it.

Unfortunately, the brave little girl died that same summer. But by then, her cause had so much life that it was impossible to stop.

"Liz said, listen, if we continue what Alex started, we have a chance to help a lot of kids," recalls Jay.

And so, on what would have been Alex's ninth birthday, January 18, 2005, her parents and friends established Alex's Lemonade Stand Foundation for Childhood Cancer to keep the campaign going.

Alex had given the foundation very strong momentum—besides that million dollars, an additional $2 million came in following the news of her passing. But now that she was gone, others had to take the lead. Her parents recruited a group of professionals to help as they worked out the way ahead.

"We steered the train, but she was the one who fueled it," says Jay. "She's still the reason many people get involved and donate. They get involved in her story. When we do a telethon and tell her story, the phones light up. People can relate.

"I can't tell you how many people email us and tell us they've named their kids after her," he adds. "She's inspired many people to do things they never thought they could do. There are lemonade stands for all kinds of charities now, which we think are great."

Alex has been an inspiration not only to fund-raisers but to patients and their families. The fact that she lived so long after the discovery of the cancer (such a long survival rate was rare at the time) surely encouraged others to seek early treatment. And it continues to give hope as new therapies are discovered and perfected.

Today, Alex's Lemonade Stand is a giant help-children-fight-cancer machine, acting as a middleman and goodwill processor connecting local fund-raisers—mostly kids—with people who can use the money to fight cancer in different ways.

The Scotts remain very hands-on with the foundation. Besides the foundation's own fund-raisers, it helps several thousand fund-raisers a year, and Mom and Dad often write personal thank-yous to the kids who hold them.

"We want donors to be part of the family," says Jay. "Most aren't 'once and out.' They keep raising money."

As deeply involved as the Scotts are with the foundation, the group is just as close with its scientists, who get personal phone calls when grants are awarded and generally remain in close contact with the organization and the Scotts themselves.

More than eight hundred research projects have been funded since 2005. The research is fundamental and complicated. There's one titled Novel Approaches to AML Differentiation Therapy, which aims at helping kids with acute myeloid leukemia (AML) by figuring out if "unwinding" DNA may be contributing or causing the cancer, and possibly finding a way to target cells with the unwound DNA as a way to combat leukemia.

Not exactly your average grade school term paper. Yet this elevated science is made possible by grade school kids all across America.

More than money is involved in the research, of course. There's hard work and a lot of trial and error. Proper development of a therapy can take years, if not decades.

But sometimes things come together quickly, with a little luck.

Not too long ago, a scientist funded by the foundation made a genetic discovery based on a phone call about a family that had three cousins with neuroblastoma. With that as a clue, she found a genetic defect common to a subset of the disease. She then found a drug used in lung cancer that went after the same defect. Within eighteen months, she had a clinical trial under way. Almost immediately, her team found incredibly positive results with a certain dose.

"That's the type of thing that gets us excited and keeps us going," notes Jay.

Families in some of the trials occasionally reach out to the Scotts to talk about how the trials have helped. They appreciate that immensely. It helps make their effort more personal, not just for them but for their staff and the donors. Stories of cancer victims are often chronicled on a website the foundation hosts.

"Our donors love . . . getting to meet the families that we've helped," notes Jay.

Not every research program or clinical trial has positive results; that's the reality of science, especially when it touches on cancer. But even prolonging life by a few months can be positive.

"If you can extend the life of a child a few years, that is tremendous," says Jay. "We're going for cures, but we'll take time."

Alex's Lemonade Stand branched out in 2017. Acting on the advice of its scientific advisory board, the foundation began a "big data" lab, designed to gather data on childhood cancer.

The Childhood Cancer Data Lab is not the kind of laboratory that has test tubes and beakers; rather, it's a gathering and processing place for data—information about cancer and its victims that may help provide insight into strategies for fighting the disease. Currently, its scientists are compiling a database of nearly two million tissue samples that have been DNA sequenced. While the sequencing is already done, the data has to be "harmonized"—in other words, put into the same sort of format so that it can be processed together. The next step will allow researchers to compare their own tissue samples to that database, finding new connections.

The Data Lab will immediately give scientists a larger data set to work with, opening up new areas of inquiry and testing. For example, a researcher might find similarities in two very different types of cancer, or similarities in the generic makeup of patients with very different ailments, and work from that parallel to find a cure. Perhaps a drug combating cystic fibrosis will have an impact on a certain type of cancer.

Very theoretical at the moment, but very exciting.

While the primary focus of the foundation's funding is research, Alex's Lemonade Stand also has a special program to help children and their families travel to the hospitals where they can receive care. One of the unfortunate realities of cancer treatment is that it is not conveniently located in every community. Advanced treatments are available in very few hospitals, and even if you happen to live near a major metropolitan hospital with a research facility, that facility may not specialize in the type of disease you have.

Having been parents of a cancer patient, the Scotts realized that the need to travel for treatment might be an obstacle for many, even if insurance covers other costs. And so they and the foundation board established a program that provides grants through local agencies to cover some of these expenses.

"The first family we helped was eight years ago," says Jay. "He's still in treatment."

All of this because one little girl decided to open a lemonade stand in her front yard . . . and because thousands of other kids decided to copy her.

But how does that part work? How do kids start fundraisers to help Alex's cause?

Like this:

In 2013, a second-grader named Adam—full disclosure, he's Jim's nephew—was working at a computer in his classroom when he happened to see a pop-up ad talking about Alex's Lemonade Stand. Curious, he clicked on the link, and within seconds, he was reading all about Alex and her fight with cancer. Even though none of his classmates or friends had cancer, he was still very touched by her battle with the disease.

Then, reading on, he saw how other kids were raising money to keep her fight alive.

This is a great idea, thought Adam.

So great, in fact, that he wanted to start his own lemonade stand. Maybe at lunchtime, when a lot of kids would be thirsty.

He raised his hand and called the teacher over to show her. She thought it was a good idea, too. She spoke to the principal, and the principal called Adam down to his office.

Was he in trouble?

No way. Just the opposite. The principal wanted to hear Adam's idea.

As soon as Adam finished explaining, the principal gave it a thumbs-up. The kids in Adam's class pitched in, as did Mom, Dad, and other parents, donating lemonade and cups. The principal designated a lunch period for the lemonade stand. The kids advertised the event with flyers and by word of mouth. When the day came, the students took turns manning their stand in the cafeteria.

They hoped to get $250. Instead, they raised about a thousand dollars.

Grateful for the donation, Alex's mom sent Adam a handwritten thank-you—a personal touch greatly appreciated by him, his classmates, and his family.

The event is now an annual one in the district, and after a few wrinkles and adjustments, it has followed Adam to the new school he attends.

Adam offered a few tips for anyone interested in starting their own lemonade stand. First, don't charge a set price—this way, donations are likely to be higher per cup.

Get your classmates and teachers involved. Adapt to changing circumstances. And if you find a good cause—like childhood cancer—keep at it.

Alex and Adam didn't start out knowing how their efforts would grow, how long they would last, or what would come of them. They only knew she had an idea and were inspired and wanted to do something with it. As Jay Scott says, "Anybody can make a difference when you set your mind to it."

Couldn't agree more.

Alex's Lemonade Stand makes it easy for children like Adam to not only get involved but to contribute and keep contributing. They can open accounts at the foundation's website and use those accounts to make and keep track of contributions. When someone wants to support a local lemonade stand but can't get there to collect their lemonade, that person can go directly to the website and make a contribution.

There's a lot more on the site, including a blog with entries about researchers and others involved in the fight against childhood cancer. One of our favorites is the story about Dr. Jean Mulcahy-Levy, of the University of Colorado Denver, who is studying auto-phagy in hopes that it can be used to combat brain tumors. (Autophagy is the process of cell recycling; the body naturally breaks down and recycles cellular material, and it's possible that this process may be of use in fighting cancer.) There are also stories about kids who have cancer and ways for kids to strengthen their bodies and stay in generally good health.

As the foundation has grown, it has gone beyond lemonade stands. Its own events raise millions each year. It also still gets money from direct donations. Visitors to the website can buy T-shirts, socks, color-ful bow ties—as my husband, Chris, would say, half the battle of fighting cancer is looking cool while you're doing it.

All told, about $20 million is raised annually. A bit under 15 percent goes toward overhead, with the rest being dispersed. Having a nonprofit of my own, let me tell you, that is no small feat.

The battle against childhood cancer is a multifaceted fight. It has to be, because there are a wide range of cancers that primarily affect children. While a great deal of progress has been made over the past several years, much remains to be done.

According to the National Cancer Institute, a little more than fifteen thousand children under the age of twenty are diagnosed with cancer each year. More than 10 percent of them will die.

Alex's cancer was neuroblastoma, relatively rare compared to leukemias, which are the major type of cancer diagnosed among children. Brain and central nervous system cancers, lymphomas, soft-tissue sarcomas, and kidney tumors are among the most common cancers diagnosed before children reach fifteen.

For comparison's sake, the most common cancer first diagnosed among adults is breast cancer, with well over 260,000 cases projected in 2018; about forty thousand people are expected to die from it. Lung cancer is the second most common cancer among adults; more than a quarter million cases were diagnosed in 2018, with more than 150,000 deaths expected. These statistics do not count nonmelanoma skin cancers; roughly three million people are diagnosed with some form each year. In general, skin cancers are far easier to treat than others, but several thousand people still die from them each year.

The National Cancer Institute estimates that there are more than four hundred thousand childhood cancer survivors in the U.S. The survival rate for the disease in general has moved slowly but steadily upward. So even though we all know there is much more work to be done, there are very firm grounds for hope.

The "Sweet Feet" Girls
Caressa and Marlee

Kids and lemonade seem to go together, but sweet drinks aren't the only things kids use to help others. Being resourceful and creative, children come up with all sorts of ways to contribute to others . . . like socks.

Socks?

It's true. This is a darned good tale.

Sorry for the pun. I'll put a sock in it from now on, I promise.

It all started a few years ago, when two friends, Caressa and Marlee, were having a sleepover at Marlee's house in a small Texas town—not too far from where

I live, by the way, though I didn't have the pleasure of hearing about these young women until we started working on this book. Like many ten-year-olds, they were playing with Barbies but for some reason got bored. Dresses, makeup, hair—it did not hold their interest that evening.

What to do?

There was a whiteboard in the bedroom, and they started writing down ideas. One floated above the others:

Help people.

And not just any people. There were two nursing homes in town, and they'd heard that some of the residents were lonely.

Could they help them somehow? Was there anything they could do for them?

The word *socks* went up on the board.

Hmmmm . . .

The magic of creativity took over, and before the girls drifted off to slumber, an idea was born: they would gather socks and give them out to the nursing home residents. Christmas was coming up, but there would be plenty of activity then; better to make it a present on Valentine's Day, in the dead of winter, when warmth for feet and hearts might be in shorter supply.

It's one thing to come up with an idea and quite another to make it a reality, especially when you're still in elementary school. But Marlee and Caressa shared their idea with their parents, siblings, friends, and classmates; they stood up at church and told the congregants of their idea; they offered it to local businesspeople and teachers.

While a lot of adults thought it was a good idea, it was the manager at the local Dollar Store who really championed it. She helped collect donations at the store and talked it up to anyone who would listen. By the beginning of February, it seemed as if the entire town was in on the project. People donated money or socks—Marlee's aunt even sent some from Germany. All told, between two hundred and three hundred pairs of socks were ready to be given out by Valentine's Day.

On February 14, the girls filled a small wagon and went down the halls of both nursing homes, handing out the socks they'd collected. Some people had also donated blankets, which they gave to residents who couldn't use the socks for health reasons.

"It was great seeing the smiles on their faces," says Caressa.

"We love seeing the smiles," agrees Marlee.

They had so much fun, the girls decided to make it an annual event. They gave it a catchy name—

"Sweet Feet"—and it's become a veritable institution in town.

One year they held a contest at school: the class that gave the most socks would win a prize for their teacher.

The prize was a pedicure. Socks, feet, toes—it was a natural.

Over the years, the girls have become experts on socks. Most of the donations are pretty plain: no-nonsense white. But there have been some extraordinary donations. Socks with little hearts are nice; purple and brown stripes—well, it takes all kinds. Their favorites are thick, fuzzy socks with aloe woven into the threads. On the other hand, many nursing home residents prefer ones with grip pads on the bottom.

Blankets have also become a favorite at the yearly event. These, too, come in many different varieties, including camouflage patterns—a hit with the men, as you'd imagine. There are so many donations that this past year, the girls made up little "goodie bags" with several pairs of socks and a blanket.

In my family, we love crazy socks. When you put on a pair with your business suit, it brings an element of fun to the most mundane activities. I'm already searching for the perfect pairs for this year's donation. The only thing I know for sure is that I won't be knitting them myself—that much crazy is too much for anyone.

What I love most about the idea isn't just that it was thought up by a pair of ten-year-olds—although that in itself is special. It's that a really simple idea on a whiteboard rippled big in the community, brightening days and encouraging others to be generous. A search for something better than playing with Barbies and, dare I say, cell phone entertainment, turned into a way to show people that they're not forgotten, which morphed into a town-wide phenomenon—and, in the process, reminds us all of what's important.

Everyone Deserves a Family
Jim and Lori Word

B ut for kids to give back to the community, they need to have strong roots themselves. That usually means great parents—which Nick, Ulises, Alex, and many of the hundred I've had the privilege of meeting have.

But what about the kids whose parents aren't there? Whether they've passed away or had some other tragedy that prevents them from raising their children? Who helps them?

People like Jim and Lori Word.

Jim and Lori met back in the late 1980s, when they were attending Ozark Christian College in Missouri.

They went to the school because they were called to the ministry—and fell in love with each other along the way. Lori was the daughter of a pastor, and as fate or God would have it, her father's church was in need of some help right around the time the pair graduated.

They went to work there. At the same time, the family was hit with personal strain, as Lori's mom was diagnosed with cancer, which she soon succumbed to.

Jim and Lori ended up staying at the church and in the area for some eight years, raising a daughter as well as helping the church grow exponentially; Jim describes his job there as a "putty ministry"—he filled the gaps wherever they were needed, whether working with youth or the underprivileged or some other needy segment in the community.

The pair might have stayed there until retirement, except for a phone call from a friend that caught Jim out of the blue one day. It went something like this:

Friend: I need someone to lead the children's ministry up here in Indianapolis.
Jim: I'll keep my ear to the ground for you.
Friend: No, actually, I'm thinking of you.
Jim: I have no desire to wear a balloon on my head.
Friend: It's not like that.

Jim tried to beg off, claiming that he really didn't think he had a gift for ministering to children. But his friend convinced him that the critical part of the job was supervising the two hundred or so volunteers who worked with the kids.

Somehow, that seemed easier. Or maybe higher powers simply intervened. As Jim puts it, "When God calls you to do something else, you just have to do it. There's a bit of heartache to it, but you jump . . ."

New town, new job, new responsibilities—but same old enthusiasm and progress. The program grew quicker than an Indy car charging off the line. Though busy with their daughter, Lori worked beside her husband as the church expanded its reach in the community. In fact, to hear Jim tell it, she was the "encourager and butt kicker" in the marriage, using her high energy to motivate him as well as half the congregation and its staff while still focusing on their daughter and the family in general.

And then, their lives took another turn.

In June of '02, Jim got an email from a church staffer telling them about a little boy from an Eastern European country who'd been adopted by a mother who was now so overburdened she felt she couldn't go on.

The adoptive mom was desperate—if she couldn't find someone to take the five-year-old child, she would have to turn him over to the child protective services system.

Could anyone help?

Jim read the email a time or two, then called his wife and read it to her.

"We can do it," she said immediately. "We can take care of that child."

In truth, the idea didn't exactly come out of the blue. Years before, the pair had both sat in on a class for foster parents, at Lori's urging. Then as well as now there is a tremendous need for foster parents—families who, to generalize a bit, temporarily take in children who either have no parents or, more often, have been taken from their parent or parents for some reason. To throw out some statistics at you, it's said that there are as many as four hundred thousand kids in foster care (or in need of foster care) in the U.S. The average age is eight, though the population ranges from infant to twenty-one. Foster parents may eventually adopt the children they care for. I wish that were always the case, but that's not the general rule. Maybe a quarter of the children have relatives as their foster parents; in that case they often stay with the family or are reunited with birth parents. Some portion of the others—there are no firm statistics—will go back to their birth parents or be adopted by families seeking children.

Many, however, fall through the cracks or have to be institutionalized for one reason or another. Their "forever home" is a hard-pressed system that may rotate them through a series of foster families until finally abandoning them as soon as they are considered adults, ready or not—mostly not.

In any case, there are heavy demands on both sides. But the Words weren't thinking about the difficulties at that point. The decision to act as foster parents came straight from the heart, and within days, their son-to-be had joined the family; because of the circumstances and people involved, he was formally adopted within two and a half months, which is extremely quick, even for a private adoption.

Their son had been born and raised overseas in another country and been institutionalized for his entire life. There were certainly difficulties to overcome, but their experience in the church with other children had given them enough experience to know how to deal with much of those problems.

Not that things always went smoothly. He was—and remains—very high energy.

"When do I get to put him in time-out?" asked the Words' ten-year-old daughter on his second day with the family.

Far beyond parenting tools like time-out, the Words discovered that the real key to raising a foster or adopted child is patience. You can have all the rules you want, all the understanding you need, and all the prayers in the world, but patience is what gets you through the day.

Shortly after they adopted their son, Jim and Lori were invited to start a new church—something they'd been contemplating for quite some time. They made their way to Texas, where they started a new church in the Dallas–Fort Worth area, which was underserved at the time. Coincidentally, Jim had grown up in the Plano area, nearly right next door, which made the move a little easier.

Going around the community, they visited different churches, trying to get an idea of what needs weren't being fulfilled. During one of those visits, a church member complained about their son's energy level.

That convinced them that *their* church would have to accommodate high-energy children, whether they were diagnosed with something like attention deficit hyperactivity disorder (ADHD) or were simply not used to sitting still for adults. That notion evolved to a ministry that took hyperactivity and other things kids do in stride. Beyond that, children with behavior problems, big and small, were welcome as well.

Candidly, not all churches are that accommodating, even in their children's ministries. But the Words adopted a motto that sums up their attitude: "We have a line item in our budget for paint and spackle. Don't worry about it."

But it was adopting their second son, in 2012, that really opened their eyes to the needs of adoptive and foster families. This was another case of an adoption that did not work out. A friend told Lori of a boy adopted from Ethiopia who was in danger of being returned.

"You guys have done this before," said the friend. "Maybe you would do this again?"

They would. As their first-adopted son said, "Everybody deserves family. Let's do it."

The family has now adopted a total of seven kids, all of whom were originally placed with other families. While the sheer number of kids can put an understandable strain on the budget, the flip side is that they can pitch in to help one another through different crises and difficulties.

As for the strain on them, Jim cites a Bible passage from James 4:17 to the effect of, *If you know that there is a good you can do and you fail to do it, then you have sinned.*

"You know the verses and you teach them," admits Jim. "But then you see it in real life and you can't turn away."

As their family has grown, so has their church. Named the Brazos Christian Church—the name comes from the nearby river and the Spanish word for *arms*—it boasts several hundred members. A large part of its ministry aims at helping foster and adoptive parents and children. One of the favorite programs is a combination day care and "date night"—moms and dads drop off their kids for a few hours in the evening. The kids get to play and socialize—there are age-appropriate groups and games—while the parents go to a movie or go out bowling or just spend some quiet time together. It's a very simple idea that means quite a lot to the families.

"In the last year, we've been branching out and working with biological families as well," says Jim. The idea is to help parents who are in danger of losing their children to the foster care system—a bit like preventative medicine.

Talking with the family about raising children, the word that comes up most often is *patience*. The children they've adopted are not "easy" kids, certainly not at first. In every instance, they were rejected, and without exception the youths test to see if they'll be rejected again—because why invest in something if it will just be taken away from you in the near future?

One of their sons epitomized this, berating them with constant angry outbursts after he came to join them.

I hate you.

Why would anyone want a name like Word?

I'm not becoming part of your family.

Those were among the milder things he said.

But on the day they went to court to finalize the adoption, the twelve-year-old burst into smiles, transforming miraculously into a mild-mannered and loving child—once things were legal, he figured, they couldn't back out.

Not that things were always smooth for him or any of the others. Just like other children, there are ups and downs—and downs and ups. But that normalcy is something of a victory in itself.

What the Words have besides their Christian faith is a belief in themselves to be able to persevere beyond that trial period—and a faith in basic human qualities like love and kindness, which they have seen win out over suspicion and anger that the children harbor.

Thinking the best of people under the worst circumstances—that's a lesson for all of us, regardless of our religious beliefs or cultural background. Don't get me wrong: it doesn't mean being Miss Mary Sunshine and smiling through every storm that comes along. Heck, I curse at those storms as much as anyone.

But remembering the ideal, and looking for it, can make all the difference.

Not Abandoned

Dream Makers

Talking to Jim and Lori Word about adoption and the foster care system led to a question:

What happens to children who aren't adopted when they become young adults?

The answer: they "age out" of the foster system and most programs when they legally become adults.

What then?

The Words pointed me in the direction of a group run by some of their friends: Dream Makers, a program of America's Kids Belong.

According to statistics compiled by the organization, some twenty-six thousand young people "age out" of the foster care system every year. While reaching your eighteenth birthday is a cause for celebration for most of us, in the case of a foster child, it can mean something very scary: no more support system.

No family to help you make the transition to a job or college after high school. No family to do "simple things" like make sure you know how to drive, or help you select a car or an apartment, or even discuss the pros and cons of everyday situations. Imagine not having a mom's shoulder to cry on when a relationship goes bad, or not having Dad around to advise you on some simple household repairs. No older brother or sister to give practical advice on budgeting or priorities. Grandma's hand-me-down dishes are nonexistent.

Dream Makers and its parent organization can't take the place of family or friends. But it can do "small" things like help with college costs, or fund a down payment for a car, or provide that security deposit the landlord requires when renting an apartment. It has paid for "care packages" for college students, helped buy staples like bathroom towels and baby paraphernalia, and even supported special occasions like Thanksgiving Day dinners and birthday celebrations—"small" gestures that mean a lot to the recipients. A special emergency fund has paid for groceries and gas young people needed to get by when starting out on their own.

The organization works with other groups and social workers to directly give small grants to young adults. Applications and nominations for grants can be made simply by filling out a form on the group's website at www.dreammakersproject.org.

A large part of the effort involves hooking up community "dream makers" with young adults in need. Social workers can make nominations or recommendations; the group will try to connect the two.

No program or organization springs from the dust fully formed and ready to change the world; they are created, nurtured, and run by dedicated people who take an idea and a lot of goodwill, mix it with long hours and ample perspiration, and set out to make ideas reality. There's a large team involved in Dream Makers and America's Kids Belong; one of the driving forces is Julie Mavis, the national director.

Foster parents themselves, Julie and her husband started the nonprofit America's Kids Belong to help get kids adopted. The foundation's modus operandi is to work with government agencies, religious groups, and private businesses in different communities to assist kids who need foster care or adoption to find families that can take them. While there is a high demand for infants, finding parents for older children can be very difficult; the older they get, the harder it generally becomes.

Julie's own experience reflects that. She and her husband were foster parents for an infant taken from his birth mother because of drug addiction. One day, the social worker called and said they had to talk. A short while later, sitting in Julie's kitchen, the worker told her that the baby would never be going back to his birth parents.

"Are you interested in adoption?" asked the woman.

"What happens if we don't adopt him?" asked Julie, who realized that there was no way in the world she would be able to adopt the little boy for good.

"Oh, don't worry. There'll be a long line. I just worry about the kids who are older."

The social worker explained that while it's somewhat easy to find homes for infants, the older a child gets, the harder it is to find him or her a permanent home. Hundreds of kids from grade school to high school were looking for homes in Colorado alone; each day that passed lessened the chances that they would find one.

"My heart was just bursting with this problem," says Julie.

She began working on the problem, reaching out to different organizations and government connections. Soon afterward, she started America's Kids Belong.

"I had no clue what I was doing," says Julie about

her early days. "To be honest, I just started asking people and got help."

The organization went national in 2015, thanks not only to Julie and her team but to the generous financial support of Illinois businessman John Ritchie. A key component was added around the same time by Janet Kelly, former Virginia secretary of the Commonwealth and her husband, Ryan, who brought to the foundation expertise in dealing with governmental agencies and officials along with a passion for orphans.

One of the foundation's more innovative—yet seemingly simple—ideas has been to make videos of the children talking about themselves. Seeing a face and hearing a voice makes adoption far more likely.

Dream Makers takes that idea even further, targeting young adults who have or are about to age out.

"I'd heard a lot about kids aging out," says Julie, who started to see the need only after America's Kids Belong became a success. "But it wasn't until we started seeing what happened to kids we knew that I realized how big a problem it was."

It really hit her hard when she heard stories of what had happened to some older children who were no longer eligible for care or programs—jail, drugs, just bad, bad things. And this wasn't ten years after they were no longer part of a foster family or eligible for adoption; it was a few months after their birthdays.

"I knew these kids," she says. "I was asking, hey, what happened to Jonathon and so-and-so. And I'd get answers back like, 'Oh, he's in jail,' and 'Oh, he's homeless.' And I was like, you have got to be kidding!"

Actually, it was more like: YOU HAVE GOT TO BE KIDDING!

"This is an injustice," she said. "This is not acceptable."

Young adults who age out sometimes have very serious problems, from unemployment to poverty, unplanned pregnancies to homelessness. Many don't graduate high school, a deficiency that will haunt them the rest of their lives. A portion end up in jail or addicted to alcohol or drugs. Suicide is, unfortunately, more common in this population than among young people in general. PTSD is also common—many of the children enter the foster care system because they have experienced massive trauma at a young age, sometimes from the foster parents who were supposed to help them. Counseling is often neglected.

Or, as Julie puts it, they don't get into foster care because their parents didn't provide fun snacks.

"There are so many problems," says Julie. "And these problems affect all of society."

For Julie, Dream Makers is kind of a plan B for America's Kids Belong: if we can't get you adopted into a family, at least we can get you some support in another way.

"I've got a lot of social workers on my team," she says. "We can talk to the kids before they age out, find out what they need, they see who we can find to help."

One of the things that makes Dream Makers unique is that the group doesn't focus on basic needs, though of course it helps get those met when needed. It's not there to take the place of government programs like Medicaid or food stamps. It isn't running a homeless shelter. Instead, the organization concentrates primarily on the unusual things, big and small, that take lives beyond the basics.

And dreams.

What are your dreams? a social worker might ask. What do you want in life? What do you dream about?

The answers can be surprising. There are the practical ones: a car to get to school, fresh clothes for a job interview. Dental care: veneers and braces, which are not covered by Medicaid, are a common request.

Laptop computers—having a computer has practically become mandatory in today's society. There's no government program for that.

The fee for caps and gowns at graduation. Not a line item in most church grant programs.

A bike.

And then there are the requests that, well, are so simple and so ordinary that they practically break your heart. A birthday cake. A graduation party. A baby shower.

Most of us take those things for granted. But Julie has plenty of stories about young adults for whom something like a birthday party is an impossible dream.

A lot of times, local people fulfill those simple but critical dreams. The helpers are ordinary people whose simple gestures mean a lot. The orthodontist down the block who remembers her own teenage self-consciousness and cures it with dental work. The baker who simply loves to create for grateful customers. It's amazing how extraordinary "ordinary" people can be.

"We know the kids," says Julie. "We find out the needs and then go out into the community and find the help."

Projects can snowball. Someone nominates a kid for help because he needs a security deposit for an apartment. The down payment comes as a grant; a hardware store donates some paint to cheer up the place. The florist hears about it and sends over some flowers . . .

Small things from a lot of people add up to a big thing for the person who receives them. They, in turn, often end up giving back, or at least spreading the word about the program and its benefits and possibilities.

Spreading that word is Julie's full-time job and passion.

"My passion is orphans," says Julie. "My second passion is getting other people to care about orphans."

To that end, Julie is a relentless speaker, encourager, and cheerleader. She's traveled around the country sharing her enthusiasm with groups such as Rotary Clubs, kindling support for local programs as well as the organization in general.

A lot of times she meets people who tell her flat out that they can't foster children, let alone adopt. Yet they feel strongly that they want to help in some way.

Dream Makers is the easy answer for them.

"People care. And we want to help," says Julie. "Whatever parents would ordinarily do to fill those little gaps, we can help."

It's a true ripple effect—one person gets involved, and suddenly there are half a dozen helping in different ways. "Multiple people get fired up helping these kids."

And so does Julie.

She was at an event when a young man—we'll call him Xavier, though that's not his name—spoke about how Dream Makers had helped him. Julie, scheduled to go on after him, was overwhelmed with emotion as she heard his story.

"He ripped my heart out," she confesses. "It was hard for me to give my speech."

But what she heard afterward hit her even harder: Xavier was, in fact, homeless; her organization was paying for him to stay in a motel as he looked for work.

"How long can we do this?" asked one of the program administrators.

On her way home, Julie told her husband, Brian, that the young man needed a permanent place to stay.

"What do you think if he came with us to stay for a while?" she asked.

"I guess that would be OK," he said after a moment or two.

"Good. Because he's coming tomorrow."

Since then, he's gone on to start a business as a personal chef. I have no doubt he'll have his own restaurant someday.

"It's really cool watching both sides of it," says Julie.

And that little boy who inspired her in the first place?

He now lives in the next town over from Julie and has some very loving parents.

It's great when everything comes together.

TWO
Getting Them There

Movers and Shakers

O ne thing Chris always said about veterans in need was that they don't want a handout; they want a hand up.

That's true of many people, I think; certainly most of those I've been privileged to meet. That hand up comes in many different forms. One of the most basic is transportation—both literally and figuratively.

In the case of many of the young people and their families, simple transportation, whether for treatment or to see a loved one, is a huge barrier. Our beautiful country is above everything else a beautiful *large* country. Getting to a place where people can treat your disease or where you can see a loved one is a physical and often mental challenge.

The amazing thing for me is that time and again, the people who provide that transportation as volunteers often say that they get as much out of doing so as the people they transport. When I first heard that, I thought it must be an exaggeration. But if so, why did people who had so much else going on in their lives keep doing it? Why would people who were successful businessmen and -women, and even celebrities, keep coming back for more?

Maybe it was more than something people like to say. Maybe unselfishly helping others in a very immediate and tangible way does benefit the giver as well as the person in need.

Getting people to places they need to be is certainly a challenge. But transportation is not always a means to an end. It can be an important part of the journey, as some of these stories suggest.

In medieval times, pilgrims traveled on foot through Europe, stopping at cathedrals, churches, and shrines to connect with the artifacts of their religion. Many of those tales speak as highly of the journey itself as the fancy buildings they visited.

That same impulse, I think, powers us today and is very much a part of the American Spirit.

Soaring for Others
Angel Flight West

It occurred to me, after hearing those wonderful stories of perseverance and heroism by children and their parents, that something was missing. In almost every case, I could see where the inspiration was coming from and how the next generation was able to tap into the wellspring of the American soul. I realized the doctors and nurses, the caregivers and counselors, the researchers and scientists, were all doing extraordinary work to find cures and apply them, shepherding kids and their parents through difficult therapies and into recovery.

But how did they get there?

Not figuratively—how did they get to the one research hospital in America where a new cancer drug was being tested? How did they get from, say, Alaska to Texas to undergo a special surgery only one team in the country can perform?

Some people were lucky; experimental treatment was in their hometown or nearby. Others drove all night.

But what about the people for whom it was too far to drive? What about the single mom who couldn't afford air- or train fare?

How do you get where you absolutely need to be when money is scarce and your resources are thin?

Angels.

Not literal angels—though I'd guess they might be along for the ride. The angels I'm talking about are the pilots of operations like Angel Flight West, a volunteer organization that transports medical patients and their families at no charge to them.

Every day, ten private aircraft—usually single-engine Cessnas, Pipers, Bonanzas, or something similar—ferry someone to medical treatment or a care facility in one of fourteen western states under the auspices of Angel Flight West. The costs of the flight are all borne by the pilot of the aircraft, who besides his or her skill is donating the plane's use as well.

That's not a small thing—the Aircraft Owners and Pilots Association (AOPA) estimates that the private owner of a comparatively modest aircraft spends between $100 and $225 per hour of flight time on the aircraft and related costs. Certainly, there are pluses to flying, and perhaps a few ways of saving here and there, but the bottom line is that these men and women are reaching deep into their own pockets to help others in need.

Angel Flight West began in a hangar at Santa Monica Municipal Airport in 1983. Santa Monica is a beautiful place, not too far from LA. The airport is small but in many ways typical of the regional airports that are the backbone of private civil aviation across the country.

There is an exception that sets the place apart—it has a phenomenal static display of old aircraft inside and out, starting with a wonderful DC-3. But I digress.

Like many community airports, Santa Monica had a small but active "family" of pilots. Dennis Torres and his wife got some friends together one year to form the Los Angeles chapter of the American Medical Support Flight Team (AMSFT). Their first thought was that the service would be primarily for organ transplants, ferrying vital organs or perhaps donors, but after talking to hospitals, they quickly realized that there was an even bigger need for what are called "nonemergency patient travel"—flying patients and their family members to treatments far from their homes and ferrying them back.

According to the group's official history, their biggest obstacle when starting out was convincing people that the flights really were free. Even so, some fifteen flights, taking organs for transplant and patients, were logged the first year.

Business soon boomed. By 1986, the group had grown large enough to split off from AMSFT. Though the idea was beyond praiseworthy, organizing so many volunteers across such a wide amount of space was a daunting task, and AMSFT no longer exists as such. But it gave birth to many similar organizations across the country, not just Angel Flight West.

Today, Angel Flight West handles more than four thousand missions a year. The bulk of these are non-emergency transport, both of patients and/or their families, for medical care. In many instances, these flights are taking patients for treatment at hospitals far beyond their homes. In many others, Angel Flight West pilots are taking family members to see their children or siblings at a facility where they are staying for weeks or even months.

Those aren't their only missions, though—Angel Flight West still carries organs that have been donated for transplants to waiting recipients. Other missions ferry blood to areas where it is in low supply. There are also trips to help relocate victims of domestic violence. And besides its volunteers' private aircraft, the organization has an arrangement with Alaska Airlines to handle long-distance transports that are beyond small aircraft ranges or are at times when weather is an issue or no volunteer is available. There are other arrangements with Hawaiian Airlines and JetSuite, a private charter company.

"Command" pilots handle the private aircraft flights. All told, there are about fifteen hundred at Angel Flight West, according to Josh Olson, the organization's executive director.

Aside from owning or renting their own aircraft, command pilots must have a minimum of 250 hours of piloting experience; most have far more. They also have to meet requirements to be "current," which translates into good health and recent time in the air, making sure their skills are fresh and proficient. While most pilots have advanced skills like instrument ratings (in layman's terms, this means they can fly in conditions other than clear, sunny skies), that's not necessary for many of the missions.

A decent number of command pilots are retired or have very flexible jobs, and so can take on multiple missions a year. "We definitely fall into the 80-20 rule," says Josh, meaning that 80 percent of the work in any volunteer organization ends up being done by 20 percent of the people. But that's perfectly OK; even pilots who can spare only a single flight a year are making an important contribution.

"Our average pilot flies 1.5 flights a year," he notes. "But we have pilots who fly over a hundred flights a year."

Among the frequent-fliers is an attorney who often arranges to help while flying to different locations for his job. Others help by arranging missions that coincide with what would otherwise be a prescheduled pleasure trip. Pilots fly everything from a Cessna 152—a small two-seat mainstay of private aviation—to a Learjet. The bulk of this air force, though, are four- to six-seat, single-engine planes.

One of Angel Flight West's command pilots happens to be a friend of Jim's—Dale Brown, whom you may know from his many best-selling techno-thriller novels. (Jim and Dale also collaborate on two series, Dreamland and Puppet Master.) Dale came to Angel Flight West after working with an earlier organization. He doesn't have a lot of opportunities to fly the missions, but he does manage to make time for the cause a few times a year.

Dale says that while the feeling that you're helping someone in need is surely part of the attraction, the enthusiasm of the passengers can light up a pilot's day.

"Most times you get kids who want to sit in the front seat," says Dale. "I give them a set of headphones, maybe let them 'fly' a little. They get excited."

Don't worry, he keeps a hand on the controls and a sharp eye on the sky.

The fact that the missions can take you all over is another attraction for pilots. Dale still remembers his very first flight with an older but similar organization, since it took him from a tiny airport in Oregon to SFO—San Francisco International Airport, one of the busiest airports on the West Coast.

He was flying a single-engine Piper Saratoga at the time, and while he had been a navigator on military aircraft like the B-52 and the B-1B, he'd never flown a small plane into Class B airspace before.

Class B airspace refers to the area around large and busy airports. Put it this way: Dale had to land his plane side by side with a 747.

The Saratoga is a high-performance aircraft, but it's not exactly in the same league as a jumbo jet. Just entering the airspace around SFO requires every inch of your attention; setting the plane down in the right spot on the mile-and-a-half-long runway is not trivial.

That's the sort of challenge a general aviation pilot, even an accomplished one, doesn't get to face every day. It's also one a lot of pilots live for.

You don't have to be a pilot to be part of the organization. In fact, there are about 750 volunteers whose "job" it is to meet the plane at the airport and help transport the patient or family members from treatment or lodging. Volunteers also serve as "mission assistants" on some flights, helping aboard the aircraft as needed.

Categorizing the people who are helped by Angel Flight West is as difficult as categorizing the volunteers. Many are cancer patients. About a third of the flights are for kids and their families.

Ages can vary—one pilot transported a ninety-two-year-old nun. The main requirement for medical patients is that they be medically stable and ambulatory, as well as have some "financially compelling reason or other need" for the flight.

There is no cost to the passenger receiving the flight. While the organization spends a few hundred thousand dollars on staff to arrange flights, oversee operations, and the like, the volunteer pilots and airlines are donating seven times that in free services.

About half the time, patients are referred by hospitals or other health professionals.

"They got into a clinical trial, and now they have to figure out how to get there," says Josh. There are also many trips by families to see loved ones undergoing treatment far away—Dad taking the other kids or relieving Mom, and vice versa.

I've often seen that one good turn leads to another and another, and that's definitely true for Angel Flight West. The group occasionally hands off to similar regional groups, part of a tag-team effort to get people to where they need to go.

Every year, Angel Flight West pilots fly kids to Alisa Ann Ruch Burn Foundation events near Yosemite in California. The Burn Foundation not only helps young burn victims cope with their injuries and the rigors of recovery, it also works on prevention. Named after an eight-year-old who was fatally injured by a barbecue fire in 1971, the California group is among the best-known organizations devoted to burn injury and recovery for children in the United States.

"Instead of getting stared at because they look different because of their injuries," says Josh, who rates the missions as one of the group's highlights, "they get to play and camp and hike with other kids. We fly them from all points of California, Nevada, and bordering states. They're always excited and talkative on the way there and exhausted and sleepy on the way home."

Flying doctors to remote locations, transporting blood—Angel Flight West volunteers help multiply the effects of different charities, rippling kindness across different communities.

When travel requests come in, the staff verify the details and then advertise the need to pilots and volunteers. Staffers match together the different components, hopefully ensuring smooth handoffs and an uncomplicated flight.

"We're kind of like a logistics company, I guess," says Josh. "We have all these volunteers and resources and people who want to use them, and we try to match them as best we can."

There are people they can't help, most especially air ambulance trips, where the patient needs more care than a private aircraft without a medical crew can provide. Long-distance flights also can be hard to arrange, even with handoffs. And unfortunately requests for funerals and the like are too plentiful to fill. The organization makes referrals in cases where they can't help.

The flights touch each volunteer in different ways. Nine years ago, the youngest child of a Montana contractor was diagnosed with leukemia and was being treated in Washington State. The contractor needed to visit the girl but was having a difficult time doing so.

Not yet part of the organization, Josh was filling in as a volunteer for his wife, who'd just given birth to their first child. He happened to take the call.

The contractor was in tears; by the end of the conversation, so was Josh.

"He was trying to take care of his daughter and be with her, but he had to keep working and keep his benefits," remembers Josh, whose own daughter was in a neonatal intensive care unit at the time. He knew firsthand how hard the separation was on the family.

"He was trying to drive his truck over the snowy passes of the Cascade Mountains," remembers Josh. "It was a twelve-hour drive each way. He had reached the end of his rope and was reaching out to see if we could help him."

Angel Flight West was able to help several times.

The child ultimately went into remission. In celebration, the family held a "princess party" for the girl and her friends with a special touch—everyone wore wigs, just like the child who'd lost her hair during treatment. The party turned into a fund-raiser, with the proceeds—approximately $10,000—donated to Angel Flight West.

The girl ultimately succumbed to cancer. But the family and community have continued annual fund-raisers in her memory and still support Angel Flight

West. In fact, Josh was able to take his own daughter a few years ago, completing the emotional circle.

"This family has been so dedicated to her memory," says Josh. "And the community has been so supportive."

"We do get close to a lot of our patients," notes Josh. Unfortunately, many pass away. Yet the families remain very appreciative of the efforts of the volunteers who helped them.

"They appreciate that we gave them that much more time with their loved ones," says Josh.

For many of the patients who make it, the only part of the treatment process that they call calming were the flights, where a stranger went out of his or her way to help. The few hours in the plane were like a respite, a calm oasis in a stark desert of pain and fear.

"There's a lot more to healing than what happens in a hospital, and we're part of it," says Josh.

Like a lot of nonprofit professionals, the director's path to the head of the group did not exactly fly in a direct line. He was an ad executive when he was first introduced to Angel Flight West, whom his agency had just picked up as a pro bono client.

It was a good fit. Josh loved aviation; his dad and grandfather were Air Force aviators. Little did he know then that he would eventually give up the ad agency—and another career as an actor—and end up employed at Angel Flight West. Starting from the ground up as a volunteer, he was eventually tapped to lead the organization; 2018 marked his third year as executive director.

An early boss "cursed" him with the title of "jack of all trades and master of none." Whether meant as a compliment or not, it does describe the light-footedness a nonprofit worker and executive has to have these days. Angel Flight West has ten full-time employees, some part-time workers and contractors for specific specialties, and some three thousand total volunteers. The organization is in the middle of a push to expand.

"We think we're at five percent of the total needs," says Josh. "We'd like to double that in five years. A lot of our challenges are awareness—and funds."

That means they need to get the word out, to both pilots and to passengers. Outreach and recruitment are priorities.

They've also launched an app for their volunteers and made other software improvements to help make the volunteer process easier and more efficient.

Angel Flight West is not the only organization of its kind; in fact, there are several covering most of the U.S., including Angel Flight East, which operates east of Ohio and north of Virginia; Angel Flight NE, which operates in nine states; Angel Flight Mid-Atlantic—

sensing a theme? Each organization has slightly different procedures, but they have two things in common: they like to fly, and they like to help. At times, they work together to transport people on really long trips.

Interested in helping? You can go directly to the group's website at www.angelflightwest.org, where you'll find a questionnaire to fill out, along with additional information about the group.

Need a flight? Go to the same place and fill out a different form.

"I always think the strength of our story is the resiliency of our patients. How strong they are," says Josh. "And then our volunteers. They walk alongside them."

Angel Flight West volunteers spend a lot of time and money to help someone they never met before and may never meet again.

"That's part of the magic," says Josh.

Magic, yes. And the American Spirit.

Bound for Glory—and Service

Brandon Gosselin

G etting to where you need to go isn't just a matter of transportation. Sometimes the hand up you need isn't one that comes on wings or wheels.

Take Brandon Gosselin.

Before I tell you about him, I want you to write down his name and tuck it away somewhere that you can find it in ten or twelve years. Because there's a possibility you'll be voting for him then.

On the presidential ballot.

Brandon was the all-American kid in high school. Gifted both intellectually and athletically, he was a top athlete and scholar at his high school in Burlington, Oklahoma, a small town on the Kansas border. Tall and quick, he was rated among the top basketball players in the region. With his senior year winding down, he looked forward to entering the University of Oklahoma. The Sooners are a power in Big 12 athletics; even more important, the university is a top research facility that each year helps more than twenty thousand undergrads prepare for careers in fields from accounting to supply-chain management.

Yes, that is a thing. Education has become far more specialized since I went to school.

"Oklahoma was a 'dream school,'" says Brandon, who was planning to take business management there. He was valedictorian of his high school class, an all-state hoop star, and one of four kids raised by his hardworking mom and dad in a very small house. The future was bright.

That future, and Brandon's dreams, came crashing down barely two weeks after graduation. Camping out with friends, he juiced his four-wheeler as fast as it would go—only to have a deer run out in front of him. Unable to brake in time, he lost control, crashed, flew from the ATV, and landed on his face. His injuries were so severe, his friends thought he had died.

Brandon lived, thanks to prompt and excellent medical care. But he suffered a severe brain injury—a

TBI, or traumatic brain injury, as they are known to the medical profession.

The general public has become more aware of TBIs of late, due in part to publicity about their long-term effects. More and more attention is being paid to concussions, which can seem deceptively minor when first suffered but in fact may be serious TBIs.

There was no question about deceptive symptoms or minor problems when Brandon was taken to the hospital. A blood vessel inside his skull had burst; the damage was obvious and excessive. He couldn't think. Literally.

As he puts it, "I went from Mr. High School to Mr. Hopeless in a matter of seconds."

His memory, his ability to learn, his cognitive abilities—they were all affected. It was estimated that he had the mental capability of a third-grader after he regained consciousness.

Worse, his sense of balance was so off that he had trouble walking. He literally had to learn how to do it all over again.

Jump?

He had to relearn how to do that, too. Where once he had been able to easily dunk a basketball, now he couldn't even come close to touching the rim.

Brandon's hometown in Oklahoma is small, but it has a big heart; people rallied to his bedside at the hospital and then to his home, offering encouragement and support.

Even so, kind words go only so far. A shadow of his former self, Brandon found himself scraping along—and worse.

"Probably the lowest point came about a month after I'd been released from the hospital," says Brandon. He knew at that point that his dream of going to college would have to be—at the very best—deferred. At the very worst, it was never going to happen.

"I was lying in bed. Depressed," he remembers. People were telling him that he had to accept his new reality.

"I contemplated suicide," he admits. "I'm not going to lie about that."

That night, scanning the web for some sort of inspiration, he came across a quote from Steve Jobs.

Life can be much broader once you discover one simple fact: Everything around you that you call life was made up by people that were no smarter than you and you can change it, you can influence it, you can build your own things that other people can use. Once you learn that, you'll never be the same again.

Steve Jobs was telling Brandon that he didn't have to be an all-American academic to be worth something. All he had to do was be who he was at that very moment.

He began turning his life around. Physical therapy. Rehab. Hard work. Perseverance. Prayer.

Slowly, with the help of therapists and therapy, he regained motor skills, coordination, memory, the ability to think complex thoughts.

Many people would think it miraculous just to recover from such an injury. But Brandon wasn't satisfied with just recovering. He wanted to get on with his life—and live out some of the dreams that he'd had before the deer appeared in front of him and caused him to crash.

Sports was out of the question, but was college?

No.

With a lot of rehab and a great deal of determination, Brandon entered Oklahoma for the fall semester of 2013 right on schedule, intent on making business a career. The first few weeks of classes were a revelation—but not in a good way. He found himself struggling simply to keep up. The former high school honor student faced academic challenges on a level he'd never experienced before. He'd never so much as gotten a B through high school; now he was failing classes.

Time to give up?

No.

Brandon doubled down with everything—rehab, studying, even prayer. He researched the various aspects of brain injuries and found strategies to either get back the capabilities he'd lost or substitute new approaches to learning and retaining information. By the end of the year, he had won an honor no one thought possible in the dark days after his accident: the President's Award for Outstanding Freshman.

Knowing that, the rest of the story may seem preordained—*Brandon crushes his classes, gets great grades, graduates, and goes on to a great job and career in a Fortune 500 company before setting out on his own . . .*

Except, things didn't work out that way.

Brandon's soul-searching in the early months of his college career led him to new decisions about how he wanted to live his life. He felt himself moved toward a more religious bent and decided that he wanted to pursue his education at a Christian college, not to become a minister but to align himself more with matters of faith. Mentors at Oklahoma helped him find a place at Freed-Hardeman University, a private

Christian college in Tennessee, to start his sophomore year.

He continued to thrive there, not only doing well academically but also reaching the point where he could compete in athletics his senior year, joining the track-and-field team.

Since graduating, he's begun working with a group of business leaders on a project that they hope will transform the economy of Haiti. It's based on a model that has echoes of his own approach to recovery. Rather than bringing food or medical supplies, they intend to help Haitians set up new businesses. These would help grow their economy, improving the country's standard of living permanently.

Brandon, who first visited Haiti as a college student on an aid and missionary trip, notes that there's a misperception that Haitians are lazy or otherwise unworthy. But just as others perceived him as diminished in value after his accident, that image of Haiti is mistaken.

"Haiti has some of the hardest-working people in the world," says Brandon. "Give them the opportunity, and they can change their country."

Brandon believes that developing water supplies for agriculture, business, and export is a promising area, one with benefits beyond entrepreneurship. By his estimate, some 250 people have expressed interest in getting involved. The water would come from wells drilled in different spots on the island. The overall budget to set up the project runs to $15 million and more, but the initial phase has a far more modest price tag of a few hundred thousand dollars. Brandon and the backers are hoping to make a "sustainable difference" in Haiti in three to five years.

Brandon's pluck and energy certainly played a major role in his recovery. But he had help—his parents and family, his friends, other community members.

And he got a hand up financially from the Jimmy Rane Foundation, an organization in Alabama that takes a somewhat unconventional approach to scholarships. Hoping to ease the financial burden on his family as he headed into his second year, Brandon spotted information about the scholarship and applied. He turned out to be exactly what they were looking for. While most college aid is granted to families of very severe financial needs, the Jimmy Rane Foundation aims primarily to help students from middle-income families who aren't really poor but nonetheless would strain to pay for college.

Now, this isn't a story about Jimmy Rane himself, but a little background on him may be illuminating.

Start with this—if you live east of the Mississippi and have a house or even leaned against a fence post, there's a very good chance you have benefited from one of his products. He's the founder of Great Southern Wood Preserving, Incorporated, a company Jimmy built with his own hands into the world's biggest supplier of treated lumber. For years he was its spokesman, known on TV and in advertising as "the Yella Fella"—a reference to the color of the treated wood.

The firm is a true American success story, all the more so because it started as a tiny factory that wasn't even being used when Jimmy took it over following the death of his wife's parents in 1970. At the time, wood was undoubtedly the furthest thing from his mind—a promising student, all signs pointed to a bright future for Jimmy as a lawyer. But he saw an opportunity where others didn't. Working 4:00 a.m. shifts before hitting the books for his bar exam, he built the company stick by stick, bundle by bundle. Not that he neglected his legal career—he did so well that he eventually became a judge and served for four years.

By 1986, the company was so large that he gave up his law career to devote his attention to it full-time. It was around then that he became known as the Yella Fella.

Trying to increase awareness of the company and its products, his marketing people suggested they create the Yella Fella character, a cowboy more interested in wood than 'rassling steers.

Who would that be?

You, boss.

Jimmy was a natural. As Yella Fella, he became so famous that the National Cowboy & Western Heritage Museum gave him the Western Heritage Wrangler award.

Quite an honor for someone from Alabama, not exactly cowboy country. (In fact, only one other Alabamian has ever received that award: actor Johnny Mack Brown, who headlined in more than sixty Westerns during the forties and fifties and has his own star on the Hollywood Walk of Fame.)

Today, Great Western has five manufacturing plants along with fifteen treating and distribution facilities. Their wood is used from South America and the Caribbean to Canada, and in at least half of the U.S., from the East Coast to Texas.

You might think that a megacorporation like that would have its headquarters in a megatropolis like Atlanta or Dallas or New York. But you don't know Jimmy.

The company headquarters remains in Abbeville, a relatively small town in Arkansas. The company is a mainstay of the local economy, and it's one reason Abbeville has retained its small-town feel, the sort of place where you can buy fresh shelled peas a short stroll from the drugstore and bank, with maybe a side trip to the barber along the way.

While their firm has an international reach, Jimmy Rane and the employees pride themselves on retaining a tight-knit atmosphere, one where it's not uncommon for the boss to know not only the workers very well but in many cases their kids. One of his favorites was the child of an associate, who from a young age was always talking about how she was going to be a doctor when she grew up.

"She never wavered," says Jimmy. "All through high school, she always said, 'I'm going to be a doctor.'"

This was more than a few years back, before the company, and Jimmy Rane personally, had been blessed with the kind of financial success they enjoy today.

The girl graduated and was admitted to Auburn College.

The girl's father owned a local tire store, and while the family was certainly not rich, under ordinary circumstances they would be considered comfortable.

College finances, though never easy, would have been doable. Unfortunately, the girl's father died from a heart attack, and the college burden suddenly became too much for the family.

"I should have been more sensitive and aware," says Jimmy humbly. "I didn't realize this would create a financial hardship."

By the time he found out, it was too late to help.

I find it comforting to know that when you miss one God-given opportunity, there's often a second chance. Jimmy got it right the next time.

"It was such a shock to me that this had happened," said Jimmy. "I felt guilty that I hadn't done anything—if I had ever met a child who deserved to go to college and live out her dream, it was her."

Devastated, Jimmy Rane decided to do something to help others in similar straits. He wanted to help "kids in the middle"—children who weren't really poor, or really rich.

"Every foundation in America tries to help really poor kids," he explains. But for children in middle-income families, scholarships and grants are hard to come by. "We have to do something about this."

Talking with some of his associates at the company and with some of their customers, Jimmy came up with the idea of a foundation funded by an annual golf tournament to raise money for scholarships specifically aimed at middle-income students. The company already had a small-scale annual golf tourney; they'd marry that with the foundation idea and see what happened.

They started small—one scholarship was awarded in 2002, the first year of the awards. By the spring of 2018, 383 scholarships had been awarded, totaling more than $3.8 million. Students all across America have benefited. The scholarships are not just one-offs—they generally last eight full semesters, the usual length of a college undergrad career.

The typical recipient will come from a middle-class family and often has at least one school-age brother or sister. Very probably both of his or her parents will be working; the student may have a part-time job as well.

"They're in the middle," says Jimmy. "A single mother making $30,000, a family with three or four kids making $50,000. College is just out of reach for them."

The size of the award will vary depending on what other resources and scholarships are available, but as a general rule, the range runs from $500 to $5,000.

Where does the money come from?

The foundation holds a banquet at the Renaissance Montgomery Hotel & Spa and a golf tournament at the Robert Trent Jones Golf Trail at Capitol Hill championship courses, roughly a two-hour drive from Abbeville. A variety of sports celebrities attend and highlight the two-day event; paying guests get to mingle as well as play a little golf. The dinner program includes a silent auction and guest speakers.

The event mixes past glory, present achievement, and future potential, all elbow to elbow. Current superstars like Cam Newton as well as past legends like Too Tall Jones typically headline the banquet and team up with guests during the tourney. Excluding the costs of the tournament itself, all the money raised is used for scholarships; the work is handled by volunteers from the company, from Jimmy on down.

(Speaking of Too Tall Jones: he called me out for awkwardly expressing a preference for Fort Worth over Dallas during my fund-raising talk. Hey, a girl's got to go with her heart. But I digress . . .)

"The inspirational part of this is that these kids became part of the foundation," says Jimmy. Students who benefit from the scholarship are invited to attend and meet with the donors. It makes the donations more meaningful, and it also helps the students express their gratitude. More than a few end up helping the foundation after they finish college; a good number have been successful in their professions and now are important contributors.

"A lot of times you contribute to things, and you don't know if it's making a difference or not," notes Jimmy. Here, "you get to see firsthand where your money is going.

"The one thing that impresses me about these kids is that the vast majority want to go back to their hometown and make a difference. That kind of matches up with my philosophy."

The foundation is now supporting just under forty students. The need, however, remains immense—Jimmy estimates they get some twenty thousand applications a year.

One of my favorite things about Jimmy is the fact that he recognized he had missed an opportunity to help someone—but didn't give up. Regret is useless unless you examine it and use that information as motivation and a guide for what to do differently, as Jimmy did. There are other chances in life, especially when it comes to doing good.

"I love sharing my story with people," says Brandon, who was featured in a special video and program at a recent banquet and is still close to the foundation. "When I do, I learn more and more about the incredible things they've gone through and what they now do for others. I love bringing those stories out, especially from people who are shy at first and afraid to share. Once they do share, they see how much good they can do."

Brandon's enthusiasm, which extends beyond sharing, has led him to tell his story to various groups. He's honing his speaking skills for many reasons—including a political career. When we talked to him, he was predicting he might run for president in 2032. To prepare himself for that, he plans on living in different parts of the country, among people from different ethnicities and backgrounds, so he can get a better idea of who he would be working for while in office.

It's an ambitious plan, but given how far he's come since his accident, I wouldn't bet against him.

The Easy Way Kills You
Micah Fink

September 11, 2001: Micah Fink is working on a telephone pole installing high-speed communication wires in Queens, New York, when the first terrorist-commandeered plane takes out the World Trade Center across the river. His perch gives him a horrifying view of the skyline.

As soon as they gather their wits, he and his coworkers cross over to Manhattan, joining the army of first responders and volunteers looking for survivors.

He finds none.

Hours later, he and his companions scavenge the remains of bagels from a demolished cart and head to the nearby East River.

"What are you going to do?" asks someone.

"I'm going to kill whoever did this," answers Micah.

At the time, Micah Fink was no one special, just a kid from New York State's Catskill region, where his parents had a farm.

"I climbed telephone poles and played in a ska band," he says, describing his life to that point.

But the 9/11 attacks touched him so deeply that he enlisted in the Navy and became a SEAL; he would serve for some ten years, including reserve duty. His service record grew to include a Bronze Star, one of the highest decorations a servicemember can receive. It was rewarding, high-risk work, but its profoundest effects on him were hard to analyze. Home following a particularly trying set of missions, Micah found it difficult to adjust to life outside the war zone.

"I was feeling isolated and alone," he recalls, admitting that transitioning from war to civilian life was harder for him in many ways than combat. "One day you're at the tip of the spear; the next day, you're at home with a head of lettuce and a box of cheddar buddies."

Still, he carried on, until one day he came down with a bad cold. He decided to go to a local VA hospital to see if there was anything he could do for it.

Four hours later, a young intern fresh out of school diagnosed him with PTSD and bipolar disorder and gave him a prescription for pills that were supposed to return him to an ill-defined nirvana similar to his pre-combat state.

"Mind you, I went there for a cold," he says now, in a voice filled with both wonder and disgust.

He argued with the woman, asking how she could possibly make such a diagnosis when they had barely talked.

"I left that day and never returned," says Micah. "I didn't take the pills; I didn't take the counseling. Two weeks later, I bought a plane ticket to the Amazon."

He ended up traveling through the South American jungle with a guide and subsistence supplies. It was definitely not nirvana. His guide spoke no English; they communicated with gestures and grunts. The pair ate rats, roots, whatever they could find. Micah felt incredibly alone.

"Days and days would go by and we wouldn't talk," he says. "I remember staring at my GPS for hours on end—and it didn't even work."

By the time he came home, though, Micah had transitioned to some deeper understanding of who he was and how he had to live his life.

He went to work as a government contractor, back

in the war zone. When he returned home after that, he realized what veterans were going through as they transitioned to civilian life. Some had it extremely hard, and not necessarily because of what they'd been through—or at least not solely because of that.

"It was like a veteran apocalypse," he notes of what he observed. In combat just a few months before, many of the men he met or reconnected with had been at the top of their game, combat-ready. Now they are hiding out in their basements, mushed up on drugs, walking zombies.

That wasn't going to happen to him, and it didn't. Moving on with his life, he relocated to Montana in 2013, along with his wife and children. They were still learning their way around the property when he planted some plants on a windowsill. Trying to help them reach the sunlight, every day he cleared a little more of the ground outside to improve the light.

The plants spurt up quickly, then, just as quickly, died.

Micah was left with the question: Had he helped them die, rather than live? Would they have been better off in the shade, struggling for light and nourishment, rather than being flooded with it?

As he thought about it, he decided that struggle was a universal condition. But it wasn't necessarily a negative one. It was hard, true, and surely difficult at times, but it was also life-affirming. He had struggled in the Amazon, only to return stronger and more purposeful.

That same summer, he went backpacking and met some cowboys riding through the mountains. Talking to them, he discovered they were veterans on a six-day trip who were part of a program helping veterans overcome adjustment problems and post-traumatic stress. The trips helped them open up with each other; they also presented the individuals with struggles that refocused them on their own strengths and identities.

"In that moment, I realized what I was doing in Montana, in the mountains, in the middle of nowhere."

Micah translated his own experiences in the wilderness and with horses into the outlines of a program that became Heroes and Horses.

Launched officially in 2013, the nonprofit takes veterans through a three-phase program that first teaches them horsemanship—basic things that are necessary to ride horses in the mountains. Following that, they take a six-day pack trip through the Gallatin Mountains, a range in the Rockies that extends through Montana and Wyoming.

Two weeks later, they return for Phase Two, which begins with more advanced skills in wilderness survival. That is followed by a hundred-mile trip through

rough country in places like the Bob Marshall Wilderness Complex.

What happens there?

Aside from the physical journey—where participants take turns planning the logistics and taking on such tasks as locating camps—veterans find themselves talking about things in a way they haven't been able to with family members or therapists. Memories, often horrific, of time on the battlefield resurface.

One common theme—guilt. Guilt at surviving. Guilt at having to struggle to cope. Guilt at not being "OK," whatever that means.

Participants tend to bond with their horses as well as with one another. There is something about relating to animals that can be thoroughly therapeutic. You're caring about another creature, responsible for them while at the same time helped by their presence and strength.

The final phase is called Integration. The veterans are placed with outfitters and others who put them to work on ranches and whatnot, using some of the skills they've learned, acquiring new ones. That lasts a month; some end up taking jobs in the field or related ones, such as working as guides or packers.

The program is still young and expanding. There are plans to buy a ranch and start raising cattle to make the program self-sustaining.

"We've got some big things in the works that will push us to the next level," promises Micah. His staff is working on analytics to show that the program can help more effectively than existing therapies. Data-driven methods and results are critical to the future, they believe, and not just at Horses and Heroes. The hope is that similar methods will be adapted elsewhere, perhaps universally.

"And at that point, I'll go get a job at Walmart," jokes Micah.

Until then, there's a great deal of work to be done, starting with weaning people off medications and changing professional minds about its proper role. Seventy-five percent of the guys who come to the program, Micah says, are on more than three medications. And that's too much.

They split about two dozen guys into eight-man classes each year. To enter the program, veterans fill out an application on the group's website, found at www.heroesandhorses.org. While there are no set requirements other than being a combat veteran in reasonable health, the group looks for people who will benefit and who understand that this isn't a dude ranch; riding horses in the mountains and depending only on yourself and the guys around you is not an easy task. Participants are not charged; Heroes and

Horses is a nonprofit and gets its money from donations and accomplishes much of its work with the help of volunteers and in-kind contributions from like-minded groups and companies.

"The environment here—I call it a high-pressure medium—is a place where veterans rediscover meaning and purpose through struggle," says Micah of Heroes and Horses. "Because the easy way eventually kills you."

While especially critical of professionals who emphasize drugs over other forms of treatment, he's equally critical of veterans who use their disabilities—legitimate or not, physical or emotional—as an excuse not to take charge of their lives. What he calls *professional veterans*—vets who go from program to program more for enjoyment than for anything else—are wasting everyone's time, including their own.

And so are the people giving them feel-good, lip-service "help."

"If I take six hundred guys out to the Super Bowl, have I helped them?" he asks rhetorically. "No. That's why our motto is 'Heroes and Horses—This Is Not a Vacation . . .'

"These guys have no idea who they are when they come," Micah adds. "They only know what they've been told."

Why is he running the program?

"We're all born with a specific purpose," he answers. "Mine is to help other people. I think a lot of modern life is contributing to the de-evolution of mankind. . . .

"Ultimately, I'm ashamed of a lot of guys in my community. What they've done is taken a free lunch—but free lunch is not free. It enslaves them.

"I had a Marine call the office," he says, giving an example. "He says, 'I miss the Marine Corps, the brothers—'"

"No problem. I'll arrange for you to reenlist."

The Marine wanted no part of that.

"What are we talking about then?" asked Micah.

The man went quiet.

"Here's what we're going to do." Micah laid out a simple daily regime—early rising, walking or running four miles. He told the man to call him in two weeks.

The Marine did. "I've never felt so great in my life."

Micah had him continue for another three weeks and, in the meantime, decide on three things he wanted to do with his life. When the three weeks were over, the Marine told Micah he had sold his house and enrolled in a flight paramedic school.

Three months later, the Marine had finished school. He called back and wanted to come into the program.

"No," answered Micah.

"Why not?"

"You already did it."

"Can I come as a volunteer?"

"Absolutely."

"Did I do anything for that guy?" Micah asks rhetorically. "No. He did it himself. . . . There's a disease. That disease is a narrative that obstacles are there to break us. They're not."

He draws a parallel between taming wild mustangs and helping veterans. The horses have to be shown what they are capable of; same with people.

"Horses are very honest creatures. They will test you in every different way." Dealing with them, says Micah, is like looking in the mirror for many men.

Both man and beast have to decide that they are going to be what they are capable of. They have to choose. The choices may not be easy, or at least not seem easy, but they are nonetheless choices.

Obstacles, though, can bring triumph.

"The greatest thing in life is that you went through hell," says Micah. "Consider yourself lucky. Because you are about to become a rocket. . . . The greater the struggle, the greater the achievement."

High Risk, Higher Reward
GearUp

L iterally or figuratively, getting to a place isn't just a matter of transportation; you have to know where you're going so you can get there.

Sometimes it takes quite a bit of help to get the destination and a map together.

Shaila, a sixteen-year-old in the Flint, Michigan, area, found both at GearUp Academy, a small alternative high school for kids with a variety of problems and home difficulties.

A self-described "people person," she's aiming to become a registered nurse. In the meantime, she's working fast food and attending GearUp, where she not only works on "normal" high school curriculum with the help of an online tutoring program but also attends sessions on social and coping skills and even leadership.

"You learn to push yourself," says Shaila, who grew up in a gang-infested neighborhood known for its crime rate and dim futures. Before she came to GearUp, she was in danger not only of flunking out of high school but simply never seeing her eighteenth birthday. "My side of town, you can't even walk to the park. Boys get guns instead of books."

Shaila is one of thirty-five students at the school. The Academy is tiny not because there's no need—it's estimated that at least four thousand young people in the area are "high risk" and need some sort of alternative program or will not graduate. A significant number are from very poor families; most are minorities.

GearUp is tiny because its funding is tiny. In fact, there's barely enough money to pay for its two administrator-teacher-do-everythingers. Along with some dedicated volunteers and board members, Executive Director Winston Stoody and Chief Engagement Officer Kelly Rodgers handle a wide variety of tasks, from fund-raising to informal counseling. While they get help from other area professionals and agencies, GearUp is very much a place where the principal knows your name.

Started with the help of a grant in the fall of 2016, GearUp Academy is an outgrowth of GearUp2Lead, a leadership program that helps inspire local young people. GearUp2Lead holds an annual conference on leadership and has developed a curriculum to help young people in trouble, hoping to buffer the bad influences of poor family situations and poor adolescent decisions. The Academy puts those two ideas to work.

Their motto is embedded in their name: GEAR stands for "Growth Empathy Action Responsibility." Those are the cornerstone values of the program and hopefully of the students who graduate.

Three distinct types of students come to the Academy. About a third are kids who have gotten into trouble with the law and are "adjudicated"—essentially sentenced to go to the school and straighten themselves out. Another third are suburban kids who, for whatever reason, are not doing well in their local high school and need a different environment to succeed. The same is true of the final third, though their hometown is Flint, where the demographics and surroundings are very different.

Those three populations aren't necessarily a natural mix. The Academy has its work cut out for it as it works to build a team-like atmosphere from the start to get everyone to get along.

"We share the fact that they have a very unique opportunity here," says Winston. "This needs to be a safe place. If there's a whole lot of drama or garbage, we're not going to put up with it."

At the same time, "kids are kids." Things happen. Flexibility and communication are probably the two most important tools the staff uses every day.

The Academy day starts at 9:00 a.m.—significantly later than most high schools, designated because it's a little closer to teenage sleeping rhythms, as any parent of an adolescent can tell you. There are a variety of project-oriented classes—say, time with a volunteer writing coach working on essays—then a couple of hours of online classes, where students advance at their own pace. Lunch, often combined with a talk, lecture, or other program, follows. Art classes follow. Then the kids go to jobs, study, or do more work on their project.

Afternoon jobs range from the trades—working in auto shops, for example—to fast food. The projects have a similar range and seriousness: among them was one called Project Citizen, which ended up with a student presenting information on curfews to the city council.

Both Winston and Kelly are devoted to their students, but they come at it from different backgrounds and résumés. Winston has a master's degree in education and extensive teaching experience; he's coached and acted as a mentor. He also started and later sold a meal delivery service and worked as a trader at the Chicago Board of Trade.

Kelly, a Flint native, worked in the automotive industry and was a board member of GearUp when, in 2016, she decided that helping young people was her true calling. So she quit a well-paying job at Nissan to become a volunteer mentor before being promoted to her present position.

Both take an entrepreneur approach to the school. Or, to put it another way, they "do whatever it takes" to make school work. They pass that attitude on to the kids, encouraging them to seek out opportunities and, if they have the temperament, aim to mold their own enterprises in the future.

Community organizations have pitched in in various and occasionally unusual ways. A twelve-week course on financial literacy was taught by an employee of a local credit union. The school is partnered with a nearby school district and Peckham Youth Services, which provides vocational programing for the students.

But teaching on a tight budget is not a thing of magic. Besides the everyday dilemmas involved with educating kids others have given up on, GearUp Academy is faced with the difficult task of raising money to fund its operation. Just keeping the lights on is a struggle.

When we were talking with them, they were looking for new quarters. The space they were using was due to be leased; after lessons, Winston was beating the proverbial bushes for a new place to call home. They have their eye on an old firehouse; to make it work, they need to raise money to buy and renovate it.

It's a daunting task, but they have plans, including a GoFundMe campaign.

Building and finances aside, one of the biggest challenges is finding businesses willing to employ young people, especially ones who have had trouble with authorities.

Successes come one at a time. Some are "big"—the week we spoke, a student had just graduated the Academy's career readiness program and started work at an eyewear firm. Others may seem "small" to outsiders: Shaila had her first real birthday party, with a cake and everything, the week before.

Flint has been in the news most recently because of a severe water crisis brought on by lead leaching from pipes in the old system. But even problems as severe as that have to be put into perspective. A dark sense of humor may help; as one volunteer remarked, "Before that we were known for our crime rate."

Hopefully, the next news cycle involving the city will be all about the success of groups like GearUp and its students fostering an economic and cultural boom.

THREE

To Help Others

Being Different

Jim has two friends we'll call Clark and Jake who often come by on summer evenings to hang out. Both are "different" in the sense that they have disabilities: Clark's is developmental, Jake's is physical. They're brothers, but their personalities are very different—Clark is a practical joker and always seems to be laughing at something, or just about to; Jake is far more serious. Neither, though, fits the stereotype of a "special" person. They're individuals, and that's all. Jake can be a bit cranky, but he is an important member of his church, often helping usher and whatnot on Sundays. He's an aficionado of classic cars from the 1950s and '60s. Clark erects the best Christmas displays in the neighborhood—in *his* opinion—and has a way with dogs and other pets. He's also the family's—and occasionally the neighbors'—prime grass cutter and the first to volunteer to help clear out a nearby senior citizen's driveway after a snowfall.

The point isn't anything special—excuse the pun. Both young men are just like everyone else despite their disabilities. True, they have and still require additional care and certainly expense because of the mixture of attributes that God gave them at birth. And no sugar coating—they haven't been given any "special" attributes to compensate for the ones that make them obviously different from others. But each in his own way is a part of the community, making his own contribution to the family and the community.

Some disabilities we're born with. Others occur after birth through accidents or genetics. But in many cases, those disabilities don't mean that the person isn't doing a lot for others.

What about those of us who don't have disabilities holding us back?

What are we doing? How are we contributing to the community? Where is our American Spirit shining through? Can we do more?

The next few people may provide some examples.

Getting Past Barriers

Jesse Saperstein

People come up against barriers at all different points in their lives. In Jesse Saperstein's case, they were there from the very beginning of his life—though neither he nor his family understood that.

Jesse has Asperger's syndrome, a cluster of disorders on the autism spectrum. The medical explanations of the condition can get very technical, and in fact, we're still learning a lot about autism and its manifestations, but to summarize in layman's terms, the condition basically affects a person's ability to deal with social situations. A person with Asperger's, as it is commonly known, tends to seem "a little off" when meeting people for the first time. He or she may appear extremely standoffish or otherwise not interactive when talking. They may become obsessive with trivial information and seem unusually focused on particular subjects. Motor skills—functions performed using their body—are often clunky. In general, they don't seem to quite fit in—they may be intelligent, even superior, but they are square pegs in round holes.

That's what they look like to the people around them. What about from the inside? What does it feel like to have Asperger's, or even to be "on the spectrum," as the common slang goes.

Jesse Saperstein knows. More than that, he's shared it with the world.

Now in his thirties, Jesse remembers becoming aware that he was "profoundly different" around fourth grade. It was then for the first time that he started becoming a regular target of bullies, pushed around, and taunted.

Though not physically small, he was very shy about fighting back. Worse, the one time he did fight back—he charged into someone who had been pushing him—it was Jesse who got in trouble. His school counselor and his parents urged him not to strike back, advice that Jesse took to heart—but which inadvertently made him an even bigger target as he grew older.

The physical and mental abuse continued through middle school and peaked around ninth grade. Some of it was comparatively mild, if being called "sketchy Jesse" and ostracized because he was different is mild. Jesse continued to grow, and eventually his size made him less of a physical target. Mental abuse continued, however, including a case where he was "catfished"—a form of cyberbullying where an invented girl- or boyfriend is created and used to taunt and tempt the victim. Aside from ridicule, targets can also become the victims of financial fraud. In Jesse's case, the idea was a cruel prank perpetrated by a classmate or classmates; it was eventually discovered, but the pain of the incident remains fresh many years later.

One of the things that made life somewhat easier for Jesse was his decision to share information about his condition with his classmates. They knew he was different, but like most people, they had no real understanding of Asperger's. And in some ways, it would have been hard to tell, as Jesse often kept to himself. His grades certainly didn't give him away, and when he did open up, even his "weirdness" had many positive aspects. To cite one of many metaphors Jesse himself uses, spending hours at Chuck E. Cheese's working on a drawing may seem strange, but if the result is a beautiful work of art, people will think you are artistic, not artistic *and* autistic. Wearing the same clothes for days on end may make you seem lazy, not autistic. Or autistic and lazy, as the case may be.

Because autism exists on a spectrum, people who are "high functioning"—Jesse would fall into that category—may just appear to be jerks, not developmentally handicapped. But they are the latter. Not only are they *not* inconsiderate, they don't know that the concept exists.

Until, of course, they are diagnosed and helped by counselors and parents.

Explaining his condition to his fellow students was one step in a long process for Jesse as he got older. Gaining acceptance from his peers was another step; those who didn't bully him gradually focused on his other personality traits and consigned his Asperger's to "different" or "weird but OK in general" categories.

People with Asperger's tend to have trouble with transitions in life, whether these are big or small. In high school, it took until Jesse was a junior to really feel more comfortable with his surroundings. When he did, he became active in school organizations, including the school newspaper, and that had a big impact on his life. The interaction with others, and the fact that he was helping a good cause, gave him confidence as well as strength to deal with or ignore the bullies. His fellow students voted him "Most Unforgettable" in the year-book, one measure of how far he'd come since fourth grade.

Getting support, increasing your self-worth, finding a community to belong in—these are all very good things, but they are not magical solutions to every problem. Jesse's Asperger's didn't go away, and while life may have become easier in some respects, he still had hurdles to climb every day. He was admitted to college, where he majored in English with a minor in peer education. He got a job as an RA, or resident advisor, which took him further out of his shell.

It was around that same time that Jesse happened to read Bill Bryson's excellent travelogue about hiking the Appalachian Trail, *A Walk in the Woods*. The book inspired him to consider undertaking some sort of physical and mental challenge that would set him on the road to adulthood. He decided on a literal road, or I should say *trail*, through the woods: the Appalachian Trail, the two-thousand-plus-mile mountain trail that stretches from Georgia to Maine.

Funded in large part by leftover college savings, Jesse set out to walk the entire trail himself, raising money for the Joey DiPaolo Foundation, an AIDS-related charity. Like many hikers, he started in the south at the tail end of winter, working his way north over footpaths that wind across rocky peaks and craggy valleys. Unlike most hikers, who complete different sections of the trail over several years, he did the entire trail with only a one-week break in the vicinity of his home.

"It's thirty percent physical," says Jesse of the long trek, "and seventy percent mental."

He learned something new every day, made some good friends, got annoyed at some strangers. But most of all, he persevered, overcoming foot sores and minor injuries, bouts of loneliness and homesickness, and the sort of bone-chilling fatigue that can overtake you after you've hiked a few dozen miles a day for days on end.

His trip lasted seven months and nine days. He was relatively lucky; he never got seriously ill. He did not contract Lyme disease—endemic in certain areas—and, miracle of all, he didn't get poison ivy, even though there were times when he feared he was "bathing in the stuff," which grows, well, like poison ivy in many parts of the trail.

"Every morning I told myself I made a choice," he says of his main method of self-motivation. "I had to get up, because I made a choice."

A choice to continue. A choice to accomplish something that few people—with or without some form of autism or other condition—don't even get the chance to try.

The hardest part?

Writing a journal every day.

The journal was important, not simply because he wanted to remember what happened but because by then he had another project in mind—a book that would tell people what Asperger's is like.

Jesse finished his trek before mid-fall snows blocked the northern reaches of the trail. He raised some $20,000 for the foundation. And he had some fresh stories for the book.

Published in 2010, *Atypical: Life with Asperger's in 20 1/3 Chapters,* covers much of Jesse's life to that point. It remains one of the few that talks about what Asperger's, and autism in general, feels like to people who actually have it. It's filled with funny stories—Jesse has quite a sense of humor—as well as bits of advice for others with the condition and their parents. It's not a how-to-live with-the-condition manual, however; Jesse's second book, *Getting a Life with Asperger's: Lessons Learned on the Bumpy Road to Adulthood,* is much more practical in that regard. Published in 2014, it directly addresses issues from bullying to getting a job and is aimed directly at others with Asperger's.

Telling others about Asperger's has become part of Jesse's mission in life; besides the books, he's now a speaker on the condition and has a website where he posts information and tips about coping with Asperger's.

Oddly, for a long time he resisted helping his peers with the condition. Maybe it was too close to home; maybe he felt they should figure things out for themselves as he did.

All that changed a few years ago, when he took a job as the social media and activities liaison with the College Experience (www.thecollegeexperience.org), a two-year, nondegree program at the College of Saint Rose in Albany, New York. Jointly run with an organization called Living Resources (www.livingresources.org), the program helps young men and women with intellectual disabilities prepare for independence by teaching them crucial life skills. It includes a specially tailored curriculum at Saint Rose and internship program with local businesses. Part of his job involves working closely with the alumni program, organizing and leading outings, and overseeing the alumni community volunteer program. He also teaches creative writing classes and helps train new employees.

"The best teachers [for others with Asperger's and similar conditions] can be people who have been through it," he notes. One thing he tries to do is advise others to learn from his mistakes, rather than making them on their own—good advice for all of us.

People with Asperger's can be very trusting, and they often fall victim to frauds, whether in real life or on the internet. Another common problem is a lack of boundaries—a boy who likes a girl may not understand that following her around is not only unwelcome, it could easily be considered a crime. And Jesse is adamant that people not use a disability—whatever it may be—as an excuse.

It's a struggle at times. Asperger's is not a condition you outgrow or put into remission. And the wounds from his youth are deep. But when someone treats him poorly, he remembers the advice a friend once gave:

You can't please everyone.

Trying to leads to bitterness and obsession, rather than improvement. And that's true for all of us, autistic or not.

"You have a right to be angry," he says. "But not to take it out on others."

If you met Jesse today, you almost certainly wouldn't know that he has Asperger's. You might think he was a little eccentric—but then what writer isn't? He tends to be precise and direct when talking, but you'd never suspect the hard work he's done improving social skills that most of us take for granted. You'll catch that he's results oriented—something the world can certainly use more of.

If you happened upon him near his home in Albany, you might end up being recruited to one of his latest pet projects—picking up trash. He is part of a local "OneLess Campaign" devoted to cleaning up the city one piece of litter at a time. The group has what Jesse calls "flash cleanups"—members gather for perhaps an hour and blitz a certain area to clear it of debris. (There's a Facebook group—naturally—at www.facebook.com/lesstrashmoresmiles, if you'd like to see what they do or want to get involved yourself.)

As part of his personal war on trash, Jesse has adopted a bus stop near his house, disposing of random bits of refuse. One less soda can, one less candy wrapper, and little by little, the street looks cleaner, and somehow the day seems brighter.

Some notes on Asperger's:

We still don't know everything there is to know about autism in general, and experts continue to study and debate the nature of Asperger's. While for the moment it is considered the "higher range" of autism—meaning that those who have it generally function better than others on the autism spectrum—there are experts who believe further research may place it in a different, perhaps separate, category. In any event, those with Asperger's generally develop "normal" cognitive and verbal skills, unlike others on the autism spectrum. Outward symptoms include extreme social awkwardness, a lack of fine motor skills, difficulty with nonverbal communication—body language and gestures, failure to understand others' emotions (as opposed to simply ignoring them), and obsessions with unusual topics or items. On the other hand, those with Asperger's often have advanced vocabularies and can be quite articulate—like Jesse. The condition does not affect intelligence.

Asperger's generally becomes apparent around four years old. Inappropriate social skills often lead to trouble in social situations and ostracization as a child. Frustration with everything from simple misunderstandings to bullying can lead to behavioral issues.

The exact cause is not yet known. There is evidence for both genetic and environmental factors. It is not, however, a result of the amount of attention or love a child receives.

The condition seems to affect more boys than girls, though more research is needed to determine whether this is due to girls not being diagnosed. It has been estimated that one out of every 110 children in America has an autistic condition and that 2.5 children out of 1,000 have some form of Asperger's. Much more has to be learned about these conditions.

There is a common belief that some people with Asperger's "grow out of it." That does not appear to be the case, though adults with the condition can and do learn to cope with the difficulties through perseverance and hard work, by parents, families, teachers, counselors, and most of all themselves.

The Blind Bikers of Central Park

InTandem

In a world where everyone suffers, it's easy to see the pain. The beauty is seeing how one spark of light, one story of perseverance, ignites a fire in others and propels them forward, perhaps at first alone, and then in tandem.

Some lives are like dramas with many acts. Artie Elefant's was one of them.

In the first act, Artie was a successful businessman in New Jersey, heading the sales and marketing department of an electrical component company. By all measures, he had a good, comfortable life.

In the late 1970s, some friends of his began running. He and his wife were inspired by their example and began running themselves. Both eventually got to the point where they could attempt the New York City Marathon. Artie ran the New York City Marathon in 1981, finishing in just under four hours, a nice achievement for a middle-age person who was relatively new to the sport.

Having done it once, he felt no need to do it again, but he stayed active, running recreationally. Life continued as before.

Then came a second act.

As Artie reached his fifties, odd things began to happen. People began appearing instantly alongside or even in front of him. He'd stop short or even walk into them, stunned that they were able to come so close without him seeing. The rooms he was in—rooms he was very familiar with—suddenly seemed very narrow, far smaller than before. At night, he had trouble seeing in the dim light, a problem he'd never had before.

Artie went to the doctor, who diagnosed him with retinitis pigmentosa, a rare genetic disease that robs its victims of sight over time.

No disease or genetic condition is kind, but retinitis pigmentosa has a particularly cruel progression, as if it were slowly torturing its sufferers. A person with the condition often does not know they have it. When they are young, their vision is often perfect, or nearly so. For many, the disease makes itself known only when they are older—in middle-age, like Artie.

It's a thief, stealing sight a little at a time—first making night vision difficult, then robbing a little around the edges as it takes away peripheral vision. Gradually it narrows what a person can see until only a small pinhole of vision remains.

Shocked by the diagnosis and alarmed at the doctor's prediction that he would quickly lose his sight, Artie decided to make major changes in his life. The most important was retiring from his job, since he had a list of things he wanted to do with family and friends before he lost the ability to see.

And so began Act Three.

In 2000, retired but still checking the must-dos off his bucket list, Artie took his running hobby up a notch and got involved with the Achilles Track Club, a running club in New York City.

New York has many running clubs. By far the best-known organization is New York Road Runners. The group sponsors the Marathon; has numerous other races; acts as a partner, mentor, and model for smaller clubs; and even has its own app and virtual races. Sixty years old, it is the granddaddy of the community re-creational running movement.

But it's not the only club in town. The others range from very informal groups of five or six people who meet on weekend mornings to run in Central Park to larger organizations that sponsor formal races on their own.

The Achilles Track Club is somewhere in the middle in terms of size and age. What makes it special is its mission: Achilles caters specifically to runners with disabilities. And while now there are many similar groups around the country and even others in New York, at the time Achilles was started in 1983, its mission was as unique as it was praiseworthy. Today, the group's members include amputees, people with traumatic brain injuries, people with MS and cancer—if you can think of a disability or serious disease, the odds are someone with it is running or has run with Achilles.

Someone who is blind or has very limited visions needs to run with a guide. As a general rule, they are connected by a tether each holds in their hand. The tether can be anything from a shoelace to a bandana; its length and width vary by pair, but the general idea is for the two runners to be close enough to stay in stride without bumping into each other.

Blind and limited-sight runners were still something of a novelty in the wider world of running when Artie joined Achilles, but there couldn't have been a better ambassador for the sport. There's a cliché in running circles about the "loneliness of the long-distance runner"—a notion based on the reality that runners often spend hours alone, running their daily workout. With Artie, that idea had no currency. Blind runners typically run with a single guide who becomes accustomed to their stride and strengths. Artie ran with a veritable army each time he ran, its members changing and growing.

"Artie's Angels," he called them.

Twenty-five years after he had run his first New York City Marathon, Artie ran his second. His pace was considerably slower and included a few stops with the Angels for chocolate and other tiny snacks—something that didn't feature into the more competitive earlier race. But this one was surely more fun. Alerted to the presence of a blind runner—rare in any marathon then—people gathered on the street corners in every borough and cheered Artie on.

Artie soon branched out. Why run "just" a marathon when you can swim and bike instead? Competing with the help of a single, dedicated guide, he undertook several triathlons in the New York area, doing so at a time when it was almost unheard of for a blind athlete to compete.

The procedure for blind swimmers in a triathlon is somewhat similar to running; he or she will usually swim with a guide, who helps keep him or her on the right path using a tether. (There are other techniques, depending on the individuals.)

Bike riding, though, is completely different. The blind rider teams up with a guide or "captain," who sits up front, steering as well as pedaling. The person in the back is often called a "stoker." Different groups and athletes use different terms, but the general setup is the same: both riders pedal like mad men while the guide does all the steering.

Artie suggested that Achilles start a bike program. Sure, said the leadership, and we know just the person to take charge.

Artie.

In no time, he raised money for the bikes and a trailer where they could be stored. Tandem bikes, incidentally, are rather special and not inexpensive. These bicycles built for two have to be extremely sturdy and, if they're used for racing, as light as possible. That hikes up the costs. Entry-level bikes start at four figures.

Artie grew the bike program over several years. But it was always a rather small part of Achilles, and with other priorities by 2013, the club decided to phase it out.

Thus began the next act in Artie's life. He began planning for a new club devoted entirely to biking. He had spectacular plans—until tragedy struck.

Besides losing his sight, Artie had battled cancer for years. He had chronic myeloid leukemia, a form of cancer that attacks the cells that make blood. In many cases, when caught early, the cancer is slow moving and can be put into remission with aggressive treatment. That was the situation for Artie, who had been cancer-free for some five years . . . until 2013.

CML can progress very rapidly, and it did in Artie's case. Within a few months of the discovery that it was back, he passed away.

And so, too, might have his dream of a bike club for the blind, except for Artie's wife, Susan, and two very remarkable friends, Stanley Zucker and Mark Carhart, both of whom had seen the plan for the bike club.

"We were shoveling the dirt over the coffin when I met Artie's friend Mark," recalls Stanley, a film producer who is now semiretired. Both men knew of Artie's cycling dream. "We looked at each other and said, we have to do this."

There is, of course, a little more to the story. To get the club off the ground, Artie had figured that they needed about $25,000, which would cover the cost of bikes, something to store them in, and other whatnot. He had not yet begun fund-raising when he died.

Mark fixed that with a check.

Meanwhile, Stanley went to work on the various permissions, paperwork, and bureaucratic hurdles. He negotiated with the Central Park Conservancy to find a place for the bikes—not as easy as it sounds in a place with literally thousands of eager though often contentious groups vying for space. He got the necessary permissions. And he purchased ten bikes and a trailer to keep them in.

Artie was relentless, recall his friends, but so is Stanley. One friend who witnessed them both at work, Jerome Preisler, says Artie was irrepressible, but Stanley (who has full sight) could give him a run for his money. Whether it was filling out IRS paperwork or getting a website together, Stanley would look up experts for guidance, do what he could himself, then find someone with expertise to handle what he couldn't.

"It was almost a reenactment of scenes I'd seen with Artie," says Jerome of Stanley's frenzied work setting up the club to honor their friend. "Now it was Stanley—frustrated but determined."

Artie knew a lot of people and was always coming up with different ways to get them together and get them involved in doing good things for the community. Stanley took the baton—or maybe the handlebars—and did the same thing, recruiting helpers as he went. Very likely he never envisioned taking on such an important role—but there he was, charging along in the path his friend had pointed out.

Within only a few months, InTandem was a full-blown organization, sponsoring regular rides not just in Central Park but in other parts of New York City. Artie would be proud. Today it has several regular programs, with a weekly ride as the centerpiece.

Each Saturday at 9:30 a.m., about fifty fully or nearly blind riders show up at the Engineers' Gate in Central Park to ride with the club. For the next hour and a half or so, they ride with volunteer guides through the park. Other events over the course of the riding season take riders farther and sometimes combine unexpected pleasures. A fall daffodil ride, for example, had club members planting the flowers' bulbs at Corlears Hook Park on the Lower East Side of Manhattan, roughly six and a half miles away from Central Park.

InTandem's DNA contains quite a bit of the man who inspired it. Artie was a self-made guy who became a success by doing whatever it took to get a job, fulfill a promise, or meet a requirement. But perhaps his greatest talent was an ability to be a matchmaker—he could somehow intuit that certain people would get along, and he strove to put them together.

That's exactly how InTandem works today. Riders—both stokers and guides—come from many different backgrounds and financial strata. A married couple from Connecticut; a kid from the South Bronx. Lawyers, shop clerks, businesspeople, housewives—there's a wide range helping and being helped.

Is it worth it?

For the riders, certainly.

"The thing that Artie would say about riding a bike," explains Jerome, "is that it's sensory. Being outside makes a difference. He would say, you could drive in a car, but biking lets you experience things differently."

The organization continues to grow; it had a $250,000 budget for 2018—"ambitious," says Stanley, who currently serves as trustee. The money comes primarily from fund-raising rides and donations. InTandem takes part in the Five Boro Bike Tour, an event that takes riders into each of New York City's five boroughs—a forty-mile trek in May that puts tens of thousands of New Yorkers on bikes.

It's all about speed for seventysomething Susan Genis, who quips that when she's moving on a bike she doesn't have to whack slow pokes with her cane.

I think she's joking, at least about whacking people. But the yoga teacher does like to move crisply through Central Park.

"It keeps me young," says the legally blind "stoker" who has been riding with InTandem for several years. "It's such a boost to get out in the fresh air and to move fast. When you can't see, everything slows down. And I like to move fast."

Susan, who gradually lost her sight to glaucoma and other ailments, first heard about the group at the library. But though she'd biked a lot in her twenties and thirties, even commuting to work through the city streets, she was reluctant to participate until an acquaintance spoke about it. There was a period of adjustment—it was difficult to learn to trust a partner she didn't know. But within a few rides, she was hooked, and now is accomplished enough to give advice to new volunteers when she pairs up with them.

The captains or pilots at the front of the bikes must learn the basics not just of riding with a partner, but of communicating their intentions clearly and ahead of time. A simple turn or stop can be unsettling if you're zipping along without being able to see what's ahead.

Aside from providing some recreation and exercise, InTandem occasionally inspires the riders with tales of others who have overcome their handicaps. That was the case when blind Green Beret Ivan Castro rode as a guest with the group.

Ivan, hit by a mortar shell in Iraq, was near death when he was evacuated from the battle site. Following scores of operations, he managed to recover from most of his wounds, even the loss of part of his hand. But there was nothing to be done about his sight. With one eye completely gone and the other severed from his brain, he had to completely reorder his life.

Being blind didn't stop him from staying in the Army, nor did it prevent him from running or biking competitively. Since being wounded, he has run more than fifty marathons, biked across America and Europe, and trekked to the South Pole with Britain's Prince Harry.

His best competitive events are in bicycling. Ivan has won silver medals in cycling at the Invictus Games and placed from third to fifth at USA Cycling's national championships in the blind category. He's an awesome athlete—not only blind but fifty years old and still going strong.

"They have great hearts," he says of the InTandem people. "It's something they're doing to show people they don't have to be limited."

As a competitive athlete, Ivan was on a different level than most if not all of the people he rode with.

But he didn't talk down to them at all. The former Green Beret is a natural coach, shouting encouragement and the occasional jokes. He yelled "You can do it!" and "Good for you!" so often that day it's a wonder he didn't go home hoarse.

But he's not a pushover, or someone who gives out compliments merely for the sake of saying something nice. Ivan is one of those guys who doesn't accept excuses, either for himself or from others. Those are the sorts of people we need more of in our lives. I believe we're only limited by our imaginations when it comes to healing, and to life in general. A person may lose their sight, but that doesn't mean they lose their spirit, or their love of activity.

One of the beautiful things I've learned from wounded warriors, is that they still have the warrior spirit and still have a lot of life to live and adventures to experience. I first saw this with Ryan Job, who managed to climb a mountain and go deer hunting after he was blinded and severely wounded in Iraq. Physical limitations don't have to limit your spirit.

Perhaps surprisingly, InTandem has more captains— sighted riders who pilot the bikes—than blind people. That's a tremendous statement about the spirit of volunteerism in New York.

It's all free, for captains and stokers, sighted or blind.

And so is the feeling as you pedal through the park, the wind slapping against your shirt, the sounds of the city muffled by the trees, the smell of hot pretzels and food trucks . . . yes, I do get distracted as I ride!

But after burning all those calories, don't you need to refuel? That was Artie's motto, after all. He was famous for taking a lead on those long rides through New York's boroughs—then stopping for a donut or even an adult beverage.

As his friend Jerome put it, even after being diagnosed with cancer, he devoted his life to helping people—and had a lot of fun along the way. What if Artie had chosen instead to feel only the pain of loss and had rested there? How many others would have missed out? That zest for living in spite of hardship, that use of freedom to achieve different dreams to overcome different hurdles—that is the true American Spirit, and it lives on with Stanley and all the other volunteers at InTandem.

You Belong Here

Brian Blackwell

As a parent, I know the pain of seeing your child suffer. I often hear from parents who are distraught with worry about the troubles their child might have in school. Each time I do, I think of my friend Brian Blackwell. Through hardship we have the opportunity to leave the world much better than we found it.

Middle school may be the roughest time for a kid. So much in their lives is changing. They're not yet adults—far from it—but they're also no longer children. Their bodies are changing, and so are their minds. Their emotions are often in turmoil as a result.

It's no wonder it can be the most prevalent time for bullying.

But this story isn't an exploration of the roots of bullying or even a guide on how to combat it. Rather, it's the story of a child who had a terrible experience in middle school and who said to himself, I'm going to do something about it when I grow up.

No one is going to have the lousy experience I did.

Brian Blackwell may not have used those exact words, but that sentiment absolutely describes the path he has taken to touch countless lives. He does it as a middle school principal: an everyday hero changing lives every day.

"I was the chubby kid called 'fat boy' all the time," says Brian, thinking back to his own time in middle school. Being called names and getting picked on was bad enough, but far more traumatic was the loss of his father to a massive heart attack when Brian was in eighth grade.

Devastated, Brian suffered through the funeral, returning to school the next day. Not one teacher, not one coach, not one counselor came up to him and expressed so much as a single condolence, let alone offered guidance or some sort of direction.

That memory still stings; you can hear the hurt in his voice when he recalls it. And yet, he persevered, bending but not breaking. He became the perfect example of why struggling can help you become stronger.

He didn't do it entirely on his own. His family and interested adults helped change his course.

Things turned around when his mom enrolled him in a new school the next year. Unlike his old school, his new principal took a personal interest in him, talking to him every few weeks and checking on him when he could. That wasn't just Brian he did that for, though— the principal made it his job to relate to everyone in his building. He seemed to actually care about his students and his school. He respected the children as well as the teachers and staff who worked with them, and it showed.

So much so that it made an impression on young Brian. He made a pledge to do that himself someday.

It took some time. Brian went to college—he was the first in his family to do so—and studied history and education. During his training, he observed at a middle school that reminded him a little too much of the school where he'd been picked on. But then he had a great experience as a student teacher in another school. And from there, the rest was history.

Well, not quite. He earned his stripes not only as a teacher but as an athletic coach, working for five years before returning to graduate school for a master's. That qualified him to fulfill that promise he'd made himself as a teenager. He got a post as an assistant principal at one school, gained experience, and moved on to another, gaining more experience until finally he was asked to become a principal.

"Not every school is a great school," admits Brian. Sometimes the problem is a lack of resources—a polite way of saying there isn't enough money to properly fund programs or hire good staff. Sometimes the problem is simply that the community is so challenged by problems like poverty and violence that teachers and staff have a herculean task just getting the doors open and shut each day.

But sometimes the problem stems from poor attitudes among the staff. And ultimately, that's the principal's fault. In Brian's telling, a school's principal is both a team leader and a team builder—and it's the team that makes all the difference.

"The most important thing is to hire great teachers, teachers who will have a great relationship with the kids," he says. "Teachers who can make learning come alive" with great activities in the classroom.

That doesn't mean field trips every day; it *does* mean presenting material in a way that catches students' attention.

If it were easy, everyone would be a great teacher. Little things as well as big enter into it. A class on fractions might revolve around slices of pie. A science lesson on photosynthesis might feature the plants being grown in the back of the room in the class nursery. And so on.

Among the things that have changed since I went to school are the sheer number of activities for kids after and even during school. The number of clubs seems to have multiplied, reflecting a wide range of interests— from a Twilight Club for kids who like to read the famous YA book series, to a video-game club . . . things I wish I had when I was their age.

The school also runs programs for parents on parenting and connecting with their kids. It's all about giving them "tools" to help their children grow and excel.

"We're here to build leaders," says Brian. Ultimately, that's what his school is about.

One thing you notice when you walk into his building is a large sign that reads, "You belong here." That's the school's spirit and mission in three words. Everyone who steps through the front door belongs there. No one is unimportant. No student is to be disrespected for who he or she is and can be.

Now you may get the idea that Brian is an easygoing guy and that therefore discipline at the middle school is pretty lax.

Not so.

Respecting others involves discipline as well as love. That, unfortunately, does mean fair punishment at times.

While fights are relatively rare at Brian's school, they do occur. There was one, in fact, just before we spoke for the book. By the time the students got to the principal's office, the boys' passion had cooled and they were very focused on their punishment. One even burst into tears.

Brian reassured them. "You're going to be disciplined for your behavior, but then it's going to be over," he said, adding that he himself had occasionally gotten into trouble as a young man, but things had worked out OK.

A fight brings a three-day in-school suspension, by the way. Good argument for talking things out before resorting to shoves and fists.

Among the principal's innovations is an outdoor classroom, where classes are often held during good weather. Another—a team of elite students called SEALs—is inspired by my husband, Chris, and other members of the Navy's elite special operations unit.

In the military, SEAL stands for Sea, Air, and Land, an acronym made of all the places the teams operate. At Brian's school, it stands for Service, Education, Attitude, and Leadership—the qualities all the students must display in order to belong. Brian's SEALs are a special volunteer force that rallies when work needs to be done—delivering meals to the hungry around the holidays, for example.

Teachers and educators who are really passionate make an important difference. That one teacher who encourages you, or excites you about a subject, can set you on a course to change the world.

It's a nice thought, but how do you work it into the daily routine? How to remind busy teachers and active students that caring for each other is more than just a nice slogan? That's where a good principal comes in. Brian has many tools. Some simple, some unusual. Walking into the school staff lunchroom, I was surprised to see a picture of every student on the walls. On closer inspection, I saw names scrawled under most— teachers' names, I realized. It turns out that each time a teacher has a meaningful interaction with a student, they write their name under the student's photo.

The people in our lives who are important are not the ones we see on television or even the ones who have books written about them. They're the people who are there every day, making a difference in small but meaningful ways.

I'm grateful that Brian was able to take that horrible experience he had as a child and turn it into something very positive for others.

He's not alone. I sometimes think the world would be a much calmer place if every parent dealing with a problem his or her child is having remembers that things can turn out for the best. Would we be less anxious parents knowing our children have the potential to grow as Brian Blackwell did?

I think so.

I met Brian at a time when I was hearing from a lot of other parents that they were anxious about their kids entering middle school. They worried about things like not making a sports team, establishing new friendships, or experiencing the heartache that is adolescence. But when I saw what Brian did with his heartache, I realize the incredible power that can come from suffering if it is channeled in a positive direction.

Maybe that's a reason not to be afraid in life—good can come out of anything. God can bring light through darkness.

Schools should be training grounds, shaping our kids to be stronger emotionally as well as intellectually, with character and responsible attitudes toward freedom. With people like Brian running those schools, our future will be secure in the hands of leaders who have overcome hurdles and difficulties, small and large. One small hurt—and even the large ones—can turn into a lifetime of achievement, if the conditions are right.

Flipping the Pig

Amanda Kloo

Her goal was to walk barefoot in the sand with her twin boys.

It doesn't sound like much, but for Amanda Kloo, it might as well have been walking on the moon, for Amanda had been born with cerebral palsy and walked with the aid of a cane. She was perhaps a hundred pounds overweight; sports and strenuous physical activity of any kind were foreign to the thirty-something recent mom.

Which is not to say that Amanda was unaccomplished. On the contrary, she was an excellent teacher, skilled in working with children who had disabilities. Beyond that, she had a PhD and excelled in teaching other teachers how to teach. No one could say that she had not contributed greatly to society or that she was not an example to others.

But she wanted to do more. After the birth of her twins—born without her ailment—she felt pangs whenever they played. More than anything, this mom wanted to play and keep up with them as they moved through toddlerhood into the typical run-and-tumble years of early childhood.

Never underestimate the power of motherhood or the determination of a mother motivated by the love of her kids.

And so, one day she ventured into a gym not far from the college where she worked and changed her life.

Eventually, she would change others' as well.

Cerebral palsy—known colloquially as CP—is the general term used to describe a number of related or similar disorders that affect movement. They involve the brain, specifically the cerebrum (which is where "cerebral" comes in) and its ability to govern movement. The condition effectively paralyzes movement, affecting everything from posture to strength (where "palsy" comes in).

While the condition probably has existed before recorded history, it wasn't until the 1830s that it began to be studied in a scientific way. William John Little, a British surgeon and a victim of childhood polio, is credited with the first important discoveries and study, naming the condition spastic diplegia. Little's work covered a range of conditions, including muscular dystrophy.

Little advocated early intervention and therapy to improve motor skills, an approach that today is standard. Among the important distinctions between Little's early theories and what we now know is that he believed the problems developed after birth. Today it is recognized that the problems generally have to do with the brain's development beforehand, although about 10 percent of the cases are estimated to be due to birth injuries. Prenatal care and monitoring can reduce the risks of CP, though they can't completely eliminate it.

Symptoms generally relate to muscle coordination and movement. In many cases, parents first notice that their baby is missing milestones—failing, say, to grasp objects or sit up. Diagnosing the problem at an early age can be daunting, since every child develops at his or her own pace. Early intervention, though, which usually involves physical therapy to develop muscles and motor skills, can help a child greatly.

One thing that's important to note: CP does not

generally bring mental disabilities or make a child un-intelligent. Nor does it lower life expectancy in the absence of other factors.

In Amanda's case, the disorder primarily affected the left side of her body. She needed to walk with as-sistance support—leg braces, a cane. She was clever and resourceful, planning ahead when she went some-where. If she and her husband were going on vacation and wanted to stay in a hotel, she tried to reserve a room on the main floor so there would be no stairs to descend in an emergency. Such are the subtle conces-sions one makes to the conditions that constrain our lives and freedom.

As a result of some of these compromises and her sedentary lifestyle, Amanda gained considerable weight; she weighed some 230 pounds at the time her twins were born. Given that she stood about five foot three, that was grossly overweight. More alarming, she was often in pain, even when not exerting herself. Between the cerebral palsy and her weight, her body was under siege.

In 2013, she decided to do something about it and found that gym.

Now, in truth, she was secretly hoping to hear some-thing along the lines of:

*No, sorry. Can't help you. You're beyond any assis-
tance. There's just nothing that can be done. You have
CP; you're overweight. Ain't gonna happen.*

But the exact opposite happened. Amanda met Ken
Crowder, the gym's head of member education and experience. He sat on the floor with her and talked about
exercise and living philosophies, how she might fit into
those philosophies and work on her body, and what a
possible first goal might be.

They came up with wiggling her toes.

You take it for granted. So do I. But it was something Amanda had never been able to do.

Just by chance, the gym that Amanda had gone to
on the advice of a colleague was CrossFit 77, part of the
CrossFit network. This international network of gyms,
founded by Greg Glassman, is based on ideas somewhat
different from traditional exercise facilities and their
cardio and strength-building machines. Their program
revolves around the idea that fitness means increased
functional ability and is not limited to, say, how much
iron you can pump or how fast you can run a mile.

To greatly simplify their philosophy and practices,
exercise at a CrossFit facility involves a wide range of
activities, from classic weight lifting and rowing, for
example, to pushing weighted sleds around a yard. A
high level of intensity—and community—are involved.

Where in a traditional gym clients will generally work on their own or perhaps with a dedicated trainer, the typical CrossFit member is considered part of a team or family. It's a "we're all in this together to succeed" mentality rather than "I do my thing and go home" head. CrossFit also uses a large number of analytics or measurements of time, speed, weight, etc. to track performance. These are built into the program, as opposed to being something an individual at another gym may or may not track on their own.

Functional exercise—the heart of CrossFit—is very similar to many of the techniques teachers working with disabled children use. The more Amanda listened to Ken and his staff, the more she felt the ideas not only made sense but meshed with what she already knew.

But it's one thing to agree on a philosophy and another to live it. So when Crowder told her, "See you tomorrow," her reply was, "Oh, crap."

She kept the words to herself.

It took three weeks before she could walk barefoot on an unstable surface—something most people take for granted, but something Amanda had never done. Standing, sitting—she moved on, strengthening her core muscles, toning her arms, legs, work, work, work. . . .

My kids have inspired me to heal more than anything else in the world. My drive to give them the lives

Chris and I wanted has spurred me on even when I would have otherwise given up. As Amanda shows, this drive is a powerful force of nature.

Roughly six months after starting, Amanda was able to reach her first milestone: taking her boys to the beach.

She didn't stop there.

Her workouts continued. She learned what a burpee was. She learned to jump.

High-intensity exercise—working at a very strong pace and with maximum effort—pushed her beyond what she thought her limits were. She lost weight—a lot of it.

She bought new pants—many times.

Finally, after months of work, she played ball with her kids.

No achievement could be better than that.

But there were more. In 2015, Amanda progressed so far that she took part in a national CrossFit competition at the Working Wounded Games. In truth, she was overwhelmed at the meet. Many of the unconventional events baffled her at first—how do you move a forty-five-pound "Atlas rock" from one point to another without dropping it on your toe?

And when you do that, how do you move a ninety-pounder?

Or flip over a pig (actually a weighted box)?

Easy?

Not if it weighs five hundred pounds. I know I couldn't do it without help.

Her appetite whetted not only by the competition but by the camaraderie she found at the meet, Amanda returned. In 2017, this mom who once couldn't even wiggle her toes took first place in her division.

Her cane? Gathering dust in a closet somewhere. It's been quite a while since she needed it to get around.

As remarkable as Amanda's physical achievements are, they're not the real story here. What's truly remarkable is her decision to help others the way she was helped with something she calls Project Momentum.

Unlike some of the other organizations we're profiling, Project Momentum is not an organized charity—not yet, anyway. (Amanda is working on the process, which involves considerable paperwork and organization.) The project is basically her, with help from her husband, friends, colleagues, and like-minded individuals at gyms and organizations around the area of Charlotte, North Carolina, where she teaches at Belmont Abbey College.

Her checkbook helps out as well. She's funded a lot of the project herself, along with generous in-kind donations from local gyms.

"It's my attempt to pay back the blessing I've had," says Amanda. "To pay back what Crowder and 77 offered me."

Many people with disabilities or other difficulties are reluctant to exercise. They're afraid of being made fun of, afraid of failure.

They're also fearful that their disability means there is no hope for them to live an active life. They may have gone through therapy to assist with coping with the basics, but that's as far as they feel they can go.

Just like Amanda, they think they're beyond help.

"In a world where you're used to being told no," she says, "we try to say yes."

Her nascent organization functions as a conduit for people with disabilities, connecting them to gyms or other facilities depending on their needs. In a typical case, someone with CP might want to see what exercise can do for them, but not know where to start. After contacting Project Momentum either through a referral or the organization's website, they meet with a counselor to evaluate their needs. They are then referred to a gym and a trainer.

The program was working with sixty-seven people when we caught up with Amanda in early 2018. Besides those individuals, Project Momentum has also started kids' programs with about a half dozen kids in each.

Aimed at children with disabilities, these exercise programs are helping about seventy, all told.

The people she's helped have a range of disabilities. Probably because local media coverage has mentioned Amanda's CP, that's the most common affliction. But there's also a seventy-year-old who's recovering from a stroke, a person with autism, an amputee working out with a new limb—there are no real limits on what sort of disabilities qualify a person for aid.

Amanda's assistance is free. In many cases, the gym workouts are also free or provided at a reduced rate, thanks to the enthusiasm and generosity of the local gym owners. This is a big boost: typical gym costs can be relatively high, since one-on-one training is usually an additional cost beyond the gym membership fee. Thirty-minute sessions with a trainer a few times a week quickly add up. Even small charges can be difficult to shoulder for people with disabilities, whose finances as a general rule are even more stretched than most.

Ultimately, Amanda knows she has to get full nonprofit status and build up Project Momentum to succeed in the long term. Given her track record, I have little doubt she'll do just that.

"I'll keep on until they take my credit cards away," she quips.

Besides teaching, being a mom, and running her fledgling organization, Amanda works as a personal trainer and presents a professional conference about once a month. These conferences are aimed at spreading the word about what disabled people can do with their bodies if given the chance and motivation.

Amanda's story wouldn't be complete without at least a nod to her husband, Rob, who has not only encouraged her but is a true partner in their marriage, actively involved in the give-and-take that all moms with busy schedules have to live by. He's also a marathon runner—though so far he hasn't won Amanda over to his particular sport.

Then again, she hasn't won him over to hers. Even when it comes to exercise, there are always boundaries in a successful relationship.

For the most part, someone with a disability doesn't struggle with life so they can act as a motivational guidepost for others. Amanda's physical and intellectual achievements weren't done so people without CP could say, *If she can do it, so can I.* Her goal was to make her life, and the lives of her kids, better.

She's achieved that. And that part of her story is inspiring, certainly, even if inspiration was an unintended by-product. But what is truly worth emulating is the idea behind her program, the notion that she should selflessly share what she learned with others. That's what really good teachers do, and really good teachers are inspiring, because they instruct us and remind us of the American Spirit.

Called to Be a Hero

Mona Ratelle

Not many of us can say we saved a life.

Fewer still can claim to have done it by literally giving part of themselves to someone else.

Mona Ratelle is one of them.

You might not guess that this feisty, straight-shooting San Diego native is a hero, but in 1999, she gave up her kidney to a man she barely knew because . . . well, because it felt like the right thing to do.

The year before, Mona and her husband met Mac and his wife at a Valentine's Day party. The couples hit it off, exchanging stories about how they had met and become a couple. They had good cocktails and a pleasant time.

By all rights, that should have been the end of the story—Mac and his wife went back to New York State where they lived, and Mona went on with her life.

But a few months later, Mona got word that Mac was having serious health problems. His kidney was failing, and he needed dialysis.

I'll pray for him, said Mona.

She did. And that might have been the end of the story as well.

Weeks went by. She heard about him again. The dialysis wasn't going well. Mac needed a kidney transplant. They were testing family and friends to look for a match.

I'll pray for him, said Mona again.

She did. Nightly. And asked others to pray for him as well.

Then more news: Mac was having trouble finding a donor match—someone whose blood and tissue type were close enough that Mac's body would accept that new kidney, rather than attack it as an invader.

Even today, kidney transplants are relatively rare procedures; a few thousand are done each year. While that may sound like a lot, the waiting list is estimated to be more than one hundred thousand.

At the time of Mac's illness, designating your organs

for donation upon death was not a widely discussed option, nor were the procedures as advanced as they are now. And getting kidneys from living patients—especially those who were not related to the patient—was far rarer than today. The procedure was long and not without risks beyond those normally associated with surgery. Still, having a live donor had and still has several advantages for the patient, the most obvious being availability—they don't have to worry about long waiting lists.

Mona prayed again. And kept praying.

Then one day she went to her doctor for a routine checkup, and in the course of the checkup, she found out what her blood type was—something she'd never known. That night, she heard that Mac's relatives had all turned up negative at the early stage of screening: they had the wrong blood type.

When she asked about the blood type, she realized hers matched.

Was God nudging her?

She couldn't escape the feeling that, yes, He was.

Oh, she denied it at first, or tried to, asking others about their blood type. But the feeling inside her grew—*Maybe I'm the one who's supposed to do this.*

"That was all I could think of," she confesses. "Here

I'd been praying for someone else to step up, and I'd gotten a God wink."

She decided she had to act on it. A blood type match was only the first hurdle; she volunteered for further tests.

Truthfully, she didn't think she'd be the right person. But her faith and instincts pushed her to find out.

"I went in," she remembers. "I was such a good match, the doctors thought the test was tainted."

More tests proved that she was perfect.

Would she do it?

Mona balked, wondering if others in her family might need a kidney in the future. But she kept coming back to the idea that she was the one meant to step forward.

"I'm a coward," she confesses now, laughing. "But I knew God was calling me to do this."

If He was, it wasn't because of Mac's religion—neither he nor his wife was Christian. But their beliefs weren't important; Mona's was. And so, she went to New York City to meet with them and the doctors.

Mac's surgeon played devil's advocate, telling her not only of the dangers to her but of the fact that transplants might not work, that Mac might not live very long even with her new kidney. As the conversation went on, it sounded to her like the doctor was trying to talk her out of it.

Mac, sitting nearby, certainly seemed to think so.

"I looked over at Mac. Tears were running down his face," she remembers. "I told the doctor, I don't mean to brag, but I've never had a man refuse anything I've offered."

With a laugh, the doctor agreed to go ahead with the operation.

There was one more complication—the night before the operation, the hotel she was staying at had a fire. Mona and her daughter had to evacuate in their PJs. The emergency left them in the street for hours.

When they didn't show up at the hospital at the appointed time that morning, Mac's wife called the hotel. The clerk told her they had checked out.

Moments later, Mona walked into the ward—still dressed in her pajamas.

Whew.

The surgery went well—for Mac. Mona's recovery was more arduous than she'd thought it would be—a fact she hadn't quite prepared for, having studiously avoided the information the hospital had sent her.

But it worked out. Mona recovered, and Mac thrived, thanks to Mona's kidney—"Little Monie," as he called it.

For sixteen years, a record at the time, Little Monie kept him going. Then another disease took its toll; his transplanted kidney began to fail. Mac luckily found another donor—a man Mona knows only as "Eddie"—whose kidney not only helped Mac but kick-started Mona's donated one as well. Today, Mac lives with two donated kidneys: Little Monie and Big Eddie.

His wife passed away a year or so ago, depriving Mona of a strong friendship that had developed over the years. But the experience has left her more committed to life and her faith.

"I feel honored to have saved someone's life," she says. "I just know this was my purpose. Being a Christian, we're supposed to be there for someone. This is extreme, but how often can you save someone's life?"

If that's what you're called to do, how can you refuse?

Today, there are various mechanisms to arrange to donate your organs after death. Some states even allow you to do it through the auto licensing procedures; check a box, and you're done. The federal government even offers information at www.organdonor.gov.

Checking a box. It doesn't seem like that big a deal, and yet . . . how many of us can say we saved a life?

FOUR
Moving Past Grief

Beyond Our Burdens

Some people seem blessed with a special bliss, destined by God and Fate to glide through life without a blemish or hiccup. They appear privileged to barely know obstacles, to have tragedy be a complete stranger. From a distance, their lives seem an uninterrupted journey of reward, pleasure, and tranquility.

Up close, I'm sure things are very different.

Other people have lives that seem like that not only from a distance but to them as well. I'm not sure they're paying attention, but I'm happy for them nonetheless.

Then there are the rest of us. Every day we face burdens big and small. We see them, feel them, and somehow manage to go on. We stumble, we fall, and somehow we get back to our feet and push on. Most of the things standing in our way are mere annoyances, some random act of inefficiency that gets us off-track—the traffic jam that makes us late for the kids' dismissal, the lost mail that delays the credit card payment. Under the right circumstances, we may not even notice them or their effect.

But sooner or later, these burdens accumulate and weigh us down. They sap our time and energy, making life seem as if it's an uphill slog.

And then, tragedy strikes.

When my husband, Chris, was murdered, I felt as if my soul as well as my body had been pulverized. My despair was so deep that I wished God had taken me as well. And perhaps the only thing that kept me from joining him in heaven was the knowledge that my two children needed me more than ever. They were my only reason for living; thinking of them was the only way I could get out of bed in the morning—and honestly, there were many mornings when, after somehow getting them off to school after only an hour or two of sleep, I retreated back to bed.

I wish I could claim that my experience of that despair provided me with great insights into survival. I wish it had given me a magic formula that I could share with others that would cut short their suffering. If I could say that my great tragedy enabled others to avoid or at least shorten their own despair, surely my grief would be justified.

But no magic formula revealed itself to me. No words of wisdom made it possible to fill the void. Every day was a struggle. Many things and people helped: Family. Friends. Grief counseling. Prayer. Color therapy.

Normal things—exercise.

Extraordinary things—the massive outpouring of sympathy from strangers who were touched by Chris, either in person or through the book, the movie, or the stories about him.

Each helped in some small way, but none were a magic formula for expelling pain.

But I got through. And I learned this: in the worst of times, if we can survive another day, that's enough. If we can do even a small healthy thing to heal, even better.

I outlined the path I took in *American Wife*, so I won't overshare again here. What's important is that the path was my own. Even the detours were of use in some way or another. Looking back, I know there was progress each day, even if at the time I thought I was sliding back. Because sometimes stopping and resting is just as important as pushing for progress.

One of the key events in my road back from the deep pit of grief was participating in the Patriot Tour with Marcus Luttrell, something Chris had committed to prior to his murder. Marcus and the others were enormously kind, telling me I didn't have to join them, or if I wanted, I could appear without making a speech. But that just didn't feel right. It seemed to me that the right thing to do was to honor Chris's commitment—that was what our marriage had always been about. When he was alive, he would back me up and I would back him up. Wasn't this the same thing?

Now, to that point, giving speeches wasn't my thing. I don't consider myself shy, exactly, but I would have understood if the organizers said something like, *No offense, Mrs. Kyle, but we're going to have several thousand people and, well, speeches are for the professionals.*

But they didn't. Maybe they just couldn't turn down a widow. In any event, I went and gave the speech.

Chris was with me that day. He wasn't a polished speaker himself—he'd started talking to groups only after the book came out, and even then most of his remarks were brief and off the cuff. But they were always, always from the heart.

I remembered that and took it as my example. I could certainly speak from the heart.

And I could speak about Chris, who then as always weighed heavily on it.

So, I did. I talked about his spirit and how we need heroes in everyday life—something he truly believed. I talked about how our veterans are among the country's greatest asset, how they give our country a blank check, and how we should honor them by doing our own bit for the nation. It was about patriotism and community—values dear to Chris's heart and dear to our family.

Maybe my first talks weren't the greatest ever. Definitely they weren't. But by the end of the first night, I realized that my words and Chris's spirit had moved the crowd. It wasn't me. It was the message—resilience, good and evil, the need to pay forward acts of kindness, the value of life and love. The words resonated with the people there because they, too, believed in those values.

Their strength jump-started me. I was able to push on, push myself, and then share that message with others. I can't say that I made it past grief, repaired all the damage that had been done, or even filled the vast hole Chris's murder left in my heart. But by learning to share, I learned to move with my loss.

Some of these stories are also stories of grief and loss. But they're also very positive. I can't call them happy stories—loss is loss, and I know for myself I would gladly trade anything and everything I've done since Chris's death to have one more day with him, even a single moment.

Yet these stories of survival inspire me like few others.

Finding Meaning in Loss

Lorraine Ash

L ate May 1999.

The new millennium was ahead, and the future was bright for journalist and editor Lorraine Ash. The head of the features department at an important daily newspaper in New Jersey, Lorraine was a successful professional with a long list of achievements. She had a strong marriage to her husband, Bill, who supported and encouraged her career. She also had deep roots in the community where she lived and worked.

And, at forty years old, she was nine months pregnant, eagerly waiting to give birth to her first child.

Lorraine and Bill had picked out her names. Her first would be Victoria, a tribute to several of Lorraine's family members. Her middle name, Helen, would honor Bill's side of the family. Bill had a pet name for her: "Sweetlet."

They had everything: a room, a crib, toys, and, most important, dreams. They mused with friends and family on her possible future—a romance writer? A celebrity fit to visit Buckingham Palace for high tea with the Queen?

Lorraine was deep into planning how to juggle the demanding dual roles of manager and mom. Everything was ready, but little Sweetlet was taking her time. Lorraine would visit the room they had set up as a nursery, imagining her daughter's future, dream-living her family's coming years, and thinking encouraging thoughts in hopes of speeding the baby along.

Finally, about two weeks past her due date, Lorraine's labor pains began. It was a Tuesday, early June. The pains were still a bit irregular, but there was no mistaking what they were—every mother knows, even the first time.

Mom-to-Be made her way to the doctor's office with her husband, excited, of course, but logical, determined, completely in control . . . at least to the extent that such things can be controlled. The office was only a short distance from their home and the hospital. The plan was simple: get the checkup, then ride across the street to the delivery ward and their new future.

The doctor asked how she felt.

Fine, she replied.

Then, in casual aside, Lorraine mentioned that she hadn't felt the baby move recently.

No?

No.

Are you sure?

. . .

Slowly but inexorably, the world around Lorraine and her husband began to change. The obstetrician put her on the examining table, began a Doppler exam, listened for a heartbeat.

He didn't hear one.

He spoke softly, calm but urgent. It was too soon to jump to conclusions. His equipment there was not as powerful as the hospital's. There were so many variables, so many possibilities. . . .

A deep quiet settled around the expectant mother and father as they made their way to the hospital. Life now moved in excruciatingly slow motion. Sensations stung, digging deep into memory—a cold floor, cold instruments, cold air.

Grief had already begun to stalk them. Birth became death. Lorraine knew before she heard the words from the doctor. Victoria had died in her womb.

Where there is life, there must also be death, but I know of exactly no one comforted by that simple and cold logic. And in this day of advanced medical care, wonderous drugs, and encyclopedic knowledge about nearly every topic, it is understandable if we are stunned by simple, cold statistics: each year some twenty-four thousand babies die before they are born. That represents roughly 1 percent of all pregnancies.

Stillbirths—the medical term for a birth that ends *after* twenty weeks of gestation—occur for a variety of reasons. Most common are birth defects, problems with the placenta or umbilical cord, and of course the mother's health. Miscarriages—defined as a pregnancy that ends *before* twenty weeks—are even more common. While statistics are elusive, some estimates go as high as 25 percent.

And yet, both events were rarely spoken of for decades. Yes, doctors and other medical professionals might warn mothers about proper nutrition and exercise and give them a list of dos and don'ts, but for the most part, that was as far as it went.

Lately, that has begun to change. While the topics

are still uncomfortable for many, there is now more information available both on the web and from hospitals, clinics, and doctors. There are counseling services and peer groups devoted to preterm loss of babies. The grief of mothers and fathers who lose children before or at birth is now recognized; with that recognition has come new methods of healing.

Lorraine is a big part of the reason.

Lorraine and Bill's baby had died after an infection caused Victoria to have a bowel movement; her amniotic fluid had become contaminated, in effect poisoning her.

"It wasn't that anything had gone wrong, which is the insidious part of it," says Lorraine now. The infection had come from a type of strep, called Group B, that is extremely common among women of childbearing age; many live life with it, and it has no effect. Except in pregnancy.

Mothers-to-be were routinely tested at thirty-seven weeks when Lorraine was expecting. She went through the test and "passed"—meaning no infection was found. But for various reasons, Group B strep infections can occur later on, after the test but before birth. At the time (and even now in many places), medical protocols did not require additional checking.

Detected, the disease is relatively straight-forward

to deal with, though anything that threatens life at an early stage can be treacherous. Undetected, it can be deadly for both mother and child.

Lorraine subsequently caught the disease herself, and besides the pain of both grief and a C-section, she spent the days after Victoria's death struggling to recover. Pain, grief—it was overwhelming.

And yet, she didn't give in to despair. Somehow, she found the strength to struggle and claw back. Trained as a journalist, she began recording details and random thoughts in a rough and informal journal.

It was not an easy path. There were reverses, stalls. Some of those closest to her had a hard time accepting the loss and an even harder time talking about it. The stress and pain didn't stop there. Lorraine and Bill experienced and expressed their grief in different ways. Ultimately, their marriage became stronger, but surely both would have traded anything, even their own lives, for a healthy birth.

It's not surprising that Lorraine explored spiritual possibilities across a variety of teachings, but she did so with a broad and open mind, as much a student as a believer. Her Catholic upbringing was important, but more as a ladder or even a springboard. From Rabbi Harold Kushner (*When Bad Things Happen to Good People*) to Jesuit theologian Pierre Teilhard de Chardin to

Buddhists to New Age philosophers, Lorraine investigated and considered a wide range of spiritual thoughts and perspectives.

"I remember being in a Buddhist temple, with an old Vietnamese monk and a translator," she says, "and asking him, 'What does this mean in your tradition?'"

She wanted every perspective she could get. One constant: she realized that spirituality must be a positive force, not a negative. Her baby's death was not a punishment from God for something she or Bill had done.

By Christmas, Lorraine had begun to rearrange her mental life. She readjusted her perspective on her personal tragedy as well; she was able to accept the kindness of others, something that had been impossible in the immediate shadow of Victoria's passing.

Most important, the writer wrote. Despite returning to her full-time job at the newspaper, she felt compelled to tell Victoria's story as well, on her own time and in her own way. It was a story that she realized could be told only in first-person, with the pronoun *I* rather than *her* or *them*.

She had to go inside herself and speak from that center, rather than being a mere observer. This was something she had always told herself she would never do: journalists write from the outside, always; they don't want to infect the narrative with their own opinions and feelings.

But here those opinions and feelings were the biggest part of the story.

Lorraine transformed her journal and ongoing experiences into a wonderful and eloquent book entitled *Life Touches Life: A Mother's Story of Stillbirth and Healing*. She takes readers through the painful and difficult experience of grief, acceptance, and the first hopeful signs of peace.

"The act of writing helped me make sense of it," she says now. "You want to come to some sort of understanding, and writing helps."

When she was finished, she made an amazing if depressing discovery: no one wanted to publish it.

Not because it wasn't well-written. On the contrary, she received many compliments. It was the subject. Even in the early days of the twenty-first century, people simply didn't talk about stillbirths or miscarriages. Certainly not as openly and candidly as she did in the book.

Many authors, of course, experience rejection. But the excuse in this case was unique.

It wasn't as if there was no market for a book that would help others through the same experience of loss, grief, and recovery. In purely commercial terms, there was a large market and little competition.

But there was a simple answer—though generally unspoken—to the business logic:

Dead-baby books don't sell.

One author told her it was a great exercise in dealing with depression but not something others would read. Another was far blunter. "Stillbirth is something that didn't happen. Go write about something that happened.'"

The book was neither about "dead babies" nor an attempt to exorcise depression. Publishers and others in the business were misinterpreting both the market and the need of grieving families, along with Lorraine's motivations. What she wanted to write about was healing—and the simple fact that these unfortunate, heart-rending tragedies are still part of our lives, even if they go unmentioned.

And, maybe most important, some of these tragedies can be prevented with different medical practices.

"You just have to hold your center" and get on with it, says Lorraine about her focus and relentless pursuit of publication in the face of rejection and negativity. She eventually did find a publisher, who released the book in 2004. She'd been right about the book's market; many women, and a good number of men, who had been through the same experiences wanted to read it.

What she hadn't predicted, though, was the outpouring of emotion. She and her husband were inundated with messages of sympathy. People sought her out to share their own stories.

Lorraine was invited to speak formally and informally all across the country, sharing Victoria's story and at the same time raising awareness of the realities of stillbirth. She attended medical conferences and spoke to nurses and other professionals about what her experience had been like. She discovered to her surprise that nurses were generally not trained to deal with patients who experienced a stillbirth; in fact, there was precious little information about it at all in most medical textbooks.

Lorraine's talks had a profound effect on raising awareness in the medical profession about how to help families. There were also many spiritual moments, not just for her and Bill but also for other women and families who had lost a baby. At a session in Las Vegas, some five hundred people stood on a mountainside as a multitude of candles floated in a pool, blazing in the night, each one a silent tribute to a deceased infant. Bill brought his trumpet to his lips and played "Somewhere Over the Rainbow," his own eloquent tribute to the dead.

The outpouring of thanks from readers and people she met was heartfelt and overwhelming. "Your book was given to me by a dear friend when our dear son

Dylan was stillborn," wrote one correspondent. "I have read so many of the chapters over and over again, and I wanted to thank you for helping me carry on so many times when I felt like giving up."

"I just finished reading your profoundly touching book," said another in an email. "As I read the last page, before closing it, I kissed it. . . . One and a half years ago . . . I gave birth to a most beautiful baby boy weighing 9 pounds 2 ounces, not alive, delivered by cesarean section due to a sudden unexplained placental abruption. I lost more than half my blood volume. Thank God my life was spared. I hold this perfect baby of mine every second of my day. I have several girls, thank God. We waited fifteen years for my beautiful boy. Although my heart has grown to hold this pain, I see my little boy before me every moment of my life. . . . Reading your book has been nothing less than therapy for me."

The book tour extended to four years. "Exhausting," she admits, "but also so rewarding."

Lorraine's courage in sharing her story inspired others. Along the way, medical professionals listened, adding and modifying training and procedures to help grieving parents. Regulations governing pre-birth practices like screenings began to change.

Slowly, though. Very, very slowly.

One of the surprising deficiencies Lorraine and others discovered was the lack of hard data on stillborn deaths. Her own state, New Jersey, didn't collect any. Such tracking is routine for other causes of death. This meant that there was no way for prospective parents to reliably know if conditions at a particular hospital might be problematic—and also no way for regulatory agencies or even other doctors to realize there was a possible problem so they could correct it.

Also amazing—at least to those of us who have had no experience with it—medical protocols do not call for additional testing after the first test for strep at thirty-seven weeks, even though it's been known since at least the 1930s that the bacteria is not only a potent danger but also extremely prevalent.

Lorraine testified before a number of groups, including the Centers for Disease Control (CDC), the nation's top health agency, suggesting that the protocols be changed. In New Jersey, her home state, she joined a fight to introduce and pass a law not only mandating autopsies and tracking of stillborn deaths but also directing state health officials to set standards for sensitive care when a child is stillborn.

Following a long, drawn-out process—not so much a fight but a slow crawl toward dealing with the deficiency—the bill was passed and signed into law in

January 2014 as the Autumn Joy Stillbirth Research and Dignity Act. Named after a stillborn baby, the law could serve as a model for others across the nation. But advocates, including Lorraine, have noted that many of the provisions have not yet been implemented. She and the others are continuing to put pressure on the legislature and the hospitals to comply.

The spiritual journey that Lorraine took after the death of her child "drives everything I do," she says today. The journey is not easy to summarize—the best account of it is in her book—but it certainly went beyond any single denomination; the result was a deep spirituality that is inclusive rather than exclusive.

"It's the way I view life," she says. It caused many changes in her perspective: the difference she sees between Nature and God, the spiritual well inside all of us. The need to "get outside" the drama of trauma.

"Now I understand," she says.

In the best possibility, the searing intensity of grief gives way to a stasis, a state not necessarily of relief or even the absence of pain but of tentative peace. For many of us, real peace comes from purpose. Regaining purpose—helping others get through what you went through, changing things for the better so that what you experienced will not be duplicated, simply doing things for other people without the need for praise or compensation—for many, purpose becomes the path to personal renewal.

And it touches the deepest strains of the American Spirit—perseverance, resilience, charity.

Lorraine has reached a point where there is a valuable sense of peace. She and her husband can talk about their daughter with a bit of whimsy—gently making fun of themselves for making her "perfect" in their fantasies of what she would be doing now had she lived. That doesn't mean that the ache has disappeared completely and certainly not that they disrespect her or themselves. But it does show that they have found the strength to persevere.

While Bill has continued his musical career, Lorraine has shifted her focus away from journalism. Along with her husband, she now works with other writers, both amateur and professional, helping them write memoirs or prepare works for publication. The pair have started a small publishing house of their own, concentrating on memoirs and inspirational stories. Lorraine also holds writing seminars; many of the attendees have gone through various traumas, and she works with them to get beyond.

"Many people are inside the trauma. They have to get outside it," she explains, adding that knowing the larger context of one's life can often help. Writing can mean healing for many: "When you push the story through the narrative form and infuse it with new insight, it changes the story and it changes the storyteller. And we call that change healing."

Lorraine's own story continues to touch people deeply. Much of the correspondence she gets now is from people who say the book helped save the life of their baby—an incredible tribute to Lorraine, Bill, and their daughter.

And to this day, Victoria gets birthday cards and gifts from strangers. It's a wonderful tribute, and one sign that the American Spirit shared with others can take on a life of its own. It can even bring life where life has been lost. That is true power.

Among other organizations devoted to improving procedures for dealing with Group B strep and preventing stillbirths is the Jesse Cause, named after a little boy who nearly lost his life when born. Information about the group and the cause are available on the web at www.thejessecause.org.

Don't Be Inspired;
Be Exceptional

Barbara Allen

He was the answer to her prayers, the man the college coed met not two weeks after feeling so desolate she prayed to God she'd meet someone nice—an echo of what I did before I met my future husband, Chris. The moment Lou Allen took Barbara's hand as they were introduced in a bar, she knew he was the one, even though she'd come to the bar at her sister's insistence to be fixed up with someone else.

Within months, they were talking about what their wedding song would be. They were married in the snow and ice in March 1996, picked up by a horse and carriage hired to take them to church.

"The poor horse was so skinny he couldn't lug us all up the hill," Barbara remembers, "so everyone but me had to get out and walk. We laughed our asses off as a tape played a constant loop of "Going to the Chapel" and a line of cars piled up behind us."

Tight finances, a miscarriage, 9/11—they got through the worst with mutual love and support, enduring and even flourishing. Lou found a dream job in a local school district and became a popular science teacher, bringing stability to their financial situation. On Barbara's thirty-second birthday, they celebrated not only the passing of another year but what they justifiably thought was a rich and wonderful life. Four kids, a great marriage, a nice house in New York's beautiful Hudson Valley. What could be better?

There was one slight complication—besides being a well-loved teacher, Lou was also an officer in the National Guard. And that night, of all nights, he told Barbara he would be deploying to Iraq as a member of New York's historic 42nd Infantry Division, known as the Rainbow Division.

Most servicepeople, especially lieutenants like Lou, don't have an option—the Army says go, you go. But in this case, he had a little bit of leeway, which must have made the decision harder for Barbara to accept. A friend at the 42nd needed a man with exactly his expertise and had asked if he wanted to transfer and come to Iraq to help straighten out what looked to be a mess in the unit's supply system.

Lou agreed. There were many reasons—his own unit was likely to deploy soon anyway, and this looked like it would take him away from his family for less time—but the most important reason was his love of our country and his devotion to duty. I'm sure it didn't outweigh his love for his family, but I know from my own experience that husbands and fathers who sign up for the military believe they can balance both and that service to America doesn't contradict their love and responsibilities to their family.

It's one thing to believe that and another to live with it easily. A lot of the burden fell to Barbara. Their oldest child was barely of school age; their youngest still in diapers. And separation aside, Iraq in 2005 was a very dangerous place.

But Lou was enthusiastic, and there was never a question of her talking him out of it. He had joined the National Guard in 1998, and ever since the 9/11 attacks, Barbara knew in her heart that someday he would have to deploy as part of the war on terrorism.

That day came several months later, as the wheels of Army bureaucracy turned very slowly. On May 1, Barbara and Lou took the kids to their favorite pancake restaurant, then with tears and hugs bid good-bye. Lou set off to the new unit's post; roughly two weeks later, he flew to Iraq.

On June 8, Barbara woke up at 6:00 a.m. to a loud knock at the front door. There she saw a sight every wife of every deployed soldier dreads—three men in Class A military uniforms who could be at her home at this hour for only one terrible purpose: to tell her that her husband had been killed.

There were extra complications in Lou's case that made Barbara's ordeal even more difficult. He and his commanding officer were killed in what authorities suspected was a "fragging incident"—an assassination by a fellow soldier.

Army investigators soon charged a soldier with the murder. Nearly two and a half years later, following a long ordeal for Barbara, the man would be deemed not guilty by a court-martial. No one else has been charged in the murder; the case remains open.

By the time I met her, Barbara was far from the shell-shocked young mother who opened the door to so much grief that day in 2005.

That first time I met her still stands out. She and a group of other Gold Star women were attending an event connected with the Miss America pageant where I was to be a judge. She had heard of my own story and wanted to meet me, but she was so shy that she texted Jim—she'd met him and his wife about a year before—and asked if he thought . . . I don't know, that maybe I would bite her head off if she said hi.

He assured her I wouldn't, texted me, and a few minutes later we were introduced. Barbara went on to introduce me to some of the Gold Star mothers with her. I was impressed by their strength. Like me, they had all lost their spouses; our grief and recoveries were our bond.

We talked together for well over an hour, before I had to leave for other appointments.

Possibly I was a little late for those. But as many people who know me well will tell you, I believe some things are more important than the clock.

What struck me at that first meeting was how poised and energetic Barbara was. Here was a woman who had gone through a deep tragedy, a mom carrying a full load on her shoulders raising four boys while helping others, and yet she was full of life and strength. I sensed immediately that she was the kind of person who attracts a network of helpers around them.

You never really get over a loss like Barbara's; at best, you find a way to keep living. Barbara has done that and more. She's launched a project to encourage others to overcome their own tragedies and reach out and help others.

Not that it was easy. After the trial exonerated the man she'd come to believe had killed her husband, she fell into a deep hole. Things were made worse when, seeking some support, she rushed into a bad relationship.

"When I got myself together," says Barbara today, "I was finally able to look behind me and analyze what had gone on. I realized that once I turned my mind-set around and got rid of the beliefs that were holding me down, I could move on."

The beliefs were a range of bad feelings that many people go through after losing a spouse: worthlessness, victimhood, a feeling that they are no good or unworthy.

A feeling that the universe or God Himself is against us.

A belief that nothing we do will make any difference.

A conviction that life is hopeless, and other people are all part of the problem.

And then there's the "No" voice inside, saying nothing they do will work, that things will never get better, that it doesn't even make sense to try. No, no, no.

But back to Barbara.

Barbara struggled to carry on with her life after Lou's death. For months, she was in a bad place—depressed, desperate. As solace, she fell into a relationship that seemed not only stable but potentially healing—only to discover that the man she thought was strong was using her and had his own demons.

Instead of leaving, she sank deeper into the hole. She told a few close friends but took no action. She felt emotionally abused and believed she was being manipulated in a seemingly endless cycle. Finally, a friend told her that she would continue to listen only if Barbara was willing to do something about the situation.

"I had to realize that I was valuable enough to save," Barbara says now. She also had to realize that her kids didn't deserve to suffer because she was unwilling to take her life into her own hands.

In essence, she had to fight. For herself and her kids. She was more than valuable enough for that.

After everything I've been through, losing my husband, the trial, everything, you're going to take me down?

No way.

No way!

Barbara finally broke off the relationship and started rebuilding her life. She got a job working with veterans. The more she did for herself and her family, the better she felt. The more she helped others, the more she attracted the kind of people who didn't need help.

Gradually, she climbed out of the hole. The dark fog that had enveloped her spirit lifted. She found a new boyfriend. She found new joy and times of laughter with her kids. She kept moving forward with her life. Along the way, she began reading stories about women and men who had gone through difficult times and persevered.

Inspired, she read more.

Then she started meeting some of the people in those stories. Her spirit soared.

Like me, and I'm sure like many of you, Barbara found the news she saw on television, in newspapers, and on the internet very negative by contrast. Everything seemed political, and everything political was a flash point; more, it was anger-inducing. Bile begat bile; tempers escalated to a boiling point.

One day she mentioned this to her boyfriend, who agreed.

What can we do about this? they asked each other.

In the past, Barbara might have said nothing. But having turned the corner from darkness to hope, she found a positive response.

Let's put the stories out there.

And so, she and her boyfriend, Dan, established a website called American Snippets (www.American Snippets.com), with a sister Facebook page (www.face book.com/americansnippets).

"Don't just be inspired. Be exceptional," says Barbara. "Our mission is to provide a meaningful platform that encourages national pride, promotes the American Dream, emphasizes the upshot of giving back, and supports all who honorably serve."

The site includes podcasts of interviews and articles that Barbara has done with a variety of people whom she finds inspiring. It's a wide range—authors and actors, entrepreneurs, disabled veterans—anyone they meet or hear about with a positive message is potentially a subject.

And then there are the stories like the one of Heather and David Mosher.

The day David planned to propose they marry, Heather found out she had breast cancer. He went through with the proposal, and she accepted—but their lives were quickly consumed by the ordeal of treatment, surgeries, and chemo. Heather's condition deteriorated rapidly, but they went ahead with the wedding, even as she was confined to a hospital bed and had to speak her vows through an oxygen mask.

It was the happiest day of her life, but it was also her last—she succumbed to the disease eighteen hours later.

The wedding, Heather's courage, and that of her husband made their love story one of inspirational triumph for those around them.

"The common theme in our stories is that everyone is giving back in some way," says Barbara. "We want to reverse the trend of all this negative news. . . . I felt this country was really doomed, because the only things I read were bad."

Some of the stories are of people they knew or have met in their travels. Others Barbara contacted out of the blue after hearing about them. The stories—told in podcasts and videos as well as in articles—are little sprinkles of good news in an often dark landscape.

"Personally, I carry something away from each one I interview," says Barbara. "I'm hooked on it—what am I going to come away with?" she wonders before each interview.

Sometimes it's a little quip. Other times it's a kind of role modeling that comes through when she asks herself what the person she interviewed would do in a similar situation.

"We're still figuring out the dynamics of it all," she notes. Some of the web stories will get hundreds of shares; others none. They've revised the site, updating and reorganizing—everything is a work in progress.

The stories of inspiration Barbara heard convinced her to do more than simply retell them.

"It's great to be inspired and maybe smile for an hour, but inspiration is valueless unless you do something with it," she says. She'd often been inspired by a speech or a story—only to crash later when she returned to the real world.

Inspire people *and* give them tools to do something with that inspiration—that was the way to help them move on.

"I started trying to encourage groups [helping Gold Star wives and mothers] to put hands-on things into their events," she says. "Self-defense workshops. That was huge to me, both for the physical aspect and the mind-set. There's a psychology involved."

The psychology is simple: your life is worth fighting for. And the physical activity is practical on many levels.

But the organizations she spoke to were reluctant to offer those sorts of programs. So, with the help of her friends and boyfriend, she put on her own event.

With support from the nonprofits Got Your Back and the Committee for the Families of War Veterans, along with help from ShopRite and in-kind donations,

Barbara set up a weekend that would provide both inspiration and some practical tools. It was aimed at military families, especially—though not exclusively—widows.

Military families often face a double loss when a spouse dies. Not only do they lose their loved one, but they also may be hard-pressed to find a support network. Service families move often, which can make friendships tenuous. At the same time, many women with young families have devoted themselves to raising children. Some lack job experience, but many others have simply taken time to put their family first. Until the people hiring see a lapse in employment to manage a home as valuable, these women will continue to face insult and injury as they work to support their family after the loss of a bread-winning spouse.

Barbara enlisted the help of professionals who volunteered their time to help educate others. She signed up an entrepreneur to talk about starting businesses in practical as well as inspirational terms. She found a martial artist who would give some basic self-defense instruction. She lined up a real estate broker to talk about how to get into that industry and a movement instructor to add some basic physical fitness ideas and practice.

She held the program in a rented house in a small

town not far from where she lives. Ten women were selected—Barbara wanted to make sure people attending were likely to benefit. The mix blended widows with Gold Star moms and a fiancée. One had lost her spouse just three months before. They all shared a common goal of doing something positive with their lives.

"I was so impressed by how everyone just jumped in and went with it," she says. Different backgrounds, conditions, they all supported each other. Most slept in a large room, slumber-party style.

Three of the women have begun serious careers in real estate investing—a bit of a surprise for Barbara, who wasn't sure what to expect out of the first session.

"We want to continue doing these events, and learn from each one," says Barbara, who was planning on a new one for later in 2018 when we talked to her.

There are limits. Neither Barbara nor her boyfriend plan on starting a full-blown nonprofit; it involves so much work that they fear they would be consumed. They're looking for a mix of helping others while living their lives for themselves and their own families.

It's a good strategy for us all to follow.

"I know if I had been able to recognize my own strength, that guy would never have gotten past my front door," she says, looking back on her life since widowhood. But the dark hole of grief robbed her of that strength—just as it has robbed other women in the same position. Her goal now is to help others recognize their strength and give them the tools to stand up for themselves, literally and figuratively.

Helping Families Recover

Erin's House

The grief when you lose a loved one is almost unbearable. As adults, we struggle to cope. Even with help, the process is long and painful, with many twists and turns. But what about young children? What do they go through when they lose a parent or sibling?

Not only do they lack adult tools to deal with loss, depending on their age they may not even understand the most basic aspects of what they are going through. Aside from sheer anger or outright despair, most will lack the ability to articulate what they feel. We may call them "resilient," but often that's a function of our own ignorance about their grief and how they process or hide it.

Until very recently, programs devoted specifically to helping very young children get over the loss of a parent or sibling or other close family member were nonexistent. That was certainly the case in 1987, when five-year-old Erin Farragh died. Her death touched the Fort Wayne, Indiana, community deeply, but perhaps no one felt the loss as painfully as her younger siblings.

A family friend, Tracie Martin, and a group of women from the Junior League realized how difficult a time the children had had. That experience inspired them to help other families by starting a program specifically aimed at helping children grieve in a group setting. They named it Erin's House, in honor of the little girl who died.

It was a unique idea at the time—there were maybe a few dozen centers devoted to grieving children in the country. Today, there are ten times that—though helping children outside of traditional one-on-one and family counseling settings is still somewhat rare. There is still a misperception that very young children, especially if they are not yet school-age, don't really grieve.

That is not true.

"You go to the funeral, and little Johnny is sitting in the corner with a coloring book," says Erin's House executive director Debbie Meyer. "People say, oh, they'll be all right; they're too young to know what is going on. But those little ears hear everything. They know exactly what is going on."

Kids are amazingly perceptive, and while they can be very resilient, they are always affected by tragedy. Even when parents attempt to keep information from them—which is often the case when someone dies because of a homicide or suicide—the children generally know exactly what happened. Being able to express their feelings, however, can be extremely difficult, even though that is often a necessary step to dealing with grief and preventing it from crippling their own lives.

"Kids deserve the truth," says Debbie. "Unresolved grief can result in all kinds of things," from truancy to far worse.

Erin's House exists to try to head off those problems.

Some grief centers are faith-based. Others are primarily places for one-on-one counseling. Erin's House works with peer-based programs, which is to say that groups of children gather with trained counselors and talk about how they feel, what happened to their loved ones, and in many cases just about normal kid stuff.

There are tearful moments, and even precious ones. Like this one, from not too long ago:

In the room for three-to-six-year-olds, the kids gathered around the table in a circle and took turns introducing themselves and speaking. (Taking turns is encouraged by a device called a *talking stick*. It's a great idea, dating back to some North American Indian tribes. Basically, there is one stick, which is held by the person talking. He or she can speak as long as they want; the stick is then passed on or returned to the center of the circle, where the next person can take it. It's an easy way of reinforcing the idea of "one person at a time" for children without getting cranky about it.)

This was Tommy's first visit, and he spoke first, introducing himself. (Tommy is not his real name; we've changed it for privacy's sake.)

"I'm Tommy," he said. "My dad died."

He passed the stick to the girl next to him, who said her mother died. And so on around the room.

"Why are you people all copying me?" Tommy burst out as the stick came back to him.

The facilitator patiently explained that they weren't—everyone in the room had lost someone close to them. Tommy was stunned—he literally didn't know that other children also experienced loss.

That made sense to him. No one in his class at school had lost their mother or father. When he sat in the school cafeteria for lunch, none of his friends at the table had lost a parent or anyone close to them. Worse, for the most part, they'd stopped talking to him—not because they didn't like him but because they simply didn't know what to say. A lot of the adults in his life were the same way.

Now he was in a room with other kids—and two adult facilitators—who had gone through many of the same things he had.

Did this instantly cure his grief? Of course not. Did it make it easier to bear? We can only guess at that—but obviously something positive was going on, because after the session he told his mom that he wanted to go back. I know from Chris's and my own experience that there is tremendous value in simply knowing you aren't alone. I had no idea how big that is until I experienced it myself.

While we often think of home as a "safe place," for grieving children, it can be a place full of land mines, at least when it comes to talking about loss. If Dad cries when they start talking about missing Mom, they may feel they shouldn't talk about her at all. The grieving center becomes a safe place to express those feelings— and a place where they can learn that they're not really hurting their dad.

Children's grief can take different and unusual forms. Children in some of the groups have spoken about having lost a pet goldfish—but in reality, there was no goldfish; he or she was talking about losing a loved one in a way that was easier or safer for them to express.

Besides the group rooms, there are special rooms for different moods or activities: a quiet room, with stars on its ceiling where children can remember their loved ones; a volcano room, where a kid can explode in anger if he or she feels the need. There's even a hospital room, which is designed to look exactly like a hospital with a bed and medical equipment. Kids get to play at being a doctor or patient, making the sometimes-scary things one finds in a hospital not quite so scary.

At the end of each session, everyone joins together for what is called a hand squeeze—a giant circle where everyone physically reassures each other that someone cares.

The program isn't just for preschool and elementary-age kids. Teenagers can feel loss very deeply, even if it occurred several years before. It's often the little things, or seemingly little things, that can provoke the most hurt. A girl getting ready for the prom without her mom to help her pick out a dress, a boy learning to drive without Dad to share advice—those moments can sting worst of all after the initial shock and recovery periods.

"This is a way for the kids to talk and share memories," says Debbie.

Friendships often start at Erin's House, and there's even been one marriage between children who went through the program.

Aside from weekly programs, the group runs three weekend camps throughout the year, kind of mini-vacations where families can make connections with others who have had similar experiences.

There is also an adult group for parents, aimed at sharing tools for dealing with the "new normal." Counselors also provide phone assistance during the day. Besides six full-timers and four part-time employees who have degrees in the field, there is an army of volunteers trained as facilitators for the programs. Most of the volunteers have experienced profound grief themselves. One caveat: while they go through an extensive training program, they do not provide counseling themselves.

Erin's House staffers present assemblies for schools at no charge. Sometimes these are prompted by tragedies—a car accident claiming the lives of high school students, for example.

"Part of it is explaining to the kids that they can still play and have fun," says Debbie. Sometimes we need to be reminded that it's not disrespectful to go on living while still remembering the dead.

It's also important to explain that there are many ways of expressing grief—some people cry; some don't. Some react immediately; others take a long time. Some deaths might be a trigger point for grief about other losses, multiplying the hurt and complicating the recovery.

"All of these feelings are normal," says Debbie. That's the most important message.

The programs cater to the school's needs. Some simply want to get back to normal as quickly as possible. In other cases, the counselors are available after presentations to talk in-depth with anyone who feels the need.

Besides traditional counseling methods, staff members employ strategies like grief activities—say, crafting simple items such as bracelets or key chains to commemorate the loss of friends. And then there are the marshmallow shooters—kids literally shooting marshmallows back and forth, sharing laughs as they talk about how much their friend used to like to do the same.

"It's a way for them to share memories and talk

about it," says Debbie. "Sometimes it's hard to talk about, especially at home."

One of the things that impressed me about the building was that it felt very much like a home, not a counseling center. There's pizza in the kitchen and fun and games out back.

I've learned that there's so much power in knowing that you're not alone in your grief. Erin's House does that in a very organic way, trying many different approaches for the many different people. When you don't have a specific solution for a problem, you can become the solution for the problem—I felt that when I walked through the door.

I know true healing comes from different avenues. Every room seemed to hold a different path toward healing—the room where you could throw things, the room where you could meditate. The room for crafts, where creativity helps foster solace. And then the room where kids learn that grief doesn't have to stop you from playing and having a good time.

By helping someone else you can help yourself at the same time. It was so impressive to find that many of the people helping others there had been through grief themselves. No map can show you which road to take to heal yourself, but traveling and sharing your choices with others can help you find peace.

When I visited, the kids and staff let me join in a simple ceremony releasing balloons in memory of their loved ones. It took me back to the day we did that for Chris. It's a small yet meaningful gesture, a way of re-membering yet letting go at the same time. I couldn't help but think of all the good things these young people will accomplish, thanks to the efforts of their parents, staff, and peers.

At Erin's House, there really is no time limit on how long kids can come. The end comes when they them-selves decide to move on.

Baseball practice is more important?

Great. That means the program has been successful.

If there's a trigger point down the line, the kids are welcome back. Most don't, except perhaps to visit. Generally, kids average two visits a month. They stay between eighteen and twenty-four months on aver-age, though certain kinds of deaths seem to take much longer to process. Children who have lost parents in homicides, which generally involve trials and many other events that provoke memories, may stay for three or four years.

Four families and the basement of a church—that's where the program started. Now there's a fourteen-thousand-square-foot building that the organization owns outright, with 660 families helped a year. Families are never charged for the services; all the money for the $800,000 annual budget comes from donations, grants, and fund-raisers. One of them is an annual Common Bond breakfast, where I was honored to be invited as a guest speaker.

"When the kids are first walking up to Erin's House, they're very timid and hanging on to Mom," says Debbie. "When they're done that first night, they don't want to leave."

Debbie's involvement with Erin's House came about through a series of coincidences—lucky ones, we'd say. She was working as a marketing executive with a local firm and considering relocating when another executive who was on the Erin's House board insisted she interview for the job as executive director. Though very reluctant, she went to see the programs and immediately fell in love with the kids they help. Since taking the job, she's managed to move the organization from a mall storefront to its own $2.7 million facility.

People sometimes think that her job heading a grief program must be depressing. It's not.

"It's a lot of fun. I think to know that you're making a difference in these kids' life is just . . ."

Meyers pauses.

Just rewarding?

Just fulfilling?

Just something you feel you need to do?

The way she laughs, it's clear it's all of the above.

"Riding around in a corporate jet was cool," she finally answers. "But oh my gosh, this is important work. It takes a whole team and a whole community to bring it all together."

As she says, everyone is going to have grief at some point in their life. Helping one another work through it is an important and very human thing to do.

FIVE

A Roof Over Their Heads

Giving Shelter

We live in the most advanced country the world has ever seen, one with an abundance of food, open land, and opportunity. Historically, there has never been a society as well off for as long as ours.

Yet every night more than a half million of our fellow citizens go to bed on park benches, under bridge trestles, behind a garbage dumpster.

It's a sin, certainly.

And yet, curing homelessness is not an easy thing. We've put men on the moon, taught silicon chips to make music selections for us, built robots that can build robots. But putting a roof over someone's head is a far more complex task.

How big a problem is homelessness in the U.S.? Here are some statistics from the National Alliance to End Homelessness, as of January 2017:

- Total nightly homelessness: estimated at 553,742

- Ratio of homeless to total population: 17:10,000

- Of the total homeless population, 360,867 live in shelters; the rest live on the streets or in buildings that were not meant as homes

- Veterans account for about 7.2 percent of the homeless

- About a third of the homeless are family units, often just a single parent with one or more children

- While homelessness overall has declined on a percentage basis since the 1970s, it increased by just under 1 percent in the last year statistics were available, from 2016 to 2017.

The causes of homelessness are myriad, which is one reason that the problem remains so persistent. While drug and alcohol abuse, as well as mental illness—often together—are major factors, families often become homeless because of financial catastrophes that have nothing to do with their behavior. The bad luck of a car accident or cancer can easily wipe out a young family's life savings, even if they have insurance; miss a rent or mortgage payment, and a sad cycle begins.

There is help, both through government and non-government programs that pay all or part of a month's rent. But real solutions have to attack the actual problem that led to homelessness; otherwise a person can't escape the spiral that led him or her downward.

But there are groups and individuals taking a shot at doing just that. And I've been privileged to meet and speak with a few.

What impresses me most of all is their humility. Not one person working on the problem ever told me, "This is the only solution; my idea is the best." What they say instead is something along the lines of "This is one possibility."

This might help some people.

We want to try this and see if it works for others.

They're also amazingly optimistic—you have to be to work on the problem.

Little Houses, Big Hearts

Safe Haven

I f you've spent a few hours watching shows on home decorating and improvement channels like HGTV, you undoubtedly know that among the hottest trends in American homebuilding are tiny houses.

Also known as micro-houses and mini-houses, the category is so new that definitions are up in the air. Generally, a tiny house is small—"tiny"—compared to most American suburban homes. Something in the area of three hundred square feet would be considered the ideal tiny size. (Tiny houses are definitely bucking a trend. According to the U.S. Census Bureau, the average home built in America in 2017 was 2,496 square feet. If you were to go back to 1973, the average size was 1,660.)

Tiny doesn't mean rustic or plain, let alone deprived. Most of these houses are well-appointed, albeit with an extremely clever use of space. High-end appliances, granite countertops, elaborate lighting and sound systems, decks—the square footage is small, not the amenities. They come in a number of shapes, from A-frames to saltboxes; some are even on wheels. The models featured on some of the TV shows are truly phenomenal.

One of those TV shows was playing in the background one day when Pastor Donnie Davis sat down at his New Jersey home to have coffee with a friend of his. Donnie is a former Air Force veteran and law enforcement officer who found himself overwhelmed by post-traumatic stress back around 2000. The stress had accumulated over the five years he worked as a cop in the Washington, D.C., area. It pushed him from a job and into some addictions; he took two years off to recover.

He did more than recover. Working past his difficulties, he set his life on a new direction as a minister, with a mission to help other cops and military veterans, especially those with PTSD. His quest took him back to the southern stretches of New Jersey, where he'd grown up.

"Everybody I served with in the police department thinks it's crazy that I'm a pastor now," he confesses. "I was the guy everybody wanted to be on a call with. I was crazy. But you just hit rock bottom, and you look in the mirror, and you realize there's more to life than this."

You can take the pastor out of the police car, but you can't take the policeman out of the pastor, at least not this one. He jokes that he's more comfortable patting someone down than praying for them. And many of his close friends are still law enforcement officers and veterans.

"I'm still in that mind-set, serve and protect," says Donnie. "Now I can do it in a different aspect but still take care of my brothers and sisters. . . . All of a sudden you find yourself helping others, and it's not a choice. You just have to do it."

Skip forward to 2016, when Donnie and his friend Ron Koller sat down for coffee. By that time, Ron was senior pastor of Amazing Grace Ministries, a non-traditional Christian church based in New Jersey about eighteen miles southeast of Philadelphia. By *non-traditional*, we mean that while the church did not have its own church building, it catered to congregants and believers in a variety of ways, with services at a local high school, for example.

An immense offer had suddenly come the pastor's way—a 277-acre camp complete with a lake was available to purchase at a relatively low price.

What would you do with it? his friend asked.

House the homeless.

Build houses? Too expensive.

Then a television show playing in the background caught their attention. It featured tiny houses.

Small houses? Just the thing!

And so, Operation Safe Haven was born.

The church purchased the property for $1.3 million, with Donnie and his wife cosigning and guaranteeing the loan. Unused for a decade, the camp property was beautiful but overgrown, with buildings in need of repair or removal and a dam that had to be fixed. And there was the matter of building the houses. Donnie started a GoFundMe campaign, asking for donations to purchase pre-built homes.

The public responded. One of the largest pledges, given anonymously through the website, was for $50,000; there were several other five-figure contributions. But nearly 1,200 donations that had been given when we were working on this book were $100 or less; often much less.

Among the most poignant donations was one from Pedro and Ida Gonzalez, who lost their son Michael to an IED in Iraq in 2008. The family and a nonprofit started in his honor provided enough money to purchase a house in Michael's name.

A total of $259,000 had been raised when we spoke to Donnie recently, putting the project past its halfway point. As the money came in, so did volunteers. Besides church and other area community members, companies like Home Depot and Comcast sponsored daylong work sessions for employees at the site. Contractors donated work and supplies. Local television stations and newspapers helped out by doing stories on the project, encouraging more volunteers to join the effort.

The property was bought in June 2016; the first micro-house arrived shortly thereafter. There are now four homes; the group adds them as money is raised, avoiding debt. The homes are built by a modular builder and delivered to the site; sometimes they include donated items, like granite countertops in the case of the first batch. The homes are then furnished by Operation Safe Haven, with everything from beds to spoons, all new.

The floor plans are fairly simple, with a kitchen, bathroom, and sleeping area in a twenty-by-fifteen-foot space. The door to each home opens toward a common area centered around a fire pit; the back of each house is private and looks onto the woods or the lake. Plans call for modest porches at the front of each home, large enough for two rocking chairs.

"Because we're volunteers and rely on donations, it

moves slow," admits Donnie. "Our goal is to be self-sustaining."

Along those lines, there are plans to install solar panels, eventually supplying enough electricity for all the homes' needs.

The first resident arrived with addiction problems; whether they were a contributing problem or not, he had lost his house and was without shelter. He is now clean, working with a local company. The second occupant was a Korean War veteran whose original home had slowly deteriorated until it was uninhabitable. And so it goes. The first residents have all been men, though there is no gender or other restrictions, aside from them being veterans and homeless.

How many homes will they have eventually?

As much as they can pay for, says Donnie. "They're all lakefront homes, and we have a big lake."

Besides the GoFundMe page, the church has benefited from fund-raisers, including a concert featuring the '60s group the Temptations. The ultimate goal is to do more than just create housing; Donnie, the congregation, and his friends want to help the people who move in recover from the circumstances that made them homeless in the first place. Peer counseling, job help, and other services are available as part of the project, whether directly or through referral.

Donnie points out that while there is a government program to help low-income veterans get housing, the income level is so low that it makes it almost impossible for a veteran to hold a job and get the help. It's a perverse catch-22—which do you want: a job or a place to live? If you take the job, you lose government help . . . and can't afford your home.

At Operation Safe Haven, there are no income limitations. In fact, the aim is to encourage veterans to work and advance in their job or career so they can move on.

"It doesn't matter if you make zero dollars or a million dollars; you can stay," he promises. With the help of on-site counselors and referrals, "We'll get you squared away."

Aside from the problem of homelessness, one of the motivations for the pastor was the number 22—reputed to be the number of veterans who take their lives by suicide every day. The cause in many instances is untreated or poorly treated PTSD.

Post-traumatic stress is said to affect as many as 15 percent of all Vietnam War veterans, some 12 percent of those who fought in the first Gulf War (1990–91), and between 11 and 20 percent of those who fought in Operation Iraqi Freedom and Operation Enduring Freedom (Afghanistan).

The suicide rate among policemen is also high, though not as well-known. Being at the intersection of those two communities was a powerful motivator for the New Jersey man. "Most law enforcement members know what the barrel of their gun tastes like," says Donnie woefully. Operation Safe Haven aims at reducing the numbers, one at a time.

Donnie handled his PTSD through therapy as well as a service dog. He also credits his work with veterans, especially those with PTSD, with helping him cope with his own demons. Peer-to-peer counseling—or just talking to others who have been there, done that—seems to help many people.

But it can be hard, especially taking that first step and admitting that you need help.

"You've been trained to be this invincible warrior," says Donnie, "and now all of a sudden there's a chink in your armor and you can't figure out why."

As Donnie's story shows, though, PTSD is not a life sentence. It is an obstacle. Getting a hand up and not a handout helps veterans and other PTSD sufferers feel empowered and hopeful about the future.

Just over forty thousand veterans are considered homeless across the country, according to the U.S. Department of Housing and Urban Development.

Forty thousand is too many for Operation Safe Haven, even in Donnie's relentlessly optimistic assessments of what the program can do. But others can fill the gap—inspiring others is nearly as important as getting more homes on the ground there.

"We'd love to inspire others to do what we're doing," agrees Donnie. "I can't help every homeless vet. But if I can inspire others, I'll be happy."

"It's not that hard to get the vets off the street, the ones who want help," he adds, noting that the actual outlay of money is far less than some might think. "If we can do this at no cost to the vets in New Jersey, one of the most expensive states, we can do it anywhere."

Interested groups and individuals from Missouri, Florida, and Delaware have already looked at Operation Safe Haven's operation. With their own local modifications and inspirations, I'm sure there'll be a ripple effect across the country.

"In this day and age when you have, left and right, so many divisions, this is really something that brings everyone together," notes Donnie. "Everyone can get behind taking care of our veterans."

Amen to that.

Get Up, Suit Up, Show Up

Solutions for Change

Because Chris Megison couldn't finish a few more push-ups, hundreds of homeless families now have shelter, jobs, and a path toward a better future.

What do push-ups and helping the homeless have to do with each other?

Let me explain. . . .

It was in Southern California, shortly after the end of the first Gulf War. By his own admission, Chris and a bunch of his fellow Marines were goofing around and doing some "stupid stuff." Their commanding officer decided that some changes were in order, and being a creative leader, he wanted his Marines to undergo a little more than physical discipline as part of his correction for their misbehavior.

It happened that he wanted some volunteers to go into the community and help with things that needed to be done. Specifically, the CO needed a volunteer to work in a soup kitchen. His motivation may have been part humanitarian and part public relations; in any event, it was a good cause and something he expected his Marines to jump on.

In fact, they were so eager to volunteer that they made it into a contest: the least number of push-ups wins . . . the job of volunteering.

Not particularly auspicious, maybe.

Now, Marines can do *a lot* of push-ups. So the fact that Chris Megison lost that contest doesn't mean that he had poor chest or arm strength. On the contrary. Compared to the rest of us, I'm sure he was a beast when it came to push-ups. But he was in with a pack of beasts. Or, I should say, Marines.

After losing the contest, he did his duty, reporting as a "volunteer" at the soup kitchen in town. While he was there, he spooned some soup into a bowl of a local known to the volunteers as Wolfman.

The name wasn't necessarily a compliment or only a description of his beard-covered face and unkempt manner.

"What's your name?" asked Chris as he served the man.

Wolfman stared at him, his lips clamped together.

Chris chattered a bit, trying to get a smile out of him, or at least some sort of acknowledgment. What he got instead was something halfway between a sneer and a snarl.

Undeterred, the Marine finished giving out food to the line, then went over with his own bowl of soup and sat down next to Wolfman, who had plenty of empty seats around him.

Twenty minutes later, Wolfman revealed his actual name: Steve.

Then came a bit more of his history.

"He had jumped into a bottle of Jack Daniel's about fifteen years before I met him," remembers Chris. It was a tragic situation—Steve had lost his mom and dad when he was young and had drifted through life and into addiction and homelessness.

As they ate their soup, Steve began talking about how society was reacting to him. Feeding him, sheltering him, giving him money—but in truth, admitted Steve, none of these things were specifically helping Steve, the person. Kindhearted though these gestures may have been, they did nothing to touch the core of his being. Or his problems.

Intrigued, maybe a little troubled, Chris went back to the base, thinking about everything the homeless man had told him.

What is it really like to be homeless?

What would I need if I was in that situation—beyond the obvious things like food and a place out of the rain? What would really improve my life?

He decided to find out.

"I had a 96," says Chris, referring to a four-day pass that gave him time off from his duties. Normally, Marines use those to visit family or friends or just take a little vacation from the rigors of military life and discipline. Instead, Chris used the time to find out what it was like to be homeless, wandering the streets. The American Spirit was nudging him to do some good. "I went out to see for myself what Steve was telling me. It really made me mad. Society was just responding in a way that hurt people."

Society thought it was helping, but what it was really treating was symptoms rather than the root cause, and inadvertently helping to keep people homeless. Rather than giving a hand up, their handouts kept people down.

His pass expired, Chris went back to base. A ten-year veteran, the Marine had planned to reenlist; the papers were already filled out. Instead, he left the Corps and began working with the nonprofit where he'd met Steve, assisting the homeless and others, trying to find ways to help the person rather than merely treating the symptoms.

Get up, suit up, show up—that became his mantra, and he preached to pretty much everyone he helped. Get out of bed, get presentable, attack the day by going to work, or looking for work, or doing whatever other necessary thing had to happen to move your life along.

One day in 1999, Chris, his wife, and their two young sons were helping out at a homeless shelter. Though designed for men, the facility was being increasingly used by single mothers and their children.

Momentarily distracted while working, Chris suddenly felt a tug at his side. He looked down and was surprised to find a little girl staring at him with a quizzical look on her face.

Her name was Jessica.

"She yanked on my sleeve real hard," recalls Chris. "Jessica asked if I lived in the shelter with her and her mom."

Hey, Mister? Do you live here, too?

Nine years old, Jessica was at the shelter with her mom and baby sister. The family had been assigned places to sleep on the floor.

This is not right, thought Chris.

"I'm looking at this nine-year-old girl, beautiful little girl, asking me if I live on the floor."

The way she asked it told Chris that she didn't realize there was anything out of the ordinary with living on a concrete floor in a homeless shelter. That being without a home, at the mercy of the elements as well as others, was a normal thing.

Chris got down on one knee and looked into her eyes.

"I don't live here," he told her. "But I am going to make you a promise. We're going to get you out of here and back into your own home with a bed and your own pillow."

That was the start of the story of Solutions for Change.

That moment led him to what he calls "a divinely navigated journey." A deep believer in God, he takes Jesus Christ's admonition to feed the hungry and help the poor as a personal commandment. But he gave the message both an American entrepreneurial spin and maybe a Marine Corps "get 'er-done" mentality tilt as he outlined plans for what became Solutions for Change.

His idea was to do more than provide a shelter, or food, or clothing. He wanted to provide the means for someone to get those things for themselves, to contribute rather than consume.

You've heard the saying *Give a man a fish, and he'll eat for a day. Teach him to fish, and he'll eat for a lifetime.*

That's Solutions for Change in a nutshell.

"The Corps taught me the importance of serving others," says Chris. "Society thinks that serving just to serve is cool. But I will tell you that one of the hidden problems we have in society is where compassion is just put out there and it turns into enabling.

"It should be serve to solve."

His battle plan—that's what he called it—was completely different than most of the plans for helping the homeless at the time. Rather than answering part of the problem and leaving the rest to other programs—say, opening a shelter and maybe handing out flyers on where someone could go for job training—Solutions for Change would be a comprehensive, one-stop program to help a person fully engage with society as a contributing member. It would, in effect, partner with the homeless to help them reach the goal of independent living.

Chris launched the project without looking for a federal or state grant. While that ruled out a potential funding source, it also meant that the project could be "outside the box" of other programs. Too often potentially good but new ideas get shoehorned into old forms, which limit and even strangle them. That wasn't going to happen here.

Then again, nothing was going to happen without money, an unfortunate reality whether you're a social entrepreneur like Chris or not. It took several years before the group he founded and now serves as executive director was able to open the door on its own, permanent facility.

"We went from a church to a small building where we could help ten families a day," recalls Chris. "Then we built a place in 2004."

The facility cost about $6.5 million, paid for entirely with donations and forgivable loans; there is no mortgage. A big portion of the funds came from seven different municipalities that resolved to help solve the homeless problem in their communities.

More than money, enthusiasm was important. Chris had plenty of that.

"In those early days, I would get up in the morning and fist pump," says the retired Marine. "I couldn't wait to get out there and help."

He's a touch more laid-back these days, but just as enthusiastic about helping people. His optimism is tempered but not diminished by realism and experience.

"Humans are messy," he says. "The people we're working with as homeless folks, there's lots of drama, lots of other stuff."

Addiction, broken homes, poverty, broken relationships—helping people overcome those things still gets him out of bed every day.

If Operation Safe Haven shows what can be done on a micro-scale, Solutions for Change shows what can happen on a larger scale. The process works roughly like this:

Homeless families—the average family is a mom with two kids—apply for a position in person at the Solutions for Change offices. They can come on their own or through a referral, but in either case they are interviewed by one of the organization's staff and given information about the program. If they're willing, they are placed on a wait list, which may mean several more weeks in whatever temporary housing they've managed to obtain.

Once admitted, they enter the first phase, or "university," as Solutions for Change calls it. In a lot of ways, it is just like going to college, except the graduating degree is a PhD in a new, productive way of life.

Parents attend classes that are aimed at developing simple life skills, progressing to leadership. Financial literacy, parenting workshops—the curriculum ranges from very basic to sophisticated classes and discussions aimed at improving job skills. After early-morning classes—alarms are generally set for 5:30 a.m.—the students head to work at various places, either in the community or at Solutions for Change's own enterprises.

While the organization does not proselytize, it does offer residents an introduction to religion. Chris is a Christian believer and sees a broken relationship with God as one of the key problems people in poverty struggle to overcome.

"People are so disconnected today in society," notes Chris. "One of the big reasons we've been successful is that we help repair that connection. We tell our people they are loved. We are glad they're here. To be able to demonstrate that level of care and love with another human being is so important. We get a like on Facebook and we're like, woo-hoo."

Solutions for Change University is a thousand-day program—but it's one thousand days not just to independence but of service to others.

"We teach people to get two or three clicks above the mediocre," says Chris. "They get on fire."

The first phase lasts six months. Newcomers meet and live with other families and begin taking their classes. There's always a bit of adjustment for the families coming off the streets—"shell shock" is how Chris describes it.

Three months of intensive job training leads to a full-time job; residents start paying a modest rent.

Residents are also required to put away a third of their salary into a savings account that they own.

Six to nine months later, residents reach the five-hundred-day mark, celebrated with a formal ceremony Solutions for Change calls Commencement. At that point, they graduate to housing off-campus, so to speak—affordable housing in the community, still owned by Solutions for Change.

From this point, the graduates begin helping others in the program.

According to Chris, 74 percent of the people who come through the front door at New Beginnings, the official name of the program's first phase, make it to Commencement; from there, 93 percent of them hit the thousand-day mark and officially graduate out of Opportunities, though they may come back as volunteers.

"That is about three times better than government programs at about a third of the cost," says Chris. "It costs us about $24,000 a year per family, versus the containment model that governments use."

Federal government data shows that poverty programs, not including Medicaid, averaged about $35,779 per family in 2016. (The bulk of these programs help families that are not homeless, though of course that can change rapidly with a job loss or some other unfortunate event. The figure for a homeless family is higher but varies greatly.)

Solutions for Change is now one of the largest nonprofit organizations helping the homeless in the state of California, which makes it one of the largest in the country.

To put that into perspective, though: with a budget in the $4 million to $4.5 million range, Solutions for Change is a minnow in the vast sea of organizations aiming to fight poverty, homelessness, and related problems. While size does limit what they can do, it's also a bit of an opportunity, or at least an attitude. Chris sometimes takes a Marine's attitude to the vast network of groups, government and otherwise, calling them collectively a $200 billion poverty-industrial complex.

"We're the rebel camp," he says proudly.

His goal is to disrupt the status quo—just like any Silicon Valley entrepreneur. Solutions now oversees about two hundred thousand square feet of housing and other space in some eight cities in California. There are about 150 families in the program at one time; the waiting list to get in had about 350 on it when we last spoke. Staff totals about forty, with another 350 volunteers. "These are people in a network we've built who are giving hundreds of hours a year."

Ninety-three percent of Solutions for Change's money comes from donations and its two social enterprise programs, Solutions Farm and Solutions in the Community, which themselves count for 40 percent of that number. The rest comes from donors—or as Chris calls them, "investors." They range from foundations to corporations to small businesses to individuals. The other 7 percent of the fund at present comes from different government programs; Solutions for Change was poised to lose that money when we spoke due to changes in program requirements. (The organization gave back some $600,000 due to changes in regulations relating to addict recovery and housing. A good portion of that money was made up by donations when the community found out about the loss.)

According to Chris, Solutions Farm is the largest aquaponics farm in the western United States. The seven-thousand-square-foot greenhouse at the center of the operation was retrofitted from traditional nursery use with the help of volunteers and in-kind donated services. The charity computed that a total of more than three thousand volunteer hours over a ten-week period were involved in getting the facility ready.

Aquaponics farming doesn't use traditional fertilizers and soil. As the name implies, it's water-based, but there's a lot more to it than simply growing herbs and vegetables in special containers. Fish are raised to supply nutrients as well as food stock. There's a delicate interplay between all the elements; the concept is still relatively new, and the industry has had fits and starts in the U.S.

Chris, though, is as optimistic about it as any entrepreneur in Silicon Valley. The people managing the farm are veterans, and the farm doubles as a training program and employer of residents in Solutions for Change University. The food is certified organic; plans call for some 1.6 million servings of greens to schools and the like.

The revenue from the produce sales is then reinvested in Solutions for Change, reducing the need for outside donations and grants.

"The farm is an amazing social enterprise," says Chris. "There are so many bells and whistles to it that it's hard to describe. It's basically the most environmentally friendly farming method in the world. It uses ninety-five percent less water than natural farming, and there are no pesticides."

Solutions in the Community is the parent organization's real estate development arm. Solutions for Change buys properties that are in disrepair and either rehabs them or knocks them down and rebuilds from scratch. They become housing complexes for people in the University, or in some cases, people who have already graduated.

"I don't believe in shelters," says Chris. "I want them to live in apartments."

Residents pay rent, which helps support the project and ultimately the entire enterprise. Taken together, Solutions for Change represents a cross between social welfare and capitalism, or as Chris calls it, "social entrepreneurship."

Chris grew up in the Detroit area. He had an experience early on that told him he wasn't going to stay there. While he talks about God helping him along his path in life, it was actually a blizzard that set him on his course.

"It's 1978; I'm standing on the roof of my house in a blizzard. I look at my dad and I say, I can't do this. I'm not going to live here. I can't do blizzards."

That revelation led him to the U.S. Marines, who took him all over the world, including Beirut in 1983. This was during the attack on Americans there, and he witnessed firsthand the almost unbelievable horrors humans can inflict on one another.

"I was a pretty hardheaded kid. I didn't have a lot of discipline. I didn't have a lot of purpose. The Corps taught me how to have a higher purpose. Now, I have [another] higher purpose. I am serving God and the guy next to me."

"When I was in the Corps, I always wanted to fix stuff. . . . I was always seeing things in my own way. I was an entrepreneur."

That caused a little friction in the military, but once out, his creativity married the drive the Corps had given him. At the same time, his extended family's own experiences with addictions made him acutely aware of how devastating those could be.

"The beast—it became the enemy that I would later fight," he says, referring to the fact that a good number of the homeless are substance abusers. College courses in counseling and related courses "weaponized" him to fight the problem. You can still hear the Marine in his voice as he speaks about fighting addiction, homelessness, and other problems; he's attacking them with a well-thought-out tactical plan aimed at a strategic goal.

It's just that his weapons no longer include M-16s and machine guns.

While Solutions for Change is fairly unique, it's a likely model for the future. "We've won enough awards where it's going to be replicated across the country," says Chris.

It's the ripple effect, on a national basis.

I met Chris Megison at a fund-raiser for Solutions for Change a few years ago. Talking with him, the staff, and people they'd helped, it was impossible not to be impressed by the long-haul approach the organization was taking. I was very impressed by a young woman who had gone through the program and was now giving back—that's what happens when you empower people. The organization's name is true—they looked at the problem and all its complicated levels, and came up with a series of solutions. They taught people to fish rather than giving them fish.

Short-term help in the form of soup kitchens and emergency shelters are very important, of course. The first priority when you're hungry is food; if you don't have a roof over your head, you want and need shelter.

But long-term help can be much harder to find and trickier to stick. Chatting with some of the graduates of the program, I was convinced the approach works, if not in every case, then in many.

"If you're with our people in a room and meet them," Chris tells others about the program's graduates, "you would be in a sense of awe."

I was, and I can attest that he is right.

Or as he puts it, "it blows your mind."

P.S.: The little girl and her family who inspired Chris managed to escape homelessness soon after meeting him. Jessica went on to community college, a job, a home, and a family of her own.

"That look in her eyes told me everything I needed to know," says Chris. "She launched the movement. If I ever write a book, it'll be called *Everything I Needed to Know in Life I Learned from Wolfman and Little Red Riding Hood.*"

He's So Fly
Melanie and Marcus Luttrell

Government and nonprofit groups are critical in the fight to end homelessness. But individuals can provide solutions as well. And not just by sharing their couches.

Toward the end of August 2017, meteorologists warned Houston that a hurricane was headed their way. Among the residents battening down were my friends Marcus and Melanie Luttrell.

You've heard of Marcus, surely, whether through his book *Lone Survivor*, about his battle with and escape from the Taliban in Afghanistan, the movie of the same name, or his prominent role in the Patriot Tour. His wife, Melanie, isn't famous, but those of us who know her value her seemingly boundless energy and open heart. Marcus would agree; she keeps his life and everything else together.

The Luttrells live on relatively high land outside the city, and so their house was a gathering point for friends and family in the area looking for a relatively safe place to ride out the storm. Things got a bit dicey when the clouds dumped so much water that the creeks on their property washed out their driveway and its two bridges, leaving the contingent stranded for six days without formula and diapers for friends and families with infants. Fortunately some police were able to bring in supplies and no one at the house was in any particular danger. As the waters subsided, a neighbor came by with a tractor and helped restore the bridges and driveway.

Overall, while not exactly a pleasant experience, their days waiting out the storm and its aftermath were far better than what many in the lower-lying areas nearby suffered. The coastal area was even more heavily damaged. All told, the hurricane killed at least 106 people and caused some $125 billion of damage in the U.S.

Freed from her house, Melanie wanted to do something for others still suffering. She and her husband partnered with a local radio host to set up a clothing drive. They put out the message on social media, thinking maybe ten or a dozen people would show up at the local park with clothes, which could then be handed off to needy families. Instead, three or four hundred donors came out; so many clothes were collected that some were later shipped to Florida and Puerto Rico following hurricanes there.

Melanie was still marveling at the size of the response when she got a text from her teenage son, who was out with some other high school students helping recovery efforts. The kids had found a ninety-nine-year-old World War II veteran whose house had been devastated by flood waters. The man didn't want to leave his house. He'd built it with his wife as their retirement home more than three decades before, and as she had recently passed away, the home represented pretty much his life.

And his independence. To his way of thinking, if he gave up the house, he'd spend the rest of his days in a nursing home among strangers or be passed around to relatives' spare bedrooms. Either way, he'd be a prisoner in a gilded cage.

The man's name was Bill Fly; he'd served in the Army–Air Force during World War II. When Melanie met him, he was understandably distressed; the sodden weight of the world was pressing down on his shoulders. But his nature was anything but depressed; he was sharp and witty and above all humble.

Maybe a little stubborn as well. He hadn't left his home until the water was over the toilets, and even then he had to be coaxed out by neighbors from a boat at the door.

Now, facing the ruined and saturated remains of his house, he told Melanie that he wanted to rebuild but had no savings to do so.

"I don't want to give up my independence," he insisted when asked what alternatives he had.

"You fought for our freedom," Melanie told him after discussing the situation with Marcus. "We'll fight for yours."

And with that sentence, the battle was on.

Melanie called an uncle to ask for advice on dealing with flooded homes. The key, he said, was to get everything out and dry the structure ASAP. Otherwise, mold could wipe out any hope of using the original structure. The next morning, a family friend who owned a company specializing in industrial cleanups pledged to help dry the house.

"How quickly does it have to be done?" he asked.

Melanie thought about it for a moment. Mr. Fly—that's what everyone calls him—had told her his one hundredth birthday was November 11.

November 11 became the deadline—not just for drying out the house but for completely rebuilding it.

There may have been some eye rolling and smacked foreheads, but that's how Melanie does life. She follows her heart; most often, as with the clothing drive, she achieves more than she sets out to. We've come to accept that not only is the impossible possible when she's involved, but it's also highly likely. So, the overwhelming response when Melanie started talking up the idea was, "Let's do it!"

As word of the project spread, volunteers rolled in. Plumbers, electricians, other craftsmen volunteered their and their company's time to help rebuild Mr. Fly's house. An appeal on the UCare website raised money for materials—roughly $100,000, five times the original goal. A heating/air-conditioning system was donated by a local company.

"I think people all over Houston and the country wanted to help because he reminded them of their dad or grandfather," says Melanie. "Plus, he was so grateful. You can see it in his eyes."

A video posted on the web helped bring attention to the project. In the end, Mr. Fly celebrated his one hundredth birthday in his new old home. On one of the walls was a favorite picture of his wife that was rescued from the flood and painstakingly dried out by Melanie.

264 • AMERICAN SPIRIT

"Helping others is the most important thing you can do," says Melanie. Whether it's one on one, or one on many, the critical thing is to act when you can.

"The ripple effect will always spread," she says, using one of my favorite phrases. "No matter whom you're helping—a veteran, an orphan—goodness is contagious."

Where did her spirit of giving come from? Melanie supposes watching her father. Raising Melanie on a tight budget as a young single father, he took in a blind man who was hard on his luck. They would talk about the Bible as her father helped him get to the next phase in his life. Her father never asked for credit or made a big deal about it. It was just something he did, the sort of thing he continues to do with no fanfare. The ripple effect of his generous American Spirit continues on through Melanie and inevitably many of those she helps and inspires.

Mr. Fly himself is like the proverbial pebble in a pond that starts the ripple. The first time I met him, he was wearing a thousand-watt smile. We were on Patriot Tour, in the middle of a long day after just getting into New York City. There were so many reasons for him to be tired or even a little down, but instead he was the opposite—brimming with energy and infecting everyone around him with a magic adrenaline. He reminded me of my own grandfather, who had a way of living every moment to the fullest. Mr. Fly has felt the pain of life, but he knows the value of joy, and wasn't about to miss any moment of it by being less than energetic and happy. His appreciation of even the little things prompted us to share his happiness and gratitude.

The joyfulness about them reminded me of a passage in James reminding us that being joyful in spite of trials can lead to wisdom. My grandfather and Mr. Fly endured despite their troubles, and their perseverance led to pure joy for the good things in life.

SIX

Giving Back

What Do We Owe?

Once we have achieved something, do we have an obligation to give back?

I think that goes without saying.

Once our basic needs are met, once we've taken care of our immediate family, then surely it is our duty to help others in some fashion.

I'm not a religious expert, but the idea seems to be basic to all religions, from Christianity to Buddhism. And if churches often provide an easy mechanism for doing this, the idea of helping others less fortunate than ourselves is not just a religious one. Many people who describe themselves as non-churchgoers can be found volunteering at community centers and ladling soup at nearby food banks.

If you're famous or wealthy, or both, do your contributions mean more than others?

And even more critically, if you have had that sort of luck in life, what's your motivation for giving back? Is it simply to have good stories in the news media about you? Selfies on social media about your alleged unselfishness?

Most of us have probably seen gestures of charity that are clearly insincere. Of course, that doesn't mean that the money or the effort doesn't do some good. But it seems to me that the hollow core of such acts is more than just a fatal flaw. It's a kind of hidden poison that can harm not just the individual but ultimately the recipients and society at large. Helping for the wrong purpose means the help is at best insincere and won't last.

So where does true motivation come from? Why do people who seem to have all the luck in life try to share it?

One reason is that, on proper examination, it turns out that they haven't *truly* had all the luck in life; many have struggled dearly, and that struggle convinced them to ease the trials of others when they could. In my estimation, compassion, endurance, and showing up for others is part of the beauty in the ashes of our own lives. For me, it is like a light in the darkness.

Upbringing, too, plays a role. Whether you are famous or not so famous, family members and close friends set a critical example when you're young. If you come from a generous family, the odds are you'll be generous, too. And for the right reasons.

The NFL has been in the news so much lately and not always in a positive light. But, like with any group of people, they are not all bad and not all good, either as individuals or as a group. Some football players and other athletes have proven to be some of the most generous people I know. While he was alive, my husband, Chris, was an avid, even rabid, Cowboys fan; I'm sure he's still cheering and groaning from above just as he did in life. It was always so exciting for him to go to games and meet players; he was like a kid at Christmas. Some of my favorite images of his smile are due, indirectly at least, to the Dallas Cowboys.

And so my highlights of celebrities giving back will start not just with some NFL players but with a retired Cowboy who inspired Chris when he was growing up.

Partying for Hope

Jay and Amy Novacek

L ittle things affect people's lives in big ways. Small acts of charity and kindness can have a larger impact than we realize at the time.

That's been the case for Jay and Amy Novacek, who have hosted a Christmas party at their Texas ranch for the past several years.

If you were a football fan in the 1980s or '90s, you've undoubtedly heard of Jay, though your feelings toward him largely depended on how badly he embarrassed your team. Jay was a Pro Bowl tight end who made a habit of undermining defenses. With the Cardinals and especially with the Dallas Cowboys, he was a versatile offensive weapon, a specialist at getting open on crucial third downs.

Retired from football, Jay lives and ranches in the Dallas area with his wife, Amy, a dog breeder specializing in labradoodles. A high percentage of her dogs are chosen as service dogs, especially as medical alert animals. Through training as well as instincts and natural ability, the dogs are able to detect certain medical conditions and alert their owners or handlers. Amy, who suffers from Addison's disease, can personally attest to the dogs' abilities—her trained canines have alerted her to low hormone levels in her body and helped make her ailment easier to manage.

A few years back, Amy was recovering from a serious car accident, thinking about how grateful she was for the blessings in her life, including their large ranch. She wanted to do something for others, but she wasn't sure what. A friend suggested a Christmas party for the kids at Hope Farm.

Hope Farm is a faith-based after-school program that began with two men mentoring inner-city schoolchildren in 1989. Gary Randle and Noble Crawford had realized that many of the men in prison had grown up without fathers or other significant male guidance. They set out to combat that problem, first one on one, and then with a larger, more formal program. Today, Hope Farm has two different locations in the Fort Worth area of Texas. Boys without fathers in their lives are enrolled as young as five and stay with the program through high school graduation. They and their families are asked to agree to a set of strict behavioral rules; in return, the program provides everything from tutoring to recreation, free of charge.

The Novaceks didn't know exactly what to expect the first year they offered to host the party; they pretty much just winged it, setting up some carnival games on card tables, opening the gates to the farm and standing back. In retrospect, that was perfect: They had a ranch. Hope Farm had young boys bursting with energy. If ever there was a perfect match, that was it.

When they arrived for the party, the boys charged off the bus. The younger ones headed for the "bounce house," an inflatable, enclosed tent with a cushion floor designed for kids to bounce in. A friend of the Novaceks had donated it for the day.

The older ones went out to meet the buffalo and longhorns and the other animals that call the property home.

"It was controlled chaos," says Jay approvingly.

The parties have become annual events at the ranch. They now include a wide array of gifts, most donated by local groups and individuals. There are inspirational speakers, including a few football friends of Jay's, and the occasional "cool" display of things like fire trucks and police SWATmobiles.

There's also a friend of the family who comes and cooks some barbecue, taking time off from his five-star restaurant.

Oh, and a jolly fellow with a white beard, huge belly, and red suit shows up to hand out goodies.

But the real attractions are the open space and the animals. And while the kids are having a blast, the adults are getting a lot out of it, too. A dialogue happens, especially in the case of kids and adults who come from radically different backgrounds.

"I realized the first time, this isn't just a Christmas party," says Jay, noting that they had invited a few friends from the local police force to interact with the kids as guests, not cops. "I saw some of the policemen doing some roping, showing the kids how to do it." They were having fun—the cops doing something they hadn't done in years, the kids trying something for the first time.

But more than that: they were breaking down stereotypes they might form of each other.

"If there was a situation in the future, where a policeman might face a young man," says Jay, "if he looks into his eyes and remembers the kid he was roping with, maybe he'll say to himself, I'm going to give this a chance to calm down.

"And reverse that—the kid sees a guy in uniform and not run away, not think he's the enemy."

I attended their first party and every one since, and I've been privileged to see this happen over and over. I never grow tired of seeing the kids pile onto Jay's lap as he powers up the tractor and sets out with them across the field.

There are definitely stereotypes to overcome. Amy's heart nearly broke when one little boy at their first party asked if the bars on the stalls in the barn meant that was the jail. But each year the parties have helped break down at least a few barriers.

Others around town have started helping in big and small ways. Coming out of a toy store last year, Jay ran into a man who asked what he was up to. When Jay told him he was helping Santa, the man volunteered to buy footballs for the kids as presents. Others learning about the party have made donations to cover various expenses or to add to the experience.

"You don't have to do something big," says Amy. "Do what you can do."

Personally, I've been known to overplan for parties, but I've learned that the best parties are the ones where you make some plans, open your home and your heart, and have fun. Hope Farm Christmas parties are a perfect example of good people coming together with love and whatever else they can. The results are extraordinary.

The Novaceks enlist the help of their kids and a couple of friends. All pitch in to help set up or make things right if needed. But take them all away, and the parties still would be a success, because the basic things the kids need—space to run around in, a pasture to do some roping or throw a football in—are already there.

That's not so much a metaphor as a reminder that what we do for others doesn't have to be perfect or huge; it just has to be done.

"Kindness is contagious," says Amy. "It catches on like a wildfire and spreads in ways we can't imagine."

MVP at Giving Dysphagia

Randall Telfer

There are crystalline moments of decision in every life—points at which we gain insight and make a decision that will propel us far into the future. Many of these opportunities to set our fate are lost, passed by at times out of cowardice but more often from simple ignorance of their significance. For they are easy to miss. They don't come with flashing lights or boldfaced capital letters. Generally sirens aren't blaring. They're most often experienced as unexpected opportunities or tricky turns, random bits of a day that blur into the normal chaos of life. They may occur anywhere—a deli, a cathedral, the basement of a department store, the back alley of a city.

Even a hospital room.

It was in just such a room that Randall Telfer met a little girl we'll call Emma back when the NFL tight end was in college.

Randall's college football team had been brought to the hospital to meet with patients. It was, to be honest, more photo op than charity, a chance to show that the college cared about the community. True, the players were cheering up many, especially the football fans. But it would be an exaggeration to say that they had a lasting impact on lives.

Except . . .

Randall stepped into one of the rooms and began talking to the girl about why she was there. It was a heartbreaking story. She'd been stricken with a severe case of scoliosis, a curvature of the spine that can be crippling. The cause was unknown.

"Out of nowhere, her spine started curving," recalls Randall, telling the story. "It made me look at things, at my own life, completely differently."

Randall ended up keeping in touch with the family as the girl underwent surgery and began to get her life back. When he got to the NFL—drafted by the Cleveland Browns—her inspiration pushed him to do more than just go on photo ops advertising what a kind-hearted person he is.

Don't get me wrong. He *is* kindhearted. But he's also a person who tries to make a real impact, one conversation or gesture at a time. In recognition of that, the Browns nominated him in 2017 for the Walter Payton NFL Man of the Year Award.

Randall, who retired before the 2018 season, was never one of the big money players of the league, let alone someone who can donate half his salary and all his endorsement money and still be a multimillionaire. He gives something more valuable than money to the people he helps: his attention.

He kept thinking about Emma: "I had injuries myself that set me back. Hers was greater than anything I'd ever had."

Other children touched him as well, like the kindergarteners he read to as part of Read Across America in 2015, just after he was drafted. He started realizing that taking the time to talk with someone, either to brighten their day or to hear their problems, could have an impact for more than just a few minutes.

Donating sweatshirts to a shelter for battered women was just a nice thing to do, he thought. He didn't realize at the time that just by going he had a powerful impact on the women, reminding them that not all men are abusers. People can be kind without wanting anything at all in return.

Conversations with people—genuine conversations, not things done in front of a camera for publicity or marketing—were what he learned to value.

Small things. One on one.

"Tuesdays, we get off in the NFL," says Randall. Without big family commitments, he started using every Tuesday to do something in the community: bringing bagels to the fire department, shooting hoops with a local high school, helping a nonprofit raise money to fight diabetes.

"After some games, I'd be so beat up, I wouldn't want to go out," he admits. "But after I saw the first person that day, my whole attitude changed. It sounds weird, but it was almost like a high, connecting with people."

Just listening to everything Randall does during the course of the year is impressive and pretty exhausting. Some are small things, others big. Some have personal connections, some don't. There's no history of spousal abuse in his family, but he doesn't need that example to know it's wrong. On the other hand, his grandma has diabetes, which is one reason he has worked with both the American Diabetes Association and the Junior Diabetes Research Foundation, or JDRF.

Would you believe that a guy big enough to play in the NFL was bullied as a kid? Yes, Randall was, though he says it was mild compared to what children go through today. But those memories are still strong and inform much of what he does for Boo2Bullying, a national effort to decrease bullying among youngsters.

Randall's efforts not only caught the attention of his team but may have inspired others to make their own efforts. Soon after inviting the Browns' other tight ends to get involved in one of his small events, he noticed other players hosting their own community efforts.

"Whether inspired by me or not," he says with a laugh, "I'm not asking questions. I'm just enjoying it."

To me, Randall is one more example that you don't have to set out to change the world with every single gesture; a genuine conversation with someone can ripple goodness outward in ways difficult to map. The important thing is to make the thing you do genuine.

There's nothing inherently wrong with having your picture taken while you're doing good or even showing up at a soup kitchen with the TV cameras rolling. But if you want to make a real difference, you have to ask yourself what Randall does: *What is the real value of my actions?*

Who is truly benefiting from what I'm doing?

Your motivations don't have to be entirely pure, and most of us find that we get a lot out of helping others. But the more genuine your connection, the more impact ultimately it will have—for you as well as for others.

Tie One on for a Cause

Dhani Jones

There are many ways to help others, sometimes directly, sometimes indirectly. It can even be done as a business, if your heart is in the right place.

As an NFL linebacker, Dhani Jones was an expert at knotting up offenses.

Now he knots ties. Bow ties, to be exact. Ones he designs for a variety of charities, including his own. They're just some of the many products of a life that marries an entrepreneurial spirit with a philosophy that demands you make the world a better place than you found it.

Dhani played for the New York Giants, Philadelphia Eagles, and Cincinnati Bengals from 2000 to 2010, ending his career with more than six hundred tackles and a couple hundred assists. Throw in nine and a half sacks and five interceptions, and you have a solid career, one that lasted a lot longer than average at a position notorious for the wear and tear it puts on a body.

More of a hugger than a tackler these days, Dhani has an open, generous spirit, and in many ways he is the personification of someone who has achieved success while at the same time dedicating himself to helping others. An entrepreneur and cable TV star, Dhani is a man of many talents. Maybe you saw him on the Travel Channel with his series *Dhani Tackles the Globe*. Or on CNBC in *Adventure Capitalists*. If you've been in Cincinnati lately, there's a chance you've had coffee at his café.

Raised in Maryland, Dhani adopted Cincinnati as his home when he played for the Bengals. He's been very active in the local community. Among other things, he's a board member of the Cincinnati Art Museum and Breakthrough Cincinnati, a tuition-free summer program that aims at helping middle-grade students, particularly minorities, prepare for higher education.

But his bow ties are what draw the most attention.

The bow ties began as a private challenge.

In 2000, his good friend Kunta Littlejohn was diagnosed with stage 4 leukemia. Among Littlejohn's many attributes were an eye for fashion and a thing for bow ties; they were more than just a fashion statement— they were a commitment, a statement:

If you want to be somebody, you have to rock the bow tie.

Dhani started wearing a bow tie as a sign of solidarity and support. Littlejohn's cancer went into remission, but Dhani's sartorial passion had just begun. He began designing for himself. Soon, he was making them for others, and he eventually founded a company called Five Star Ties, which created ties and accessories for men.

The chairman of Chiquita Brands International asked if he could make a bow tie for his son, who had juvenile diabetes. Dhani worked on the tie, and it ended up being used as a fund-raising and awareness-raising tool.

The BowTie Cause was born. Other groups began contacting the company. Dhani worked with them to design ties that had a meaningful connection with their cause. The young man with juvenile diabetes had described his life as a series of up and downs; the design had up and down arrows. Blood cells populate a tie for the Leukemia & Lymphoma Society.

That tie is a tribute to Kunta Littlejohn, Dhani's friend who started him on the bow tie journey. And it illustrates how deep some of the thinking behind the design goes. From the website where the tie is sold: "The meaning behind the design is very personal. When first diagnosed with cancer, Kunta thought that he was going to die, which is symbolized by the black base of the BowTie. As time progressed, Kunta began to improve, and grew largely optimistic about his survival. This is seen in the silver lining, symbolic of optimism. The red blood droplet is actually the logo for the Leukemia & Lymphoma Society. The pattern is representative of cell growth, which is something to be largely optimistic about for anyone with leukemia or lymphoma."

Today, the company partners with groups to create bow ties to be used as fund-raisers and awareness boosters. Though particularly popular with groups dedicated to fighting different diseases, the ties have been sold by everyone from the Armed Forces Foundation to the SPCA. And not just bow ties—they've also introduced scarves and jewelry.

"I had no idea what it was going to become. I wasn't creating BowTie Cause because this was going to be the biggest business in the world," he says now. "I always thought about giving people the voice.

"You have to believe in yourself and the ideas that you have. There are always going to be people who will look down on your idea. . . . As an entrepreneur, there are days when things are really good. There are days when things are really bad. You have to be comfortable with being uncomfortable. If it's status quo, it's no go."

Helping others with bow ties inspired Dhani to start (what else?) the BowTie Foundation to contribute to some of his own causes. The foundation funds outreach programs and provides grants to organizations that "foster the personal development of underprivileged youth," such as the Friars Club.

"I don't look at it as making a difference," he says of his charitable efforts. "I look at it like a responsibility to leave things better than you found it. You live in a house, the house should be better when you leave it. These are values that you should have learned as a child."

His career in football—in the NFL, in college at Michigan where he was named a three-time All–Big Ten player, and back at the high school level—taught him a lot. But this education and growth was built on the strong foundation his parents had given him as a child.

"There are a lot of things that you learn about yourself through sport," he says. "I learned about my own resilience. My ability to work through pressure-filled situations. Through travel, I learned to not judge. I also learned to ask a lot of questions and not be afraid of what the answers might be."

His advice for others? Expand your horizons and your circle of friends. "If you do the same thing every day, if you hang out with the same people every day, you're not going to learn the things you would learn if you travel."

He preaches that as a businessman and consultant.

"I get to come in and ask big questions as a Montessori kid," jokes Dhani, referring to his days as an elementary schooler, "and hopefully don't get tossed out of the room.

"I think there's a natural good in people. To do good for others and the world. But I also think there's a selfishness in people that prevents them from doing good for others—a kind of catch-22—because they're trying to protect their families or do what's right for them. Now, as people become more selfless, expand their thinking, see things for the greater good, then the dynamic starts to shift."

A friend of mine breaks the world down into three groups: the 80, 18, and 2 percenters.

Eighty percent of people just want to do what's being done. Another 18 percent want to do what is being done but do it better. The final 2 percent want to blow out what's being done, and in so doing, change the world.

If that's true, then Dhani is one of the 2 percent. He's an idea person—a fire starter, a world changer.

"The way I look at it, this is what you're supposed to do in life," he says of giving back. "[This] should be everyday practices of people. It should be the common occurrence. . . . When you live a selfless lifestyle, you walk around smiling."

Bad-ass with a Heart of Gold

Jesse James

G randmothers can be the greatest inspiration in the world, simply by being who they are.

Take "bad boy" turned reality TV star and celebrity bike and car builder, Jesse James.

Jesse genuinely earned his reputation as a bad-ass, getting into more than his share of trouble as a teenager. But that was never all he was. Overcoming his tough childhood, he worked security for rock bands, moved on to become a master motorcycle creator, then hit the big time as a reality star. He had a series of marriages, each time hoping he'd found the perfect yin to his yang. When he married superstar Sandra Bullock, many thought he'd achieved the American dream, going literally from rags to riches, from hardscrabble childhood to adult wedded bliss.

Then things crashed and burned. His marriage to Bullock collapsed—his fault, he says in his accounts—and he became embroiled in a custody battle with another former wife. He hit bottom.

But only for a short while.

Jesse went back to what he did best, working with his hands. Turning from vehicles to guns, he began crafting high-value guns and knives that are as decorative as they are utilitarian. Today, he has a wide range of business interests but remains at heart a blue-collar craftsman. I've heard people call him the "Pope of Welding," and after watching him in his workshop, I think it fits.

You can read about his dark side and his adventures in celebrityhood in his book, *American Outlaw*. What you won't read there—or in any of the tabloid stories about him—is what he did for the homeless in Long Beach. Because while he may be a genuine bad-ass, he's also humble when it comes to things like that.

Maybe he's afraid of crashing the bad-ass image.

"Downtown Long Beach in the '90s. Post–LA riots. Shop right in the middle of it," he told me when I visited his current digs in Texas. I'd heard rumors of his helping others and wanted to know if they were true—and if so, how he'd gotten involved in the first place. "It was kind of a lesson in taking care of where you are."

His shop, famous now because of the TV show, was a renovated garage with some of the latest and greatest tools. But before Jesse found it, it was a squatter's paradise—as were many of the buildings nearby. Jesse was part of the area's rebirth.

Fixing up the area properties was great for the city and the local economy, but it did nothing for the people who'd found shelter there. Anyone arriving at the shop around six in the morning would find the streets dotted with homeless men and women. The problem was acute. And while restoration of Jesse's and others' property in the area didn't cause it, the work didn't help. What it did was make residents and property owners more likely to complain. In their eyes, the hard work they had put in was being ruined by a horde of homeless.

Things reached a peak about a year after Jesse moved in, when Catholic Charities proposed opening a homeless shelter in the neighborhood. What the group saw as a solution suddenly became the focus of the problem. Angry meetings, petition campaigns, even a movement to bus the homeless to another city—tempers rose.

Jesse started talking to his neighbors. His message was simple: "You're never going to clean up the city if you don't take care of the problem." Give the homeless a place to stay, he argued, and the problem will be less acute. Treat the disease, not the symptom.

He didn't just talk. When Catholic Charities was looking for a facility to use in their mission, he asked what their budget was. The amount was far short of what property in the area typically sold for and millions below what he could get for his building.

Jesse gave it to them at their price nonetheless, shrugging off the difference as a donation. That may not have endeared him to his neighbors—but that's one advantage of being a bad-ass.

And hey, if people are going to be angry with you, let them be angry because you did something *good.*

Among its other efforts in the area, Catholic Charities ran Project ACHIEVE, helping homeless and formerly homeless people get jobs. Jesse pitched in there, too, hiring two of the seven hundred and fifty or so the charity helped place that year. He and his kids worked as volunteers over the holidays in their shelter. When he opened a restaurant, he donated each day's leftovers to the charity.

In the course of all this, he met many of the people the program helped—and a few it didn't. "Some people didn't want the program," he said. "The drug-free life, the rules. Too much. They didn't take it."

But others were helped tremendously. One man with his wife stood out.

"A string of bad events had taken them down," said Jesse. "His wife got sick; he lost his job."

Jesse shook his head, maybe thinking that if life had taken him in a different direction, the man might have been him.

In 2010, Jesse closed down the Monster Garage. He sold it—to Catholic Charities. At last report, it was being used as a thrift shop.

Even though the group was obviously religious—it is called *Catholic* Charities, after all—Jesse wasn't drawn to it particularly because of religion. (He's Christian, but not Catholic.) Religion wasn't a motivator at all— if anything, it may have been a turnoff. Many of the people he knows personally who profess to be religious he views as hypocrites in their daily lives.

If church didn't motivate him to help, what did?

Empathy. Experience. And Grandma.

Besides growing up relatively poor, Jesse often accompanied his father when he went to inspect and buy used furniture for resale. He remembers going into countless "filthy houses" and being disgusted by the despair and poverty so evident there.

And in his own home.

"We had a house that looked like the house in *The Jerk*," he said. He didn't mean it as a joke. "I didn't even have a bedroom. I slept in a hallway on a cot for a couple of years.

"I don't think people realize how special a home, a place to be, a place where you belong, is."

But the real inspiration for his good works was his grandmother—"Nana," as he calls her.

"My nana lived on Butler Avenue in Compton right by the train tracks," he told me. "She used to make sandwiches for all the black transients and leave them on her windowsills. They would come by and take them. She would never turn anyone away.

"She died when I was twelve. I think it was the most devastating thing in my life."

But her memory lives on, not just in Jesse's acts but in the countless small mercies and kindnesses that started with her free food and rippled out as others paid it forward.

"You don't have to start a homeless shelter to be good," he said. "Even on a small level, being kind and sticking up for the underdog—there's stuff you can do to make a difference. Whether it's dropping coins in someone's cup or volunteering. Reading for the mentally challenged. There are a million ways."

At least.

"There are lots of things in every part of this country where we can really make a difference."

Jesse's life has changed for the better since the very public end of his relationship with Sandra Bullock and the high point of his tumultuous fame. He's still a businessman, has an inspiring and interesting social media presence, is still seen occasionally on TV and is married to his perfect match, Alexis DeJoria, a successful businesswoman herself. They raise their daughters, go to church, and have a bunch of dogs, a monkey, and an adventurous life together. And he still gives back, spending time with high school–age kids in industrial arts programs.

Working with your hands is often looked down on in these days of high tech. But as Jesse's own life has shown, skills like welding, metalworking, and automotive mechanics are demanding and potentially rewarding. Even if they are neglected in schools.

Jesse's show helped make blue-collar skills "cool." He still treasures a letter he got from a teenage girl who wrote that she used to "look down on" her father until she saw the show. Then she realized that he did the same thing Jesse James did.

Molding a piece of metal is not the same as molding a person. Whether an impressionable teenager, a desperate father trying to shelter his newborn, an addict who refuses to clean up and come off the streets—people are made of far more complicated ores than iron. Reaching them takes time and effort—but nothing says it can't begin with a sandwich left on a windowsill.

Summer Song

Zac Brown and Camp Southern Ground

Kids are the products of their surroundings as well as their genes. If they spend their days going from home to school and school to home, how will they expand their horizons?

Not by playing video games or fooling with the latest app on their phones. Real growth comes from actual interaction with physical things, be it nature or another human being.

Where's that going to happen?

Summer camp—especially if it's Camp Southern Ground in Georgia.

Kids from seven to seventeen spend a week at the camp, hiking, swimming, doing arts and crafts—

pretty much everything you'd find at a typical summer camp. One of the things that makes it a bit unique, however, is that the camp attempts to be inclusive, integrating children with conditions like autism into the camp population. The camp also actively recruits children of service members as a way of paying the families back for their service. The camp also offers retreats and programs for military families separate from the summer camp. We liked that idea so much that our foundation, Chris Kyle Frog Foundation, became one of the sponsors. We're excited to be hosting programs there.

The camp is the brainchild of musician Zac Brown, the leader of the popular country music group the Zac Brown Band.

Whether you are into country music or not, you should know that the Zac Brown Band is big time. At last call, the band had placed thirteen #1 singles on the country charts and taken home enough platinum to make an entire beach of blondes jealous. They have three Grammys, and I'm sure more are on the way. "Chicken Fried" is probably the standard introduction to the band's music for myriad reasons; check out one of Jim's favorites, "I'll Be Your Man (Song for a Daughter)" for a deeper listen. And their concerts, with amazing musicians and often collaborations from other artists, are eclectic, artistic, entertaining, and some of the best you will ever see.

Zac would be the first to tell you that Camp Southern Ground, which hosted its first summer campers in 2017, depends on an entire team of people. That's true enough, but he was its driving force and vision. More than that, it reflects his values and own experiences.

He first went to camp as a seven-year-old, where he came to view the counselors as role models and even kinder, gentler superheroes. His experience at Camp Michael, from roughly ages nine to fifteen, was "transformative" in several ways, including musically: while there, he saw a fellow camper flat-picking a guitar and realized there was more he could do with the instrument than he'd thought. The experience may or may not have set him on a musical course—he was taking classical lessons already, and his older brother played—but it's still a memory that he returns to after all these years of touring and top albums.

"I went to a camp with kids who had autism and Down syndrome," he explains. "I learned to celebrate differences. We saw the strength that other kids had, and that inspired me."

On my first visit, I was blown away by the serenity of the place. It's not all that far from Atlanta, but in many ways it's a world apart. The camp aims at being self-sustaining; campers grow their own healthy food. The architecture is tuned to the environment and the kids—a treehouse that looks like a spaceship serves as a conference room. A planned technology center looks like something you'd find in a science lab.

I didn't go on the rope course—but I will on my next visit. Challenging yourself physically to do something you've never done before is a great way to prepare yourself to do something emotionally you've never done before.

Of course, now that I've said that in print, I have no out.

Summer camps can provide new experiences, new friends. They can also be a place to gain acceptance as an individual. A performer-to-be might go on stage there for the first time and get encouragement; a child with autism might learn that he can interact without being ridiculed.

But Zac's ideas and hopes for Camp Southern Ground go beyond the week campers might spend there. He's hoping that it can show the way to better, more stimulating ways of educating our kids. The people who help shape programs there are working on different ways of helping children "out of darkness." Nutrition, physical activities, art—it's a mix of different things and different ways not just of reaching kids, but of encouraging and helping them to break past whatever shadows their true selves and potential.

This isn't limited to kids who have been diagnosed with some sort of disorder or physical limitation. All of us have something that limits us or makes us square pegs in round holes at different times. Zac talks about how he was always failing something or getting into trouble as a young child; nowadays, he would be diagnosed with some form of attention deficit disorder and probably given medication. But the real problem wasn't his body chemistry; it was the system that tried to impose six to eight hours of desk-sitting on that chemistry. Teachers and the system they were stuck in didn't know quite how to deal with him. He hopes to change that, long term.

"The problem in America is everybody's thinking about what's going to affect them in five years and how they can make money off that," he notes. "Instead of in twenty years, America should be a leader of education in the world. We're number thirty-five right now. We should be ashamed of ourselves."

Putting children with different physical and mental capabilities together seems to me an important step in opening young minds. Doing that opens up our future, making it something more cooperative, closer to our society's real potential. And it takes a team, not just at a summer camp or a single school. As Zac told me one day when we were talking about the camp, it's hard to accomplish big things on your own; working with somebody, or a lot of somebodies, puts some fire behind you.

Reading about celebrities and superstars, some will be tempted to think, well, they can do that because they are famous . . . rich . . . whatever. And of course there'll be haters as well—criticism is epidemic these days.

But to quote Zac, "If you do something, you'll be sure to be met with resistance. That's OK. Keep going until you find others who believe in you.

"Make a difference in whatever way you can. Everybody is an ordinary person. I'm an ordinary person. The important part is that you can do something extraordinary."

Junking for Joy

Amie and Jolie Sikes

Maybe you saw their television show on HGTV. Maybe you sought them out after seeing the bus they decorated for country singer Miranda Lambert. Maybe you found their treasures in Pottery Barn stores and catalogs, or followed their entertaining mix on Instagram, or happened into their store in Round Top, Texas (population: 90). Or maybe you are one of the thousands who swell Round Top's population during the biannual antiques fairs and partake in the sisters' Prom.

However you meet the Junk Gypsies—Amie Sikes and her sister Jolie—you will immediately be impressed by their humor and kind hearts as well as their knack for picking gems out of the trash.

The two sisters have raised "junking"—recycling junked items—into an art form and a growing sensation. They sum up their philosophy as "We believe every man's trash is truly our treasure, junking is a way of life, and garage sales are our Rodeo Drive."

TV stints aside, their main business is selling antique and antique-inspired treasures that dress up minds as well as homes or bodies. Their eclectic style combines roots with whimsey, often with a Texan slant; it's a look that inspires hugs and grins. As they put it, they set out to create a store and instead found a lifestyle.

They are doing literally what I feel we all should do metaphorically—making beauty out of the junk of life. And they do it with flair and fun.

Three of my friends bought me my "She Who Is Brave Boots"—Junk Gypsy creations. They're my favorite boots, not just because they're comfortable—that is important!—but because they incorporate phoenix designs. The phoenix is a symbol of rebirth, new life rising from the ashes. Every time I put them on, I feel ready to become a new person.

But there is more to life than decorating or television shows. When Hurricane Harvey hit the Houston area in 2017, the two sisters felt they had to do something to help their neighbors. Their home is some eighty miles west of Houston, and while the storm did considerable damage there, it wasn't hit nearly as bad as the coast.

"I felt a huge guilt," confesses Amie, "that we weren't there to help."

There were personal connections to the disaster; relatives and friends were hit hard. One cousin sent a picture showing their entire first floor flooded—they'd taken shelter upstairs, fortunately, but were stranded until the water went down.

Seeing these and other pictures of the devastation, the Junk Gypsies decided to launch a fund-raising effort, designing and marketing T-shirts they sold online. Working with their friends Miranda Lambert and Marcus Luttrell (*Lone Survivor*, Team Never Quit) and his wife, Melanie, they designed a special T-shirt with the logo "We are Texas—come hell or high water." They raised $150,000 for flood victims and restoration, eating their own expenses on labor and other overhead.

Once they had the orders, they had to produce. The sisters and their employees collected the tees from their manufacturer, then began packing. They were joined by local volunteers, including a man who had already bought a hundred shirts. The post office stayed open late to handle the bags the Gypsies kept bringing in as they rushed to get the shirts out quickly.

I'm not surprised by that. Anyone who knows the sisters can tell that they are openhearted, generous people. If you make that connection, it's hard not to be the same way yourself. Part of it may be like attracting like. Another part may be something like inspiration and leadership—leading by example is hard to beat.

It's the ripple effect in action.

But why start? Why go through all that trouble for strangers?

It's not religion or church. Amie admits she goes to church sparingly, and if anything is turned off to religion. But she still feels a need to help others, not for God but for them and for herself.

"I don't feel like I *have* to do it," says Amie. "But we just feel better if we do."

The sisters' parents owned three small restaurants when they were growing up, but their lives were middle-class-comfortable rather than rich. They both worked in the family business at an early age and watched their parents habitually "comp" those too poor to pay. And like Jesse James, their grandmother was an important influence. She had a saying: "Cook enough for the family, and the stranger at the door."

At the end of the day, a lot of threads tie together in all of us to push us toward helping others. Empathy cannot be overrated. But neither can humility.

"We've had a lot of success," notes Amie. "Part of it was just hard-ass work, and a lot of it. But also part was luck."

That goes for all of us. Knowing that, how can we fail to help others whose luck has gone bad?

Or as Amie says, "If we put a lot of love into the world, the world will love us back."

SEVEN

Honor, Memory, and Angels

Precious Resources

As the wife of an active-duty SEAL, I learned a great deal about the sacrifices that service members and their families make. Chris often said that servicemen and -women sign a blank check to the USA for a price up to and including their lives, never knowing when or if it will be cashed. They do so willingly, understanding that service and sacrifice are the greatest forms of patriotism.

Their families make similar sacrifices, but often without any say in the matter. A toddler doesn't understand the word *sacrifice*, let alone the concept, yet he or she may have to sacrifice the love of a parent. Unless they've been through it themselves, few young wives or husbands truly understand what it's like to uproot their own lives every year or two because their spouse has been reassigned. And there's no way to explain to anyone why your stomach feels like an open sore every time a news report brings a rumor of war.

As important as it is to honor the living for their contributions, we can't forget those who have gone before. We've spoken a lot about the future in this book, about children and doing things to make their lives better. But our lives were improved as well. We stand on the backs and shoulders of many generations, pioneers, immigrants, overachievers. Laborers, workers, and, yes, the occasional no-good miscreant. Intentionally or not, their collective journeys made us better.

Thinking of the past reminds us of the values that brought us here. When it comes to the history of our sailors and soldiers, remembering the past and preserving it for the future is a vital task.

Which brings me to Lee Grimes and some other wonderful folk, past and present as well.

Honor and Heal

Veterans Memorial Museum

Having been military himself, my husband, Chris, loved helping other servicemen after he got out of the Navy. And he loved to do it anonymously. Many of his friends have stories about how he'd see a sailor or soldier in line at a store or a restaurant and would arrange to surreptitiously pay for their coffee or whatever. Then he'd tell the cashier not to give him away while he made off; the beneficiary was left to wonder who to thank.

On those occasions when he was found out, Chris would always tell the soldier or sailor to "pay it forward"—deliver some act of random kindness to someone else in the future.

Paying it forward works like magic, creating a ripple effect of goodwill throughout our communities and the country in general. And we're not talking big things, either—someone unexpectedly paying for your coffee profoundly changes your mood for the rest of the day and maybe the week. Yet the gesture doesn't actually cost all that much. Even cheaper: letting someone go in front of you in traffic with a smile.

Paying it forward.

But sometimes to pay things forward, we have to look back. And that's what Lee Grimes did out in Washington State.

As a young man, Lee won an appointment to West Point, the Army's prestigious college dedicated to training young officers. But circumstances kept Lee from joining the Army; he ended up becoming an accountant and then a carpenter in the area around Centralia and Chehalis, Washington, about an hour south of Tacoma if you're obeying the speed limit; a little less if you don't.

Still somewhat interested in the military, Lee got involved in re-creating some famous battles and encounters in World War II. He was just finishing one at a July 4 celebration when a veteran came up to him and thanked him for being part of the production.

It was important, said the veteran, to let people know what had happened in the past.

"Nobody's going to remember what we did," lamented the man.

Really?

The more Lee thought about it, though, the more he realized the man might be right. While there are plenty of history books around with the basic facts, each man's and woman's war was different. Many World War II veterans had never bothered to tell even their families about what they went through, and thus their memories of the war would disappear when they died.

Something, of course, that happens to us all, but was accelerating as these World War II soldiers aged.

Lee bought himself a video camera and a VCR and went around town interviewing World War II veterans about their experiences. His library of interviews quickly grew.

Occasionally, a veteran had to be coaxed into telling their story. This was a time before YouTube and Snapchat and other social media venues. More critically, the veterans were from a generation that tended to look suspiciously at anything that might smack of bragging.

And there were also men who'd had horrible experiences and didn't want the old memories and horrors to resurface.

Every story Lee collected is poignant in its own right, but among the most moving is the tale of a World War II POW tortured by the Japanese, who went on to serve in Korea after the war. Always tight-lipped about the experiences, he finally opened up for Lee at the urging of his family.

But this isn't a story about these veterans' memories, all of which have been archived for posterity.

Sometime after he started, veterans began giving Lee mementos of their service—jackets and uniforms, medals, diaries . . . all the physical things one might use to build a museum exhibit.

Or fill a basement and an attic and the rest of a house . . .

At some point, Lee and his wife realized that they had a lot of memorabilia and no place really to share it. As the story goes, one night he woke up with a message from God—make a museum.

Lee and some friends held a meeting in December 1995 and established a board to create a museum. Shortly afterward, they got a nonprofit status and began looking for a building. They found it in a storefront on Main Street in Chehalis.

Veterans Memorial Museum opened in 1997. Lee quit work to organize the museum and raise money. He also mortgaged his house to raise funds.

There were 189 visitors that first year. Two years later, the museum was too small to handle all its visitors, let alone house and display its artifacts properly.

The board decided to move down the road, finding a piece of property right off the highway.

That was the easy part. Raising the $1.68 million it took to build the facility was harder. Grants were not available for an operation that small and without a permanent building. But local veterans emptied their wallets; by opening day, the building was entirely paid for.

Museums at the time tended to tell stories about battles rather than about individual soldiers. At the time, there weren't many museums that would make service during, say, the Civil War, "real" by talking about a specific soldier, what he did before and after as well as during the battle, and how he lived. Besides his musket, the display might have his diary or pages from it, a sock darned by his mother, and so on.

Events with veterans as featured guests became a regular and popular occurrence—dances with World War II veterans, for example. Those events helped grow a community, as did more traditional programs like lectures—but even these had personal twists, with audience members who had served invited to come up and share a few memories. In many ways, the museum was as much a gathering point as anything else.

While much of the original focus was on World War II, Vietnam veterans found a particular resonance with the museum and its mission. In some cases, the programs represented a turning point in their ability to deal with the aftermath of their own war, to accept what they had been through, or to simply celebrate their time in the military. In a few cases, the museum acted as a clearing house for referrals, helping people get in touch with needed professionals. The overall message was one that honored service—not just of the men on the frontline but of everyone behind the scenes as well.

A flood in the winter of 2007–08 nearly wiped out the museum. While the building was three feet above the worst flood the town had ever experienced, it was still inundated. Flood waters—and everything associated with them, from grime to mud to debris—surged inside, filling the building with roughly a foot of water and damaging many of the holdings. The community responded—people whose homes and farms were four feet underwater left their property and spent countless hours salvaging, cleaning, and then repairing the museum, its artifacts, and the displays.

It took three months and hundreds of volunteers, but the museum reopened.

Not only has it recovered, but it continues to grow. There are displays and information on veterans from the Revolutionary War all the way up to what the museum calls "the desert wars"—Iraq, Afghanistan, and the current period, conflicts where my husband, Chris, served. Families continue to donate items and, more important, the life stories that go with them.

The current director of the museum is Chip Duncan. Chip is the son of an Air Force officer who was a nuclear engineer and a staff officer who became a computer simulations modeler—as he used to tell his son, he fought World War III forty-eight different times, trying to figure out what the proper strategy would be if there was a major conflict between superpowers during the Cold War era. Rejected from the service because of asthma, Chip trained as an architect, but as a young man he became a missionary. Somewhere in there, though, he developed a love of history, and on a visit to the Oregon area, he happened to meet a "grizzled old Marine" who told him he had to visit the museum.

His visit to the museum left him enthralled with the museum and its mission—and in tears. The stories the veterans told resonated in many ways, not least of all because of Chip's own family history, which includes men who served all the way back to the Revolutionary War.

He met Lee and started talking. A personal tour of some of the museum's holdings not on display led to a longer conversation, and out of the blue, Lee asked if he wanted to have his job someday.

Uh, but . . .

"I'm not ready to retire any time soon," answered Lee. "But keep it in mind."

Chip left with some skepticism about the offer, no doubt, as it had been made on the spur of the moment after perhaps an hour's worth of conversation. But a few years later, when Lee contacted him out of the blue and said he was ready to retire . . . how could Chip not check it out? Besides the museum, the community was perfect—a small-town feel, but not so small that it was isolated, with Tacoma about an hour to the north and Portland, Oregon—my hometown—an hour-ish to the south.

In 2008, Chip took over as administrative assistant—just after the museum had recovered from the flood. "That's my shame," he jokes now. "I missed it, and it was one of the biggest miracles of the place."

In 2010, Lee handed over the scepter. Today Chip presides over an institution that sees some seventeen thousand visitors a year and boasts its own army of volunteers, most of them veterans who have their own stories to tell.

Unlike a lot of small institutions, the Veterans Memorial Museum operates in the black—not by a huge amount, but these days anything above break-even is a huge success.

How does it do it?

Part of the answer is a very minimal operating budget, below $150,000 a year—it surely helps not to have mortgage payments. Then there are the perspiration and inspiration of the volunteers, many of whom start as visitors and get hooked.

"We honor relationships," says Chip. "We don't just say, pay your admission and look at old stuff." People get involved and become part of the museum community. Their contributions don't show up on the balance sheet, but they are critical to the museum.

The "old stuff" the museum puts on display is always part of a story, one that tells more than just the tale of heroes or battles. Cooks, truck drivers, clerks, medics, infantrymen—the full range of the services are represented and personalized; it's as if the man or woman down the street is personally sharing the tale of his or her life. More important, the museum serves as a nexus for a veterans community, whether locals or visitors.

The museum's veterans programs have two themes—heal and honor. Chaplains are generally on hand during events in case memories become overwhelming. The museum's small refreshment area features snacks and such and often becomes an unintended blessing, as it has morphed into a sharing place for visitors telling their own stories.

"When you're looking at our display, you're making a connection to the veteran," notes Chip. "It's not all blood and guts and glory."

It's real people.

The effects are endless. There was the Vietnam veteran who wandered in one afternoon for a little peace and quiet—his grandkids were having a party, and after a while there was only so much he could take. He happened to start talking to one of the staff and suddenly opened with his tale—wounded with a buddy, he'd been triaged at an evacuation site, waiting for an inbound helicopter. The medic decided he was worse off, and so the man was put on the next chopper out. His friend waited for another flight.

The friend died there, waiting on the ground for the helicopter.

The guilt still haunted him. *Why me? Why not my friend?*

Maybe your large family, ventured Chip, who'd listened as he told the story.

"I never thought of it that way," admitted the man.

The museum has branched out beyond its display cases. It sponsors a Civil War reenactment that has become one of the biggest in the state, perhaps because so many Civil War veterans migrated to the Pacific Northwest following the war. There's also a car show, and Chip and his team are on the lookout for more ways to reach a new generation that will have less connection to veterans than those from World War II or Vietnam, where the draft meant so many families were familiar with military service and valued information about what their loved ones and ancestors might have done.

But the stories of the men and women who served remain the centerpiece. Everyone finds a different connection. Among the most poignant for Chip are the artifacts for a corporal killed in Vietnam—including a Purple Heart and another medal, as well as letters—that were found and bought in a garage sale. Contacted by Lee, who thought they might want the items, the family said they wanted nothing to do with them.

He died in Vietnam. We're done.

While shocking to some of us, it's not an unusual sentiment for a portion of Gold Star families. The pain of loss in many cases is so great that the survivors push away all memories. Attempting to do something positive with the memory can be an impossibly difficult task.

"About 2007, or 2008, one of the corporal's platoon members came through," says Chip. The man had carried the corporal's body out of the jungle. Overcome with emotion at seeing the display, he later wrote the museum a letter detailing his memories and experience. It's now on display.

Next to that display is one remembering a local Medal of Honor winner, a man who had jumped on a hand grenade. The two displays speak of the range of memory—one trumpeted, one muted—that war evokes.

Every tour Chip gives ends with the story of Jeff, a local kid from Spokane who at age ten realized he wanted to help people through first aid. He became an EMT, then a medic in the National Guard. Deployed in Iraq, he was in Baghdad, working in a trauma center, when an Iraqi doctor asked for supplies for a clinic a few miles outside of the city. On their day off, Jeff and some others went to deliver those supplies; while en route, their vehicle was hit by an improvised explosive device, or IED. Jeff took the brunt of the explosion, dying instantly but saving the others.

"To love and live with passion" was Jeff's motto. He picked it up when he was sixteen; today it is enshrined on his marker at the cemetery. He certainly fulfilled that; his service and sacrifice were made in the hopes that we, too, would remain free to fulfill it.

I drove up one day with my father, who retired as a lieutenant colonel in the Marine Corps. The visit prompted memories of his early days with my mom as well as his service. Inside the museum, Chip took us on our own private tour, filling us in on so many of the stories connected with the displays.

When it came time for the day's program, veterans came up individually to address the crowd and tell them a few words about their service. I was moved practically to tears.

As important as the displays are in teaching others what military service and lives are like, the best part of the museum are the people you meet there—not only the veterans but the people who come to honor them, to learn a little bit about them, and to pass that knowledge on to others. It's a ripple effect of information that forms a deep bond between the past, present, and future.

"We can't let these stories go," says Chip. "We have to share them."

And that's what Veterans Memorial Museum does so well.

Perseverance and Remembrance
Kim Roller and the *Indy*

Spreading the stories of veterans could be the motto of another Pacific Northwest native, Kim Roller. Not that she set out to do that, exactly.

Kim was a mom in Utah around 2003 when she booked a flight to see her sister in Southern California. The weather in California was undoubtedly beautiful—as a former resident, I know—but the weather in between was decidedly not, and Kim found her flight delayed for several hours. Wandering the airport, she happened into a bookstore and picked up a copy of Doug Stanton's book on the USS *Indianapolis* disaster, *In Harm's Way*.

The USS *Indianapolis*—CA-35—was a heavy cruiser in World War II. (Technically minded buffs will point out that the ship was originally designated as a light cruiser because of its armor displacement; it was only the size of its guns that made the Navy add the word *heavy*. But we'll leave all that to the experts.)

Cruisers were important ships in World War II. While smaller than aircraft carriers and battleships, they were swift and powerful, able to operate on their own or as part of a battle group. Among her many other accomplishments, the *Indy* served as the flagship for Admiral Raymond Spruance during the war; Spruance was a key leader in the conflict's Pacific theater. The *Indy* also played an important role in ending the war, delivering the uranium and some other parts of the first atomic bomb to a base on the island of Tinian in the Pacific.

Immediately after that trip, the ship sailed to Guam and then headed toward Leyte in the Philippines. She never made it.

Early in the morning of July 30, about midway to her destination, the cruiser was hit by two torpedoes from a Japanese submarine. Within twelve minutes, the cruiser had rolled and begun to slide down beneath the waves. Roughly three hundred of her nearly twelve hundred crewmen died immediately or went down with the ship. Adrift, the survivors were attacked repeatedly for several days by sharks and suffered all kinds of different tortures, many of them fatal. Only 317 men remained alive when Navy rescue forces finally managed to reach them.

There's one other element to the story that is important here. The ship's captain, Charles McVay, was court-martialed following his rescue, charged with failure to zigzag—basically, take defensive measures meant to make it more difficult for a submarine's torpedoes to hit the ship. He was also accused of failing to give the order to abandon ship promptly.

The court-martial was unusual and extremely controversial; McVay's commanding admiral tried to short-circuit it but was overruled. It seems likely that the reason for the prosecution had more to do with the Navy's failure to promptly search for or rescue the men than any alleged action on McVay's part. Nonetheless, he was convicted, becoming the only ship's captain (of nearly four hundred) who lost their ships to enemy action to be put on trial and successfully prosecuted. The secretary of the navy overturned the sentence but not the conviction. McVay returned to active duty, but he was forever haunted by the disaster, and it may have been a contributing factor to his suicide in 1968.

In the years that followed, many people realized that the court-martial was a grave injustice. But it was not until the 1990s when a twelve-year-old Florida student, Hunter Scott, did a National History project on the matter that public opinion persuaded Congress to pass a resolution formally exonerating him.

Kim started reading Stanton's book in the airport and basically didn't stop—not on the plane, not at her sister's. She was so enthralled by the tales of the men—their suffering, their perseverance—that she decided to include it as a lesson for her kids, whom she was home schooling at the time.

Looking for a way to make the history come alive, she wondered: What if they heard it from Scott himself?

Kim tracked down the young historian, who by that time was in college. She offered to pay his way if he'd come and talk with the kids; he gladly accepted.

And by the way, he told her, did you know that two of the survivors live near you?

Kim contacted them, and they agreed to come along and help Scott make history come alive. Elated, she told some fellow home-schooling moms, who told others, who told a high school teacher. . . .

Originally planned for Kim's home, the event was moved to a hall. When Kim arrived an hour or so before

Scott's presentation, she saw some eight hundred chairs set up.

"You have to take half of these away," she told one of the custodians. "We're not going to fill them, and it will look embarrassing."

Too late, said the man. Make do.

They had to. But it turned out that the problem wasn't empty seats—it was an overflow crowd. Word of the presentation had spread far and wide, and some eleven hundred people showed up.

Kim became friends not only with the survivors who were her neighbors but with others. She attended the crew's 2004 reunion. Then she began helping them spread their stories in presentations to schools, businesses, and civic groups. That task went into high gear after she started working as an airline attendant, which not only gave her a flexible work schedule but also made it possible to obtain low fares for the survivors.

There are possibly as many variations to the *Indy* presentations as there are survivors and audiences, but when Kim's there, you can count on her coming on stage to introduce the program dressed in 1940s garb from head to toe—even with the authentic eyebrow pencil line on the back of her calves, imitating the way young women pretended to be wearing expensive nylons during the war. There are photos, a little bit of the movie *Jaws,* where Scott first heard of the story, and the scenes drive home the danger the men faced after the sinking. The grand finale features a survivor who can tell his specific story and answer questions from the audience.

"I like doing high schools best," says Kim. "The schools freak out when I say I need an hour—no one thinks they'll have the attention span to last. But I've never lost an audience yet."

Indeed, the most common reaction from those who witness her presentations is a liquid one: tears.

Over the years, some of the most poignant tears have come from the survivors themselves, often behind the scenes before the actual presentation. The memories of their suffering in the water, the loss of their companions—the experience remains very real and immediate all these years later.

The men have also talked frankly about the toll the disaster took on their lives afterward. This was long before PTSD was recognized, let alone properly treated. Alcoholism was not uncommon among the survivors. For some, settling down to a productive life was beyond difficult; as one put it to Kim, "I drank myself from town to town for years."

But overall, the stories the men tell, and the lives they've lived, are ones filled with hope. If they could get through such an utter tragedy, what can we get through? They did it with such limited resources. We have so many avenues to healing today, it is unconscionable not to keep trying.

It's almost a certainty that whatever difficulties any of us encounter pale in comparison to spending days in shark-infested waters and seeing our best friends and comrades die. If these men can get beyond that—can go on to lead productive lives and inspire others to do the same—what can't *we* do? We're all survivors in our own way; the trick is to move to the next stage, where we don't simply survive but thrive.

As time has gone on, fewer and fewer of the survivors have been left to tell the stories. Kim has kept going, believing it's important to help while they are still alive to make that important human connection. She believes it's important for the next generation to honor those men in person, if possible. In a very real sense, the suffering that the crew of the *Indianapolis* experienced was a payment for today's freedom. The demands of tomorrow have yet to be made—but the wages will be more easily given by people who understand that they have already benefited from others.

These days, Kim does four or five presentations a year. Schools and other organizations contact her through the *Indianapolis*'s Facebook and web pages; in many cases, word of mouth leads them to her as well. As a general rule, her minimal expenses and those of any veteran are paid by the hosts; Kim has stayed in many a spare room to help keep the costs down—and it helps, too, that she can fly for free.

The youngest remaining survivor is now in his early nineties. At some point in the future, there will be no more survivors to join in the presentations.

"I'm still going to do them," she says firmly. "We need to tell the real story."

With all due respect to my friends in the movie business—and our fellow writers—you can't get the real story from a film or a TV series, or even the best-written book. There's no substitute for hearing it from the person who actually experienced it, though the next best thing is surely someone like Kim, who has spent so much time with the "real" people that he or she has absorbed the facts almost by osmosis.

During one of the earliest presentations that Kim did with some of the survivors, an audience member stood up and asked one of the sailors what advice he might give a fourteen-year-old just starting out in life.

With a tear in his eye, the veteran thought for barely an instant.

"Never, ever give up," he said.

The words reverberated in the hall, echoing in the silence that followed. They resonate with me, today and forever:

Never, ever give up.

For Kids and Country

Angels of America's Fallen

Empathy—*The ability to understand and share the feelings of another.*

Back in the mid-1990s, Joe Lewis was a young Marine officer training to become a pilot when he befriended another aviator-in-training who happened to be his next-door neighbor. The two completed the early stages of training, then transitioned to different aircraft. Shortly after that, Joe's friend died in a training accident.

The loss hit Joe hard. His friend had left a wife and young son; they soon moved away, cutting off all contact with the circle of friends that included Joe as they sought to get past their grief.

How will that boy do? Joe wondered. Father and son had been close; Joe had often seen them together, playing, fooling around, doing all the little things that a dad and boy do.

Who was going to do that with him now? Just as important, would there be money in the family for the little things like Little League or soccer, music lessons, art camp, Scouts, ball games—extracurricular affairs that don't seem like a big part of growing up until one stands back and considers the subtler influences on the way we become adults?

With all contact lost, Joe could only wonder.

Joe got on with his life. He continued his military career, excelling as a Marine Corps pilot flying F/A-18s, working for American Airlines, and then joining the Air National Guard after 9/11.

As his career went on, Joe lost friends in every service. In nearly each case, the families had young children. He noted that the families weren't abandoned, exactly; besides friends and extended families, there were different programs for big things like scholarships that helped provide for the children's futures.

But he also realized that there were gaps. There was no replacing Dad or Mom. And in many cases, no money for those little things that Joe had thought about when his friend died.

Sports, art, music—there was more to those activities than entertainment for kids. Under the right circumstances, they could become outlets for grief and constructive ways of channeling energy and emotion. They were also places where adult mentors—coaches, teachers—might provide positive role models or at least spot potential problems.

"I saw a gap," says Joe. "Between grief counseling and scholarships."

The more he thought about it, the more Joe wanted to fill that gap.

"I didn't hear a booming voice of God or anything," he notes. "But I knew this was what I had to do.

It was a big problem. Joe found that in 2010, there were more than sixteen thousand children of military families who had lost their dad or mom. The average age of the children when the parent died was seven. All the kids were at a higher risk for things like depression, suicide, truancy, dropping out of school—you name the problem, they're likely to be in danger of succumbing to it.

Since there was no organization helping them, Joe decided he would start one himself. Not entirely alone, though. His wife, Shelli, who had an extensive background as both a teacher and a financial manager, would be a full partner.

"I just asked her to write the checks," says Joe. "But she went all in."

This doesn't surprise me. I have found the best military spouses—and perhaps committed wives everywhere—are every bit the warrior their husbands are.

They called their organization Angels for America's Fallen, which pretty much summarized their goal.

Following his final separation from the service, the family took a several-month RV vacation. Joe, his wife, and their two sons traveled all across America, then relocated to Colorado in 2012. Joe went to school, literally, on running nonprofits, earning a master of public administration degree, a graduate certificate in nonprofit management, and a graduate certificate in nonprofit fund development and program evaluation from the University of Colorado. (He also has a bachelor of science degree in physical science with dual minors in business and criminal justice from Troy University.)

The first children they helped were three boys whose father had been a chaplain killed in Afghanistan.

Joe hadn't even finished the IRS process to be declared a bona fide nonprofit when he was introduced to the chaplain's widow. "I didn't know what to expect," says Joe. "Talking to them, though, I was inspired. I realized it was more than an obligation—it was an honor."

The kids wanted to learn to swim. So his nascent group's first mission was to arrange lessons for the two older boys and a "mommy and me" class for the youngest.

That set the pattern for the way Angels would work. Rather than providing the actual service itself, the organization arranges with instructors, leagues, organizations in the families' hometowns. The idea is that these providers already exist and have the expertise to help; letting them handle it makes more sense than inserting another party. Angels contacts them and makes the payment arrangements; in many cases, the children are provided for at a reduced rate, though that is not mandatory. While they accept discounts gratefully, Angels doesn't ask up front for them.

Is it difficult to talk to families who have lost their father or mother?

"It's difficult and emotional for them," says Joe, who has had many such discussions now over the years. "We honor the loss and the sacrifice. But we also recognize the parent and the kids who are continuing."

The overwhelming feeling at these first meetings is sadness. It's just sad.

But then, as they continue to talk, the mood often changes. The focus shifts to positive things that Angels—and the family—can do. The conversations end on a hopeful note. Then, over time, hope turns to genuine progress and positive things. It is truly a beacon of light through the darkness.

There are some very personal cases, including the family of a master sergeant Joe had once served with. But most often, families hear about the foundation from others in the military or the law enforcement community. They go to the website—www.aoafallen.org—and fill out a brief form there with contact information and a short message describing the need. Shelli then follows up.

It doesn't matter why or how the service member died, whether in combat, in training, on leave. Even suicide is not a barrier to help.

"To the child, it doesn't matter," says Joe. "If Mom or Dad gave all, that's all it takes to qualify."

Joe and his wife try to get to know the people who apply before the arrangements are approved. They're not counselors, but they have sympathetic ears who by now have lots of experience hearing stories of grief.

"We encourage the kids to stay in touch," says Joe. He and his wife have quite a collection of homemade music videos. It's fun to see the performances gradually improve over the years.

Currently, Angels of America's Fallen is helping more than 330 children spread all across the country. Families of law enforcement are also eligible to apply. Once enrolled, there's a long-term commitment to keep helping. The kids go through different phases as they grow; the organization tries to stay alongside them.

There are success stories—or "Angel Stories" as the organization calls them when they post videos on their website.

The group helped Boston Gilbert, for example, develop a love for soccer. His skills have now taken him to Southern Methodist University on an athletic scholarship. His dad, Major Troy Gilbert, was an F-16 pilot who died in Iraq. Boston was nine years old.

"Being on that soccer field gave Boston a way to focus on something else," says his mother, Ginger Gilbert Ravella. Boston's dad had played as a young man, and Boston has clearly inherited his athletic skills.

Boston credits Angels with having not only helped honor his father and the family but also encouraging him to do what he loves. It's a sentiment echoed by many of the others who have benefited from the foundation.

While they're raising awareness of the kids, the Angels are also raising awareness among the families in need. Unfortunately, the latter is growing more quickly than the money to help them, and there's a long waiting list for help. Joe is working on fund-raisers to bring more support so that additional families can be assisted each year.

Help comes from all corners. American Airlines contacted Joe after learning of his military retirement, asking if he wanted to come back to work as a pilot.

No, he answered, I have this cause. . . . Maybe you would support it?

The airline has, giving Angels frequent-flier miles to be used in support of the programs.

The Angel Gala is the foundation's major annual event. Originally started by one of the moms the organization helped, it has become not only a fund-raiser but a chance to show off the talents of some of the kids.

I was honored to get a chance to speak at one in 2017. What impressed me then, and continues to impress me today, is how infectious the atmosphere in the room was. There's a ripple of energy that vibrates right through the walls. And you can tell the flow continues throughout the year—and onward.

The people you meet and hear about there are not just families who have been helped, like the handful of friends who came together after a man they knew died, leaving his little girl without a dad. They wanted to help, but not one of them knew anything about girls; they either had boys or no children at all.

What they did know was woodworking.

But that's not something you can do with a girl, can you?

Sure it is!

Under their tutelage, the young girl became a skilled woodworker—a testament to her adopted "dads." It's now a pastime that brings her much pleasure—and results in some fine woodworking. Angels helped support her work in small but very meaningful ways over the years.

I heard of a study once showing that if a young person has five adults in his or her life whom they trust and know truly loves them, they are far less likely to escape into drugs and other addictions. That surely helps their odds of turning out better than OK. I guess if those five adults are skilled woodworkers, they'll turn out some great furniture as well.

Besides the big fund-raiser, there are local efforts, like a local skate-a-thon at a Chick-fil-A parking lot, where people raise money in a marathon skating session. Participants dress up in costume—Elvis has been sighted on more than one occasion. Other events held by different groups also benefit the foundation. And people who have been helped by the group give back by holding their own small events or pledging money as part of fund-raising events like races.

"What keeps me up at night is that we've made a commitment to help kids," confesses Joe, who works tirelessly coming up with ways to keep those promises. "It's only the goodness of people's hearts to support it."

Got a lot of kids who want to get swimming lessons?

A partnership with the National Swimming Pool Foundation allows Angels to hook the kids up with local instructors. How that partnership came about is a perfect illustration of what I call the ripple effect.

Joe was invited to speak about his organization at the World Aquatic Health Conference. While standing in a line, he struck up a conversation with a magazine editor, who in turn was inspired to create a category of people in the industry—or related to it in some way—who helped others for the magazine's annual selection of the most important people connected with swimming.

Joe ended up winning the award. More important, the connection he forged at the conference helped the Angels launch the national program, which served a hundred kids in its first year.

For the record, Joe is not much of a swimmer himself. "I had to take remedial swimming in the Marine

Corps," he confesses, and he claims he hasn't gotten much better.

Angels of America's Fallen remains a home-grown group—its offices are in the Lewis's home—which means husband and wife spend all day working, and a few of the nights as well. It's efficient in some ways, but there are *moments*.

"What hat am I wearing?" jokes Joe at times, speaking to his wife. "CEO? Husband?"

Or just the guy whose turn it is to take out the garbage?

"It's a passion," he says of the foundation, not the garbage. "We never turn it off."

The foundation has helped the pair over the years as they've lost friends, giving them a channel to turn grief into something positive.

As the foundation matures and the kids it helps grow, there will undoubtedly be many more success stories—and many kids who in turn help others. That's one that drives everyone involved. As Joe puts it, "I can't wait to see what all these kids do as we go on."

I agree!

Mr. Perseverance

David Goggins

If you open the dictionary and look up the word *perseverance*, you'll see David Goggins's picture next to it.

Or at least you should.

If David's life story illustrates anything, it's what you can accomplish if you put your mind to it. And that *is* the definition of perseverance.

The amazing thing about David is not the fact that he graduated SEAL training after breaking a leg, or that he went on to become one of the very few SEALs to complete Army Ranger School, which made him a rare Ranger-SEAL. His fifty-plus ultramarathons? Impressive—crazy, even—but just part of his résumé.

The fact that he lost more than a hundred pounds in a few months just to get into shape to try out for the SEALs?

Quite an achievement, but not quite as amazing as the fact that he did all this, and more, with a hole in his heart.

A hole, I might add, that had to be repaired not once but twice.

David is one of my favorite people in the world. I truly love him. Not just for his grit and perseverance, though those are unmatched. His spirit, laughter, and goodness are what make him special, a beautiful human being in spite of the ugliness of life. David and my husband, Chris, first bonded during SEAL training, and it's obvious why. You couldn't find a better battle buddy. They pushed each other to be the best, beyond all obstacles—something David continues to do not only for friends but for anyone who meets him.

I've had the privilege of working with David on the Patriot Tour, where I'm always in awe of his speaking ability. He never fails to enthrall audiences with stories of his life and hardships.

David's childhood was difficult. His father, now dead, was abusive; his stepfather murdered. David experienced more than his share of racism as a child and young man. He joined the Air Force; after reentering the civilian world at the end of his enlistment, he found himself overweight and undermotivated. He set out to change who he was.

The change was dramatic. Not only did he slim down to roughly 175 pounds (from close to 300), he got himself into shape to enter BUD/S—Basic Underwater Demolition/SEAL Training, the gateway to becoming a SEAL. Not coincidentally, he met my husband, Chris, in BUD/S, where they not only became friends but decided to partner up. They pushed each other through, achieving more together than they might have on their own.

As physically demanding as that training is, most SEALs will tell you that the hardest part is mental: the key is to keep going after finding your physical limit. In a word, *persevere.*

Where did that come from? David says he found mental strength by remembering the adversity that he'd experienced as a child. No matter what the present threw at him, he'd come through worse.

BUD/S and especially Hell Week—the legendary period of physical extremes and sleep deprivation that is one of the key passages of the early training—somehow helped him focus his mind. Rather than thinking about the pain of exhausted muscles or the cold ocean water or even the cries of others ready to quit, David was able to isolate his mind, finding peace in the stars and the vacuum that suffering placed around him. The mental abuse he'd suffered as a small child—the lies about how he was a worthless human being and worse—were a thick skin of armor against failure now. The strain of pushing his body to its limits released him from worry and pain.

Which is not to say that there were no physical consequences. He suffered two stress fractures during his first Hell Week and was therefore "rolled back"— taken from training and held out to heal, before joining a later class. That happened again, though this time with a more serious break to his leg. Rolled back again, David made it through the third time. (Because of timing with the injuries, the regulations in effect, and his status as a reservist, David went through Hell Week three times. Regulations now prevent that. I'm not sure whether it's a record—David doesn't know of anyone else who endured that—but it's certainly not an experience anyone would want to live through.)

David describes himself as a "weak kid" growing up. He acted tough, but in reality, on the inside, he was scared and unsure of who he was and what he should do. He remained that person until his first Hell Week. At that point, he realized the nutrition and exercise program he'd followed had "created a whole 'nother human being."

The realization helped him turn things up another notch. Rather than running from challenges, he began seeking them out. He saw difficulty as opportunity— the "crucible of life" was a chance to become someone unique and different. Struggle made him better.

Not that he always won; no one does. But the process of testing himself became growth.

Then came his biggest challenge: his heart.

David was already a SEAL and an ultramarathon runner when he realized he was feeling excessively fatigued. He went to a doctor, who conducted a thorough examination but couldn't find anything wrong.

Maybe it's in your head, suggested the doctor, who wondered if David had PTSD or some other mental ailment.

"It's not in my head," replied David.

One thing I'll say about SEALs—they don't go to doctors unless something is really wrong. And I mean *really* wrong. So you know David was hurting very badly.

Still skeptical, the doctor sent him for an echocardiogram—sonar for the heart. The machine watches the heart as it beats, providing a thorough image of the vital organ's functioning.

The test is fairly long; it lasted about forty-five minutes in David's case. He and the technician spent the first half hour or so chatting and joking around. Suddenly, the tech grew silent. With a serious look on his face, he excused himself and left the room.

He returned a few moments later with a doctor.

Another doctor joined them. Then another. Before long, an entire pack of doctors, interns, and medical students had squeezed into the room to check on David's tests.

The machine had found a hole in his heart, apparently present since birth, that allowed blood from one side to enter the other. In effect, "bad blood"—blood that had given up its oxygen—was taking a shortcut back out into his body without picking up the fresh oxygen it was supposed to carry. That lack of O2 was why he felt so run-down.

The condition was far more serious than David thought; there was no curing it with a nap. The wonder was how he had achieved so much with such a defect, which he'd obviously had from birth.

It took two operations to fix his heart. It was more than two years before he was released back for regular assignments as a SEAL.

Since leaving the service, David has tried to find new challenges, the Patriot Tour among them. Audiences love him, but the challenges he seems to like best are physical. When I spoke to him for the book, he was training to be a smoke jumper—one of those guys who jumps out of an airplane to fight fires.

Why?

Because he wants to do something that most people don't.

And, he says, because smoke jumpers are some of the most extreme people on the planet, and hanging out with them makes him a better person.

"It's not the Trident that makes you a superior human being," says David, referring to the SEALs' signature symbol. "It's the guys next to you."

David sees today's society as too soft and challenge-adverse. In his mind, challenge is good for individuals and for society as a whole. He's spreading that message, both in a recently published book (available online at his website), and in talks to groups. He gives about fifty a year, including the Patriot Tour. He uses his story to inspire others—his message to the audience is simple: if a severely overweight former airman with a heart defect can get himself into shape and become a SEAL, pretty much anything can happen if you work hard enough.

Set the challenge; embrace the struggle and the pain. Work through it.

There's another message in his life story, though, and it has to do with his heart. Sometimes the biggest things holding us back aren't those that we know, like a broken leg, but those we don't know, like an undetected hole in our heart. It may take deep examination to find that handicap or barrier; very possibly, it will be obvious to no one else. Finding it sooner rather than later, and then dealing with it, may be the key to your success.

David's perseverance led him to succeed despite his physical ailments. He was able to achieve a great deal largely because he refused to quit and realized as he went that he could make himself into a new person.

Also key: once he achieved that, he didn't rest on his laurels or his backside; he kept going.

David gives money that he raises from speaking to groups that help others, most recently the National Smokejumper Association, which among other things has a fund to help families whose loved ones have recently died while working. But I think the most important thing about him is that he's a one-man ripple effect, the stone that drops into the pond and pushes out the rings. Meeting him, listening to his story, people realize that they, too, have untapped strength and unrealized potential.

Maybe they'll become SEALs or smoke jumpers.

Maybe they'll sit behind a desk all their lives. But whatever their goals, if they push themselves to reach them, if they push through the difficulties and persevere, they will become better human beings, in turn inspiring and encouraging others.

EIGHT
Belief

Matters of Faith

You don't need to have a strong belief in God or be of any one particular faith or persuasion to overcome tragedy. There are plenty of examples of people from all cultures, past and present, overcoming dramatic odds to achieve greatness on both small and massive scales.

Having recognized that, let me say that, for me, faith has always been important. My beliefs have been Bible-based since I was a little girl. To paraphrase some advice my dad gave me as I was growing up, *It's not absolutely necessary to know the Bible, but it does make things easier. It's a recipe for happiness.*

The more I have looked to it for answers, the more I see he is right. It is a recipe for happiness, but it takes faith to believe it and courage to live it.

I proudly call myself a Christian and am drawn to seeing how others see God in their life.

If you've known me for any length of time, you know it goes without saying that I'm not perfect. I could be the reason for the saying "I love Jesus, but I cuss a little." I'm working on it. Often I've failed to measure up to the standards I set for myself. But one of the most reassuring beliefs for any Christian is the promise of redemption. God loves all of us, and if we turn toward Him and ask for forgiveness with true conviction, it will be granted.

Not that we won't pay for sins, just that salvation won't be denied on account of them. Not only is it reassuring, it's demanding. If we can be flawed and forgiven, we must accept the same is true for everyone. Even murderers, if they seek forgiveness.

Those are my beliefs, though. I won't force them on you or even think less of you because you don't share them. It's my responsibility to live them, not yours. You must follow your path.

Sometimes, people are tempted to measure their faith against others. They ask, does this person believe the way I do? Do they believe as strongly as I do?

Or conversely:

How can this person believe at all? Why would anyone?

Both are an attempt to judge others—a right that belongs to God, not us. The sentiment was best summed up for me by a pastor: "I hold neither the keys to heaven nor hell."

Or, to use an agnostic or atheist version: "I am not an Almighty; it is not mine to condemn or save."

I don't take anyone else's faith as a challenge. And I decided a long time ago that I am absolutely fine with my faith being challenged. I wouldn't base my life, earthly or eternal, on anything I hadn't studied and found to stand up to the challenge of science or academia, let alone the peaceful exploration of other religions. Freedom of religion, not freedom from it, is one of the best parts of America.

Lead with Love

The Collins Family

As a parent—as a mom—I can't think of anything worse than seeing a child suffer. My own kids, God bless them, are healthy, but let one of them get hurt playing or even come down with the flu—I'm sure parents everywhere understand exactly what I feel.

How much worse it must be, then, for parents of children who get a disease like cancer. Even with an array of dedicated professionals to help the family through, even knowing that in many cases there are cures—it takes extraordinary strength to persevere.

But what if the child's disease is not well-known? What if there's not an army of professionals standing by to attack the disease?

What happens then?

Susan and Chris Collins met in high school—teenage sweethearts.

But it wasn't quite love at first sight. In fact, just the opposite.

They met on Chris's first day as a sophomore transfer when he swaggered into class. His long, curly hair framed a good-looking face atop a tall, athletically slim body.

"Who is this cute new guy?" said Susan from her seat.

Perhaps she said it a little too loudly, because the cute new guy—Chris—walked directly to her and said, "The best thing you can do is sit down and shut up."

Ouch.

The mutual animosity softened in the months that followed, giving way to a grudging and then solid friendship. Romance followed, and by senior year, they were going steady. Four years of college and courtship led to marriage in 1986.

After high school, Chris became a professional ballplayer, working his way up in the Angels' organization while Susan finished an accounting degree. While still in the minors, Chris hurt his pitching arm; eventually he needed Tommy John surgery. Unfortunately, despite the operation and a lengthy rehab, he ended up blowing out his arm again and reluctantly gave up his career.

What do you do when your dream ends?

You get another one. Chris went into golf, finding work at different clubs as a pro and slowly building a new career from the bag room up.

Susan, meanwhile, was crunching numbers as an accountant in Florida, where the couple had made their home following Chris's Tommy John surgery. It was a good climate for baseball and a great one for golf.

It wasn't a bad one for raising a family, either. Susan suffered two miscarriages before the successful birth of their first son in 1990. Three years later, they conceived Christian.

At first, everything looked A-OK. Then one day during a routine ultrasound, the tech had trouble getting a good image.

"I'm having trouble with the hands," she explained to Susan as she worked the machine. "Hard to get the image."

Just one of those things, thought Susan, until the next morning. She was taking the last bite of her Wheat Chex before heading out to work when the phone rang.

It was her doctor.

"There's a problem with the baby," he said.

"Problem?"

Choking down the food in her mouth, Susan listened as the doctor told her Christian's hands were deformed.

There might be other problems, too. More investigation was needed.

They scheduled a more sophisticated ultrasound at a facility two counties away—it was the closest place available. The distance wasn't as bad as the wait; it took a week to find an opening. That week was filled with anxiety, trepidation, and pleading as Susan tried to get an earlier appointment but couldn't.

The new test showed that the fetus had no thumbs on either hand.

"You got plenty of time to get rid of it," said a doctor coldly.

Neither Chris nor Susan had given abortion a thought to that point, and they reacted immediately.

Not an option.

"We were both still processing," Susan remembers. "We were in a fog. On the way home, we passed a baseball field and it hit me. Baseball had been such a big part of our lives, and I thought, this child won't be able to throw a baseball and do normal kid stuff. How bad is it—will he be able to hold my hand?"

The doctors they spoke to weren't sure what caused the abnormalities or what else to expect. With little to go on, Chris and Susan braced themselves for other issues. The doctors made a guess that the disease might be related to a blood ailment, but they could not be definitive. The family lined up donors in case the infant needed transfusions at birth.

As Susan's due date approached, she told friends and coworkers of the baby's problems. The reaction ran the gamut, from sympathy to outright cruelty. One suggested she just "get rid of it" with birth only a few weeks away.

As cruel as that sounded to Susan, it's a common conversation during pregnancy. There are many tests mothers take to determine if their fetus has abnormalities. One reason is to prepare the parents, but the other is to give the option to abort. It takes courage to make the decision the Collins family made.

What Susan and Chris didn't get, with the problems Christian had, was the one thing she really needed: information on what to expect. No one knew, not the experts, not random acquaintances. Everything seemed a dark, unspeakable mystery.

A few weeks before she was due, Susan sensed that the baby had stopped moving. When her doctor insisted nothing was wrong, she called his partner, who scheduled a C-section for the next day.

The fact that Christian had stopped moving turned

out not to be critical, but it was definitely a sign of trouble to come. As soon as he was born, Christian was moved to the neonatal intensive care unit and given a battery of tests. They found he had an issue with his heart, only one kidney, fused vertebrae, no appreciable pituitary tissue. . . .

The list went on.

"Basically, they found problems in every system, except his eyes," says Susan. Each day brought a new test and more gloom.

His parents did the best they could to cope.

"Every time we got a new report, we said, OK. OK. OK," says Susan, remembering the onslaught and their efforts to simply keep up. It helped tremendously that Christian had a sparkling personality. "He had character, even as a little monkey in the NICU," says Susan before bragging on her newborn son's silver-gold mohawk.

He was cute but very small. That happened to be a clue to his condition, but neither his parents nor his doctors knew that yet.

Conflicting theories rose from the puzzling results of the tests. As the specialists puzzled it out, Chris found a doctor in Boston named Peter Waters who could operate on their son's hands. Though he taught at Harvard and was among the world's experts at pediatric hand surgery, he always seemed to have time to explain and sit with the family.

Acting on suspicions based on his experience, he initiated tests that revealed that Christian was suffering from Fanconi anemia. By the time the diagnosis was confirmed, the little boy was two years old and had had five surgeries to correct the problems associated with his hands.

Fanconi anemia is a genetic disease that mainly affects the bone marrow and the production of blood cells. (There is a similarly named disease, Fanconi syndrome, which is a rare kidney disorder. The two are not related.)

There are three types of blood cells. Red blood cells distribute oxygen throughout the body. If our blood vessels are a transportation system, the red blood cells are the delivery trucks. White blood cells help the body fight infections; they're like an army in our body, kicking out invaders. Last but not least, platelets are a special kind of blood cell that clots to stop bleeding— construction crews to patch things up when you're wounded.

A shortage of any one of these cell types creates huge problems. A shortage or imbalance of all of them, especially before birth and soon after, is catastrophic. Vital organs may not develop properly. Hearing and sight can be impaired. Cancer—leukemia, especially, but others that primarily affect the head, neck, and urinary system—often occurs.

The condition was first named in 1967 by a Swiss doctor, Guido Fanconi, whose work linked with earlier discoveries and really started what eventually became a wave of research into the disease and its related affects. But even by the time the Collinses' son was diagnosed, information was still relatively scant.

Chris was with his son in Boston when the doctors revealed the diagnosis. The hospital library had a single book about the disease.

Knowing he couldn't finish it before having to leave, Chris "borrowed" it and brought it back to his hotel room.

"I think there's a little more to this," he told his wife that night after reading through much of the book. The condition was not just life-threatening but dramatically life-shortening as well.

Still looking for information, Susan decided they should seek out the best experts. She found Dr. Arleen Auerbach, one of the pioneer researchers in the field. Dr. Auerbach told them that there was a wide range of symptoms and mutations responsible for the disease.

She also added, ominously, that she had never seen a child with symptoms as severe as Christian's live past four.

I don't know what my reaction would be if someone told me that about one of my children. I have no idea what I would do. I hope it would be something similar to what Susan did:

Dig in.

Not give up.

Refuse to surrender.

Fight.

Help him survive. Find a cure. If there is no cure, fight even harder.

That was nearly two decades ago now; Christian is not only still with us—he has thrived.

But we're getting ahead of the story.

Presented with a diagnosis at last, Susan and Chris searched for information that would help them be proactive or at least provide Christian with better care. They heard about Camp Sunshine, a place in Maine where families and children with Fanconi from all over the world gather over the summer for a week's vacation—and a chance to share stories and information. So they went.

They'd only just gotten there when the group gathered in a big room and sang "You Are My Sunshine"—an almost-saccharine-sweet song popular in the 1960s. (It was actually written toward the end of the Depression by Jimmie Davis and Charles Mitchell, but it enjoyed a second life decades later.)

The family felt an immediate disconnect.

"It was like a *Twilight Zone* experience," remembers Susan. Everyone was happy—something she just couldn't understand. How could people whose children had the disease be so happy?

She wanted to leave.

"Give it two days," said a counselor, reading her mind.

"I'll give it to the morning."

An hour or so afterward, the family met and bonded with the parents of a little girl. They stuck out the camp and ended up learning more from the other families than they'd found out from the experts or the book.

There were little things—the kids were often nocturnal, with far more energy at night than they had during the day. There were big, potentially life-threatening things—the kids sometimes didn't know when they were cold, which could easily lead to frostbite or hypothermia.

The list of symptoms and consequences and dangers was exhaustive. The family struggled to process it all.

Soon after going to the camp, Christian's blood counts started falling. That was bad on its own, but it could also lead to immediate drama: a minor injury with prolific bleeding could be fatal. Even internal bleeding was a danger. Bruises were easy for this active toddler to obtain and far more dangerous than they would be for others.

Regular blood transfusions helped save Christian's life, but the arrangements were complicated and the constant procedure tiresome. A more permanent solution was needed.

Chris and Susan heard about a technique involving transplanting bone marrow tissue that would allow their son's body to manufacture its own cells. While the procedure held out hope for a long-term solution, it was far from foolproof—in fact, the leading American hospital doing the operation had a shockingly low success rate.

They were ready to have the procedure done there anyway, but something didn't feel right to Chris—a feeling, a premonition, perhaps even God speaking to him. In any event, they changed plans at the last minute, pulling out of the program days before it would have begun.

"It seemed like every single doctor in the United States screamed at us," says Susan, recalling that experts felt the procedure was his only chance at survival.

Their concern was understandable. Leukemia was ravaging the boy, and even his parents felt he was approaching death. Christian's body couldn't even regulate its temperature—Susan had to bring blankets to keep him warm if they sat in the shade during the Florida summer.

With her son sinking fast, Susan heard about a new transplant protocol being developed in Germany. The method involved less toxicity than the American procedure, though it still involved deadly radiation and came with no guarantees.

It took a month to stabilize Christian in the ICU in the U.S. before he could be flown to Europe for the operation. His condition was so dire, a nurse traveled with them. The procedure went well, but the recovery was months long. It was an ordeal . . . and something of a miracle, as Christian did better than any of the other patients operated on at the same time.

All of this cost a tremendous amount of money—not just for the medical treatments but the adjustments that the family had to make to give Christian a somewhat normal life. Chris had a good job as a golf pro, but it was far from enough to finance what they needed.

His employer stepped forward to cover their share of the operation, an incredibly generous gesture.

There were many others.

Chris's fellow pro Russ Holden met little Christian and, in Susan's words, instantly fell in love with him. He decided to host a golf fund-raiser to help the family meet expenses. That led to the creation of Caddy for a Cure, a nonprofit that helps raise money for different charities. Christian and his younger brother Calen—born later with the disease as well—are now spokespeople for the organization.

Calen's birth presented the family with more complications, as he, too, had Fanconi anemia. (The family's three other children do not.) While the specific symptoms of his disease are different, much of what the family learned with Christian helped save Calen's life and make treatments far easier; it also helped that unlike his brother, Calen's blood type matched that of other relatives. Still, the list of surgeries both boys needed seemed endless.

Christian and Calen have not only survived past the four years once predicted for Christian; they've thrived. In the process, they have spread the word about Fanconi anemia to the general public, both formally and informally.

As hard as the journey has been, Susan maintains a sense of wry humor about it. Maybe that's the only way to deal with a serious, little-known disease that hits you out of the blue. There's humor, and there's poignancy, in most of her memories.

"Every birthday we thought would be the last. Dog and pony shows, the works," she says. "We literally thought this might be the last. Let's do it big."

The neighborhood *loved* Christian's birthday parties. Who wouldn't?

They're now a family joke: Christian doesn't have a birth *day;* he has a birthday *month.*

There were points when Susan literally yelled at God in a parking lot:

What did Christian ever do to you?!

But despite moments when she blamed God as well as fate, in the end, she believes her faith in God and her belief that God does things only for a reason was strengthened. The words of the Lord's Prayer, one of the earliest most believers learn, took on new meaning as she prayed. She reconciled herself to the idea that his life on earth might be short—three minutes, three years, three decades—but there would be an eternity beyond that.

"Our lives are like a grain of sand," she told herself. "But, Lord, don't let him suffer."

Susan freely admits that her faith ebbs and flows, and she hesitates to describe herself as anything other than a normal, flawed human when it comes to faith. She says she's not as fervently religious today as she was at the peak of Christian's distress. Her struggles seem like the struggles many of us have, navigating modern life as well as faith—even before great tragedies descend.

"I get up and try every day, not to be a Christian," she says, "but to live for Christ. That's the struggle, figuring out what that would look like. . . . Some days we hit the mark. Some days we don't."

In some ways, her son Christian has been the family conscience from birth, piping up from the back seat of the car as Susan complained about someone else's driving, reminding other family members of what they said about how one should behave, and just generally being a positive reminder of how to cope with bad situations.

Today, the Fanconi Anemia Research Fund supports a range of research programs working on helping children with the disease. Medical advances and simple awareness have helped families cope far better than they did a decade ago, and life expectancy is greatly improved. Bone marrow surgery is still the key to much treatment; new, promising therapies are being tested every day.

What impresses me is simply the perseverance it took for Christian and his family to get to the point where they are today. Multiply that perseverance by 150,000—the estimated number of children born with birth defects in the U.S. each year—and you begin to see a measure of human strength.

Some of these children—they total about 3 percent of the babies born each year—are far worse than Christian and his brother. Each deserves an equal chance not just at survival but to become contributing members of our society—a proposition that takes money and many helpers.

If at times the kids and their handicaps test our capacity for optimism, in the end they greatly enhance it.

"Lead with love," says Susan. "You'll find common ground."

Out of the Fire
Mel and Brian Birdwell

So many lives were changed on 9/11, including mine and Chris's. But perhaps none took quite as dramatic and difficult a turn as Brian Birdwell's.

On Monday, September 10, Brian Birdwell spent a routine day at work. The onetime ROTC distinguished graduate was a lieutenant colonel, working on the Department of the Army staff at the Pentagon as the executive officer to the deputy assistant chief of staff for installation management.

It was not by any means a dramatic assignment, but Brian had already seen plenty of dramatics in the first Gulf War and the humanitarian crisis in Honduras and other parts of Central America following Hurricane Mitch in 1998. His résumé included a Bronze Star.

By the fall of 2001, Brian; his wife, Mel; and their twelve-year-old son, Matt, were living a quiet life in the suburban Washington, D.C., area. Church, volunteer work, home-school lessons, Friday TV movie night—it was pretty much a routine middle-class existence. One might even describe it as "boring." Brian certainly does.

That changed the next day.

Since starting at the Pentagon, Brian left for work around 5:30 in the morning, arriving just before 6:25. He headed up to his office on the second floor in the "E Ring." In case you're not familiar with the Pentagon building, the five-sided structure is made up of five separate "rings." From outside, these look like individual buildings butted against each other and connected by spokes that extend from the innermost ring. The spokes contain hallways connecting the separate rings.

The E Ring is on the exterior of the building. This outer ring has grand views of the surrounding area; the offices there are generally considered the most prestigious.

Around 9:00 a.m., a coworker told Brian and others to turn on the television news. They watched in stunned silence as New York's Twin Towers smoldered. They stared in disbelief as the video of the second plane striking the South Tower was replayed. They understood this was no accident, that America was under attack— and yet that made no sense. No sense at all.

Brian excused himself and headed for the men's room, walking down Corridor 4, turning left, and entering the lavatory. A few moments later, having just washed up, he stepped out into the corridor, passing some elevators.

The time was 9:37 a.m.

Boom!

The sound was incredibly loud, even to a man who knew war. His thoughts scrambled.

Construction?

Demolition?

Bomb?

Before his conscious mind could provide an answer, everything around him turned to pain.

Blackness.

The building, so solid a moment ago, disintegrated.

In its place: fire.

Tremendous fire.

The terrorists who had taken over American Airlines Flight 77 from Washington Dulles had slammed the plane into the Pentagon, striking the E Ring a short distance from the hallway where Brian was walking when the plane hit.

Somehow in the fog of smoke, Brian managed to figure out where he was and what he had to do to get to safety. The walls around him were crumbling. Because of security precautions, Brian's ID would not unlock the doors to the nearby rings. He'd have to get to the A Ring and escape from there.

That was half a football field away.

He started moving and somehow managed to get close enough to the corridor at B Ring to realize that the fire doors there had closed. He was trapped.

Miraculously, two colonels stepped out of the B Ring around the same time and found him. But his ordeal was just beginning.

Rushed to the hospital in a commandeered SUV, Brian was admitted with burns over 60 percent of his body. Some 40 percent of those were third-degree burns.

I don't want to be too graphic, but to give you an idea of what happens to a human being in a fire:

Third-degree burns destroy the outer two layers of skin. The burns can then destroy the body under the skin—fat, muscle, bones, nerves. (When fire goes this deep, the result is sometimes classified as fourth-degree burns.)

Obviously, the pain is excruciating. I have heard many medical professionals say that severely burned patients endure pain unmatched by any other type of injury.

Besides the damage to the skin and the internal parts of the body, the fire robs the body of essential fluids, dehydrating the victim; it's common for a victim to breathe in smoke and even flames, damaging their lungs and respiratory system. In a severe case, the victim may go into shock. The damaged body may have trouble keeping its proper temperature, resulting in a host of other problems.

There's more, but suffice it to say that being burned over a significant part of your body is extremely life-threatening.

In Brian's case, the doctors and nurses who first treated him were not optimistic about his chances for survival beyond a few hours. They gave him less than a 1 percent chance of survival.

Back home, Brian's wife, Mel, was working with Matt on a science lesson when a friend phoned and told her about the World Trade Center attacks. Mother and son went into the living room to watch the news reports; after a short while, they returned to the kitchen heavyhearted and went back to work.

Then a friend called with news that the Pentagon had been hit.

Television images followed, showing the impact area—exactly the side of the building where Mel knew her husband worked.

She feared the worst—that her husband had been right at the point of impact when the plane hit.

The pair prayed. Prayer and God had always been an important part of the Birdwells' lives; its importance would increase and become more intense as the days went on.

There was no news from her husband, no call or message. Somehow Mel managed to stay calm enough over the next few hours to care for her son. But there was little she could do for him, or for her husband, for that matter, aside from praying and waiting to hear the absolute worst. Finally, she got a call from the husband of someone who'd been with Brian after he was injured, telling her that he was on his way to Georgetown Hospital.

Their story is intense and dramatic even in the details of getting to the hospital. I have been with Mel in Washington, D.C., where we inadvertently traveled the path Mel took to get to her husband. To this day it is traumatic for her to relive it. Mel's few moments of relief knowing her husband was alive were replaced by anxiety and worry when she arrived at the hospital and discovered the extent of his injuries. For several days, Brian's life hung in the balance. A full team of specialists cared for him. Slowly, he began to recover.

It took three harrowing months before he was released to return home. Miraculously, he made his way back to the Pentagon six months to the day after the attacks.

That's the simple version of the story; it leaves out the many sleepless nights, the physical pain of the injuries, the difficulty of getting off painkillers. It ignores Mel's many fights to make sure her husband got the kind of care he needed—rumor has it the staff took to calling her a pit bull. It neglects, too, the difficult emotions their son went through as he came to terms with his father's mortality, the strains that hospitalization and rehab put on the family's lives, the subtle but very real disruption of everyday life.

It fails to mention that his trip back to the Pentagon was more for show than a true return to work. It would be quite a while before Brain was capable of that.

The brief version of his recovery also leaves out the many efforts of neighbors and family and friends to try to help the Birdwells. It neglects to mention the country's response to their courage, from President Bush to random well-wishers. It skips lightly over the deepening of the Birdwells' faith and even how their trials came to inspire others.

But no matter how many details are related—the fact, say, that Brian couldn't go to the bathroom on his own or even open a milk carton when he first came home—it's impossible to fully convey the deep despair that comes when an adult suddenly finds him- or herself reduced to the role of helpless infant.

I first met Mel Birdwell in the Texas State Capitol building in 2013 when I traveled there in support of the Chris Kyle Bill, which allows governments to count military experience when considering hiring new employees. Mel was there because in the decade and a half after 9/11, her husband had given up one career and taken on another—state senator for Texas.

I must tell on myself: I almost got us kicked out for talking too loudly.

And laughing. You're apparently not supposed to do that while the Senate is in session. As Mel recalls it, one of the security people came up and told her, "Ms. Birdwell, I've never removed a senator's wife before. But if you keep on talking so loudly . . ."

We took the hint.

What intrigued me then, and continues to amaze me now, was Brian's decision to leave the Army and become a politician.

The first, leaving the Army, is understandable; he'd been injured so badly that his career and ambitions were put quite off the track; they would make it extremely difficult to advance. Many career military officers come to a point when they realize that they will not be able to advance beyond a certain level, if only because the math is so daunting—the Army simply doesn't need more than a few hundred generals. (Technically, the service is allotted 231, with another 310 of similar rank split between the Army and other branches. The Army has averaged just under 350 total members of all general ranks during the past several years.) That is out of some 475,000 soldiers; not great odds.

But why volunteer to be an elected official? He could, and in my opinion there would be no one better, teach American History and the Constitution. He has educated me a ton, and I am pretty sure that not only could he do it in his sleep, but he probably does do it in his sleep. But politics?

Texas pays its state officials very little—$600 per month, plus a per diem under $200 for each day the legislature is in session. You almost have to pay the state to do the job. This is no federal position with ridiculous pay structures. State senators can accept no favors, no payment for any legitimate speaking engagement. The Birdwells spend far more than Brian makes as a senator. They already donate time and money to other causes and constantly help charitable efforts individually and through nonprofits. So why politics?

For both husband and wife, the answers to those questions come first from their deep religious beliefs. They're all of a piece, as the saying goes. Ask Brian why he decided to talk about his injuries and recovery or why he decided to go into politics, and the answer is likely to be along the lines of "the glorification of Christ's Kingdom." Mel's answer will be a little more earthy—and don't get on her wrong side!—but along the same lines.

Brian's story of survival is filled with many happy miracles and what-ifs. Had he remained in that office for just a few more minutes, he would not have survived. Had he turned the wrong way in the corridor after the plane hit, very possibly he would have been overcome by smoke. The flames around him suddenly went out. The door at the corridor opened at just the right moment. So many coincidences, say the Birdwells, can only add up to a miracle.

What do you do when you are the recipient of a miracle? If you believe strongly in God, and it seems by all logic and emotion that you have been saved, you must ask yourself, *Why?*

Why was I saved when my colleagues died?

What debt do I owe to God? And to my fellow human beings?

What am I supposed to do with this miracle?

The answer to all these questions came to Brian while he was in outpatient therapy the winter after the attacks. One of his therapists asked him to visit a patient in intensive care who'd been burned in a farm accident. Brian spoke in simple terms of what he'd gone through and what the man would face; he encouraged him to look at his recovery like a mission, to follow the staff's recommendations to the letter, to persevere.

When he was done talking to the patient, Brian felt somehow fulfilled; he'd accomplished a mission he didn't know he had. By the end of the day, he and Mel realized they could help others who'd been injured as he was. Both could tell others what they would go through and give them ideas on how to cope.

"It's not survivor's guilt," says Brian. "It's survivor's charge."

"You don't go through something like this and not learn a lot of things," says Mel. "We can relate to burn patients and families better than other people who haven't gone through it."

"The word *invalid* might be too strong," notes Brian, speaking about the condition of burn patients immediately after they've sustained their injuries, "but as an adult with an adult brain, and you can't do a thing for yourself—in those moments, when you're thirty-nine years old and you're praying to open a milk carton. That tells you where you are in life."

It's important for people in that position to hear from someone who has been there and gotten through. In a sense, his message is a bit of tough love—no bs about how everything will turn out fantastic, no sugarcoating the pain. But that makes it more powerful—*Look, this is going to be terrible, but eventually you will make it. Be strong.*

As the informal meetings with fellow burn patients and their families multiplied, the Birdwells began formalizing their outreach. They had coins made, tokens similar to military challenge coins that were a physical reminder of Brian's visit and his words of encouragement. Brian began combining hospital visits with talks he was being asked to give about 9/11.

Both Mel and Brian stepped forward into the public arena, talking about what happened on 9/11 and afterward. They teamed with a writer and produced a book—*Refined by Fire: A Family's Triumph of Love and Faith*—and the speaking engagements multiplied.

As demand grew, the pair began Face the Fire, a special ministry that assisted burn survivors and their family. Money from the book and honorariums from speaking engagements went to the ministry, which then gave money to burn victims and their families to cover incidentals and things like lodging during treatment.

Counting contributions the charity made to burn centers and other organizations, a little more than $400,000 was distributed before it was wound down in 2017.

Before that happened, Brian had been asked a different question, this one by friends and acquaintances:

Why don't you run for public office?

A Texas native who'd spent part of his childhood in California and had also moved around quite a bit in the Army, Brian was somewhat reluctant at first, though the suggestions and offers kept coming.

Active military members are not allowed to be politically active and cannot run for office. The Birdwells were always "diligent" about politics, voting and making sure they were up on the issues, but that's as far as it went.

Once he was retired, however, he felt able to work in the Republican Party.

"I don't want to say that I was drawn to politics because I was drawn to war—that's not the quote I'm looking for," he jokes. But he does believe in Carl von

Clausewitz's famous formulation, that war is politics by another means, and vice versa.

Eventually the suggestions that he run included a chance to become a state senator. Brian ran, won, and in 2010 began his first term representing Texas's 22nd District from his hometown of Granbury. (Granbury is nestled on a bend of the Brazos River about thirty-eight miles southwest of Fort Worth.)

It would be an exaggeration to say Mel was enthusiastic. She's probably even less so now: "Watching the sausage being made, you'll never eat sausage again."

Nonetheless, she's not agitating for him to leave the Senate. His top causes include religious issues; an opponent of abortion and gay marriage, Brian has specifically worked to carve out religious exceptions on such social issues based on conscience. "If government can compel you to do something that is against your conscience," he believes, "you're on the road to totalitarianism."

More prosaically but importantly for constituents, he's worked to make college education more accessible, strengthen citizens' rights against eminent domain, and limit the power of state river authorities.

"It's easy to throw out the negative," says the senator. You have to work to keep things positive. "The political world has become so callous, so crass. There's a cottage industry of people out there who will tell you how much you suck."

Nonetheless, "duty is ours," notes Brian, citing the writings and service of John Quincy Adams, who not only was president but also served afterward in the House of Representatives. "He spent years leading the fight against slavery. He never achieved it, but he fought the good fight."

Among the men he influenced was Abraham Lincoln, who would surely have met Adams as a congressman shortly before Adams died in 1848. The point being: you serve, do your best, and have faith that your efforts will one day pay off, whether you witness that or not.

"Before 9/11, I had a good relationship with the Lord," says Mel. "After 9/11, it was intense, and personal, and real. . . . There were times I felt that I could feel God's arms around me."

In the immediate aftermath of the tragedy, both Birdwells felt their faith become extremely intense, almost as if it reached a new level. As they have gone on since the event, some of that intensity has worn off, though both clearly remain firm believers.

The senator has told his story of survival and recovery hundreds, if not thousands, of times, both publicly and privately. He feels it's his duty as a survivor: "If we didn't tell the story, and give the Lord the honor, we would be derelict. Too many things, too many miracles, too many people in the right places at the right time, too many circumstances that came together . . ."

How did he manage to recover from his wounds? Certainly, one can call it a miracle. But as the saying goes, God works in mysterious ways, and usually through human beings. The trained medical people, not only at the burn unit but those who first found and cared for him en route to the hospital, surely played a big role in his survival. The willingness of his fellow soldiers to help him, the ingenuity and training of the medical staffs, the support of his family and friends—all of these were important, too.

Brian's background and training as a soldier must have helped give him strength. His experiences in combat surely eased him through difficult moments. His innate American Spirit undoubtedly helped him through rehab and helped him find his voice as an example for other survivors.

But above all those things, I can't help but think that Mel's love and devotion was the secret to his pulling through. I can't help but think the gentle mercies of his "pit bull" were the crucial ingredients in his recovery.

After Brian was released from the hospital, Mel was more than a pit bull. She filled many roles, from literal crutch to chauffeur. For roughly a year, much of the weight of his recovery was on her shoulders.

There were many times when she was angry as well as exhausted. Her wedding vows, her memory of Brian and their times before the accident, and her deep love and faith all must have pushed her to continue her fight to help him through.

Watching both of them together, hearing them talk, it's clear that they have a tremendous love for each other. They have a strong marriage, one that saw a lot of sacrifice even before that terrible day in September.

As Brian healed, he became more of a partner again. And while they don't always agree on everything—he's far more enthusiastic about politics than she is—they still support each other, walking side by side as they go through life.

That's a testament not just to their faith in God but in each other. And to the American Spirit.

NINE

Spirit's Wings

Without Boundaries

The American Spirit doesn't stop at our country's shores. It may be our greatest export, one that can't be measured in dollars or euros or Chinese renminbi.

When Frédéric Auguste Bartholdi designed the Statue of Liberty, he placed a beacon in the copper lady's hand, a beacon to guide the world to the notion of Liberty and its connection between the Old World, then thought of as Europe, and the New. But light doesn't stay at its source. It flies out, illuminating all that is around it. Like the sun, it doesn't respect the geographic boundaries that mankind imposes; it finds a way to shine in the darkest places, fighting through clouds and chasing shadows.

Kindness, charity, concern for others—these core American values aren't ours alone. They are embedded in all humans. But sometimes it takes a spark from outside for them to thrive. The entrepreneurial aspects of the American Spirit, the impulse not just to help but to help in new and different ways, can be that critical spark.

At times, of course, we overreach. There is a danger in being arrogant—in thinking that we know best what others should do. But the greater sin is often not to act at all. Help guided by wisdom and a touch of humility changes minds and the world.

The late twentieth and early twenty-first centuries have seen terrorists attempting to set up barriers to the light. In some ways, they have succeeded even among Americans, making us less willing to share ideas, money, and time with those in other countries, especially the Middle East. But they have not and will not triumph. Even as I write these words, Americans are reaching out across the borders to do amazing things. Whether they are billionaires like Bill Gates and his wife, Melinda, reaching out to improve health and economic opportunities in third-world countries, or small bands of volunteers bringing clean water to threadbare communities, Americans are having an impact for the better, sharing expertise and the American Spirit.

Into Satan's Lair

The Exodus Road

In 2011, Matt Parker stood at the edge of one of the most notorious red-light districts in the world and said a silent prayer. Then he put his head down and walked into a brothel, about as unprepared for what he would find inside as anyone in the world.

Raised as a Southern Baptist, the thirty-something-year-old had never been in a strip club before, let alone a place where women's bodies were openly displayed for sale. He wasn't there to have sex or even to ogle the girls. He was there to spy on the establishment for the Thai police.

Matt's visit represented the end of a long journey of conscience, prodded not only by his Christian faith but also by a deep sense of justice. At the same time, it was the start of a journey that would lead him across several continents, part of a mission aimed at rescuing girls and boys, men and women, held as slaves in the sex trade.

Still, it was a strange place to be for a man whose closest encounter to a live sex display was ordering chicken wings at a Hooters.

Today, Matt is the CEO of the Exodus Road, which by early 2018 had rescued nearly one thousand people, freeing them from the bonds that held them to brothels, Russian mobsters, pimps, and madams.

While faith led Matt to that initial foray, the Exodus Road itself is nondenominational, working with governments and law enforcement officials of all religions. Its undercover operatives and social workers range from atheists to Buddhists to Christians to Muslims. Its primary goal is freedom for the rescues, though that freedom does not always lead to a perfect or even happy future.

That's the reality of working in the darker corners of the human condition.

The Exodus Road story began more than a decade earlier, when Matt and his future wife, Laura, met in high school. They fell in love and married when they were twenty-one. Their first jobs out of school were teaching gigs in Saipan, the large island in the Northern Marianas, about 3,680 miles west of Honolulu. Laura describes the year they spent there as almost an "extended honeymoon."

The island is a place of great beauty, and even with their jobs and a baby, their lives were almost idyllic. But paradise was temporary, and as their contracts ended, they decided to go back home.

Their return to the U.S. brought a variety of job possibilities—they even tried doing missionary work, again in the South Pacific. The missionary stint didn't go well, and eventually they found themselves on the East Coast, looking for more conventional jobs and lives. With a family to feed—they would eventually have three children—Matt went to work as an investment counselor with Vanguard. Though never formally trained before getting to the financial firm, he found he was good at it . . . yet he hated going to work.

"Every day I got up early and stopped at a coffee shop on the way to work," Matt recalls. "And I asked myself, Why am I here?"

The answer apparently was to wait for something better—which came with an offer to work as a youth pastor in Colorado. It turned out to provide the fulfillment of their shared interest in both serving others and sharing their love of Christ with others.

They spent five years there. It was a great job, good for them, good for the community, good for the kids Matt mentored. As part of his work, he began taking some of his groups to help children in other countries. But a tragic, rare event changed both their lives: Andrew, one of the seventeen-year-olds in Matt's tight-knit youth group, was struck by lightning and killed.

Matt was among those who rushed to the hospital; by the time he arrived, young Andrew had been declared dead. Matt had to relay the news to the kids out in the waiting room. He still chokes up when recalling it.

The young man's funeral attracted seven hundred members of the community. The death touched everyone deeply, but perhaps none so hard as three of Andrew's friends, who had been planning to spend the summer traveling around the world with him. The young men carried on with the plan, aiming to help orphanages along the way, dedicating the trip and their charitable work to Andrew's memory.

They were in the middle of the trip when arrangements for a visit to Thailand fell through. They asked Matt, who was back home, to see if he could make alternate arrangements. After he did, the parents generously offered to send him to join the kids there.

He was happy to go—even when he found out that he had inadvertently booked the kids into a hostel near one of the most notorious red-light districts in Asia, the Ratchadaphisek entertainment district in Bangkok.

Not too much room for effective missionary work on *that* street. Or so they thought. But they found plenty of work at a children's school and completed the trip in good spirits.

Back in the U.S., Matt was surprised to get a call from the school's main beneficiary, asking if he'd like to take a job as its director.

Excited by the possibilities, Matt agreed, and Laura reluctantly went along. Arriving in 2010, they found the home—a boarding school for poor children from the northern provinces of the country—to be in far worse shape than Matt had suspected. The pair threw themselves into the work needed to improve it, learning everything from basic Thai to how to build water towers and deal with the Thai bureaucracy.

They were still feeling their way when Matt was invited to a meeting dealing with exploited children—young boys and girls who were essentially sold into prostitution in cities around Thailand, including the city where they were.

Unlike most of the others at the conference, Matt knew next to nothing about the problem or the ways that nongovernment agencies were attempting to cope with it. As the participants split into groups, he and two other men ended up together in the only session devoted to intervening in the problem. (The other groups were primarily devoted to prevention and helping those who had escaped or otherwise been able to leave their masters.)

The situation was tailor-made for despair. The police, it turned out, had very little intelligence on the arrangements inside the brothels. Nor could they make arrests without hard evidence against the pimps and madams running them.

While illegal, prostitution was widely practiced in Thailand. Underage prostitutes were especially desirable by johns—the customers—but the people running the brothels were savvy enough to keep the young girls and boys hidden from anyone who appeared to be a policeman or an informant. Payoffs and corruption were rampant.

As elsewhere, prostitution has a long history in Thailand. The state even operated brothels for hundreds of years. Laws punishing prostitutes were adopted in 1960, but for many years they were rarely enforced.

As air travel became more and more common, Thailand became known as an international haven for those seeking paid sex, especially with young prostitutes.

In the 1990s, the government increased penalties for child prostitution, defining *child* as boys and girls under fifteen. There were also added strictures against *trafficking*—moving children into prostitution, whether inside or outside the country. The problem continued.

Brothels in Thailand run a wide gamut. At the upper end, hotels, massage parlors, and especially bars and restaurants serve a largely foreign clientele. Literally any sexual taste or perversion can be satisfied, for the right price. The owners of these "clubs" and the pimps are sometimes independents; more often, they are either part of, affiliated with, or work with crime syndicates from China, Russia, and elsewhere. The prostitutes generally come from the poorer parts of the country, especially the north, but also arrive from China, Laos, and Vietnam.

A few go into the trade of their own free will, seeing it as an alternative to poverty and wooed by the promise of easy money. It is also extremely common for children to be "recruited" from poorer areas with promises of a job and money to their family. The promises are lies, though the initial payments are welcome in the poor areas where the slavers ply their trades.

Upon arriving at the brothel, the girls and boys find themselves essentially slaves, unable to escape. In theory, many can buy their freedom back by paying off "debts" their masters claim they incur. As a general rule, though, it is extremely difficult for anyone caught in the web to escape without some sort of outside intervention, at least until they have "worked" for several years.

Sexually transmitted diseases such as AIDs are rampant. Corruption at all levels—from the police on the streets to the highest reaches of government—is endemic.

When the Parker family arrived in Thailand, the problem of underage prostitution, kidnapping, and sex slavery was acute. Church groups and aid organizations were starting to take steps against it, but the attitudes and practices that had permitted the sex slave trade to thrive remained in place.

Following the meeting, Matt spent about a year researching the problems that prevented effective intervention. To simplify, things basically came down to this:

Lack of prosecutable evidence.

The Thai police interested in making arrests needed concrete proof that girls were underage and being offered for prostitution. They were either reluctant to gather it, were paid not to, or were so easily spotted when entering a brothel that they might as well have been carrying neon signs that told the perpetrators to hide everything.

Matt and the other men on his committee came to a single conclusion:

We have to gather the evidence ourselves.

Unlike the police, foreigners could easily enter the brothels; they were, after all, the customers. Matt decided he'd find people to go undercover, pose as johns, and get the evidence themselves. Once they had it, they would turn it over to the cops.

After asking many men, he finally convinced two friends to do it.

As long as he went along.

It wasn't going to be a joyride. Given what they wanted to do, their lives would be in danger as soon as they passed through the door. If they were even suspected of trying to gather evidence or spy on the operation, a beating would be light punishment. The gangs that controlled many of the establishments were not known for mercy.

But the danger wasn't the biggest thing holding him back. The morality of entering a bordello loomed large.

Even if he had no intention of having sex, the bars and restaurants openly displayed their wares. Think sleazy strip club, and multiply by ten.

It was a scene that his upbringing told him was barely a step from hell itself. If you believed in the Devil, this was surely a place where you could step on his tail.

He was also concerned about what entering the brothel might do to his marriage. To that point, he and Laura had a strong relationship, based on mutual trust and affection. Would temptation on his side or distrust and jealousy on hers disrupt that?

The couple sat in a coffeeshop and discussed it for hours. Their need to do good clearly outweighed the dangers.

Still . . .

They set clear boundaries—he would not sleep with a prostitute, they agreed right off.

They kept talking. Matt remained hesitant.

What would they want someone to do if their own daughter were enslaved?

Give her the chance to be free.

"If you don't go," asked Laura, "who will?"

Not long afterward, Matt left for a suspected brothel in Bangkok, located in the same red-light district he had seen years before with the teens.

The street was madness, a collage of temptation and

corruption. Erratic traffic, drunks jostling, hookers calling out, "ladyboys"—transgender men who still have male anatomy—aggressively courting customers, the rotten smell of garbage and sweat, blaring neon lights. The sensations were overwhelming. A prostitute came up to Matt, and he froze, unable to react, unable maybe to process everything around him.

It happened again. Again, he distanced himself.

But the third time—the third time he was ready, and he smiled and fell into his role.

They talked. Maybe later, he said, noncommittally.

The men headed for the brothel, which was set up as a bar. Inside, they went in for a drink. A girl sat next to Matt. Her name was Belle—or so she claimed. She was a beauty. The only distraction to her radiant face was the paper pinned to her chest.

The number written there made it easier for a customer to purchase her services.

Matt took her hand. While he held it, she was safe; no one would use her.

Slowly, gently, he asked who she was, prodding for her story. His Thai was still rudimentary, but his two friends spoke it well enough to converse.

Belle had come from an impoverished community up north. She looked well under eighteen, though there was no way to tell what her actual age was.

By the time Belle moved on to more promising customers, she had left an indelible mark in Matt's brain. He carried her image for years, using it as his inspiration.

Ironically, the reason they had targeted that particular bar turned out to be something of a false lead. Someone had seen photos on the wall at the back; they were of young girls, clearly underage. The writing with the photos claimed they were orphans being supported by the bar and its owner; that seemed to everyone, police and Matt included, a cover story to throw snoopers off the trail.

But it turned out it was actually true. The owner of the bar, an American expat and Vietnam veteran, sent money to the orphanage to help keep it going. Maybe it was his way of doing penance. In any event, he was actually helping those girls.

That ambiguity—the mix of good and bad—was present throughout the red-light district. Matt came to discover that the people running the bordellos were generally not as wholly evil or unconflicted as he originally thought. The madams tended to be former prostitutes themselves; a few actually seemed to care about the girls working for them.

While he strongly believed that the people involved at every level should be punished, Matt nonetheless came to see the humanity in nearly everyone. Their lives were as broken as the prostitutes'. To use religious terms, they, too, needed God's mercy.

"I had this idea at the start, that brothels were filled with demons," he says today. "But when I got inside, I realized it's not true." The customers were of all ages and descriptions—a seventy-year-old woman, a twenty-something nerd who had never had sex, a father-and-son team there to end the boy's virginity.

Broken people, desperately lonely. "If you just look at their faces, that's what you see."

Not that that should keep them from being punished by the law.

That first mission was enough for Matt's two companions; they called it quits that night.

Matt, though, had found his true calling. He began working closely with the Thai police, gathering information, sometimes hitting as many as ten or a dozen brothels a night. He carried a letter in his shoe from a police chief that—he hoped—would get him out of trouble if he was arrested. Otherwise, he was unarmed and generally completely on his own.

He traveled around on a scooter, Skype-chatting with his wife as he worked his way through the underworld. His Thai grew better; his senses sharpened.

He started wearing covert recording devices, getting pictures.

Arrests began to be made. Not a lot, not nearly enough to reverse the tide. But a start.

Matt branched out, working in neighboring countries. He met others doing the same type of work, forming alliances and coalitions.

Matt and Laura started the nonprofit Exodus Road in 2012 as a way of expanding the work that Matt had begun. A loose coalition with others at first, the organization helped get equipment and funding, coordinated between the police and different groups that could provide assistance, and trained undercover agents.

The undercover work took its toll on both. In *The Exodus Road,* the short book recounting their days starting the project, Laura candidly recalls her feelings of repulsion at the smell of Matt's clothes, skin, and hair after he came from a night of pretending to be a pedophile. She also writes of finding Matt in the shower crying, overcome by the memory of a child prostitute in a brothel he'd recently visited.

But they persevered. From a two-person organization that existed primarily in their thoughts and good intentions, today Exodus Road has a budget of more than $1 million, with investigators and social workers in six countries. Some 389 offenders had been arrested as of early 2018. More important, more than nine hundred former sex slaves had been liberated.

As a general rule, the organization does not "grab" prostitutes and carry them away. Rather, the investigators will typically hand over evidence to the police. Arrests are then made.

The prostitutes as well as the pimps or madams are arrested. The prostitutes are connected with social workers who follow their case through the system. Exodus Road works with the local authorities, prioritizing a long-term solution to the problem by permanently disabling the brothels and the networks that feed them.

Liberation does not necessarily bring a person peace. In Thailand, convicted prostitutes are supposed to enter government shelters and a yearlong program aimed at rehabilitation. There are some good shelters and programs; there are some bad ones. A number of the prostitutes return to their families or stay in the cities and work at more legitimate jobs once the year is up. But many former sex slaves go back to work as prostitutes; others "disappear"—either moving away, changing identities, or simply removing themselves from the authorities' immediate attention.

Many people are disappointed to discover that so many choose to go back to prostitution. Matt, however, is philosophical. "Freedom is like an onion; there are many layers," he says.

While faith definitely moved the Parkers into this crusade and has remained a vital part of their lives, Exodus Road itself is not a faith-based organization. Its board members, operatives, and other employees include Buddhists, Christians, and atheists. Doing the right thing and being brave in the face of evil is not a matter of religious beliefs.

They're an energetic young couple, but they're far from superheroes. See them on the street, and you'll think they're on their way to a PTA meeting. I asked them if they ever felt like quitting, and they said, "all the time."

But I know they never will. Not while there's more work to be done.

And there is. While the exact number of sex slaves is difficult to determine, estimates run far into the millions. And just so you don't think that this is a problem confined to poor Asian countries, Matt estimates that there are perhaps fifty-five thousand sex slaves in the U.S.

When we spoke, his organization had just freed two of them.

To me, the problem seems daunting. But Matt and Laura break it down to somewhat more manageable levels:

It's not about the millions. It's about the one you help.

Amen to that.

Pioneer Abroad

Leslie Schweitzer

The words *pioneer woman* bring an immediate image to most minds: *a sturdy twenty- or thirty-something woman from the nineteenth century, dress to the ground, sleeves rolled up, bonnet on her head.*

She's got a skillet in one hand and a harness ready for an ox and plow in the other. Three or four kids are peering out from behind her skirt; her husband, probably with some chaw in his mouth, nods approvingly in the background.

There's nothing that a woman can't do.

Except vote, enter politics, run a business, sign a will . . .

You get the idea.

Despite their vast accomplishments and the sweat they put into building this country, women, even pioneers, have been sorely limited through most of our history.

But that has changed in our lifetime, thanks to more modern pioneer women, including Leslie Schweitzer. Inheriting fortitude and resilience from earlier generations, women like Leslie prodded and sometimes pushed their way into what was considered a "man's world" as the twentieth century wound down, making that world a whole lot better in the progress.

Leslie doesn't typically wear a bonnet, and while I can picture her hitching an ox to a plow if necessary, I doubt she's done that recently. Then again, I wouldn't be surprised if she has. She's done so much else in her life.

Leslie was one of the first American women to do business in Communist China as the country began opening up again to the West. And she didn't stop there. A cofounder of Noble Trading Company in 1977, she and her firm helped U.S. companies sell and trade in a number of countries where trade ties at the time were rare, China, Yugoslavia, Hungary, Poland, Romania, and India among them. Her clients included the overseas arms of Pepsi and GM.

Ten years later, Leslie started Schweitzer & Associates, a company that developed consumer-product industries in developing countries. She also has owned and operated clothing factories in the Caribbean and employed more than seven hundred people at one time.

As senior trade advisor for the U.S. Chamber of Commerce, Leslie created the TradeRoots Initiative, the only sustained national grassroots international trade education program in the country. The initiative has helped with free trade agreements in a number of countries and raised awareness of the importance of international trade to small- and medium-size American firms.

Those are only a few of the highlights from her résumé. I'm not going to go into more detail because her business acumen and accomplishments as a trailblazer, while they impress the heck out of me, pale in comparison to her heart.

And that's what's most important when it comes to the American University of Afghanistan, where a new generation of women—and men—are being educated thanks in part to her efforts.

Let me tell you a little bit about the university.

Known as AUAF, the school is a not-for-profit university modeled on American colleges and chartered by the Afghan government. Dr. Sharif Fayez, the country's former education minister, founded the school in 2006. It's been a revolutionary institution and occasional terrorist target ever since.

Born in 1946, Dr. Fayez is a scholar who published a work showing connections between the poetry of Walt Whitman, whose *Leaves of Grass* is considered one of the great works of American literature, and Rumi, a thirteenth-century Sufi poet and mystic. Dr. Fayez fled Afghanistan after the Soviet invasion in 1979. A leading voice against the Taliban and Islamic extremism, he joined the Afghan government following its liberation in 2001 and worked to revamp the education system.

The school accepts students from all across the country and awards undergraduate and graduate degrees as well as professional development classes—the equivalent of certificate and continuing-education programs in the U.S. The undergraduate courses, which cover majors in math and the sciences, computers, political science and the law, are all taught in English. Afghan's first MBA program is housed there, as is a five-year law program that partners with Stanford University.

There are roughly fifty professors drawn from more than a dozen countries as well as Afghanistan. Many of the students hold down regular jobs while attending.

As at American colleges, scholarships are available to help students with tuition and other costs. Eleven percent of all the students at the university are Fulbright Scholars—a sign not only of the school's prestige but of the students' brainpower and determination.

Colleges in the U.S. are more than lectures and exams; so is AUAF. The university now has a soccer field and both men's and women's soccer teams; there are plans to build a cricket field. There's a girls' basketball team—though as of yet there are no other sports for the girls to play.

The university calls itself "American" because its basic structure and program is modeled after U.S. colleges. There are differences, of course—Islamic prayer rooms for men and women, for example. The school respects Islamic and Afghan values and does offer courses on Islam, but it is not a religious school per se.

Educating women is extremely controversial in the Islamic world; when the Taliban ruled Afghanistan, it was grounds for execution. But the country does have a narrow tradition of empowering women through education dating at least to the 1970s. The American University builds strongly on that tradition, taking it further than perhaps any other school in the country.

The connection between the university and the United States goes far beyond one of style. Money from the U.S. Agency for International Development (USAID) helped launch the institution in 2005. The grant was announced by then First Lady Laura Bush during a visit to Kabul.

The Bush connection was important to the university in another way, for it led to Leslie Schweitzer's involvement.

Her role in business and national politics had introduced Leslie to the Bush family; she was friends with Laura as well as with George W. Bush. But that friendship didn't prepare her for the phone call she got in 2006.

"The president called me and said, 'Congratulations. You've been elected to the board of trustees of the American University of Afghanistan,'" says Leslie.

Afghanistan would not have made the top ten list of anyone's peaceful getaways at the time. Leslie's first thoughts were along the lines of:

Afghanistan? You've got to be kidding!

She didn't say that—that *was* the president on the line, after all. But she certainly thought it. More to the point, she had no hint that such an appointment was in the works, nor did she want one. Or as she puts it, "It wasn't on my bucket list."

Leslie had never been to Kabul—or anywhere else

in Afghanistan—and was undoubtedly looking for a graceful way to avoid going when a group of board members took her to lunch. By the time they waved off dessert, Leslie was thoroughly impressed by the school and its mission.

The pictures of its buildings were stunning as well. Her curiosity piqued, she went to Kabul to see the place for herself—only to find that the photos were actually an artist's rendering of what the university would look like when it was finished.

Hopefully. For at that point, the only thing on the undeveloped property were land mines, which had to be safely removed before anything else could happen there.

"Forty Russian mines," she recalls. "I was conned. Totally conned."

But she was also hooked. Not far away, students were already attending classes, and their smiles and determination convinced her that she just had to help.

"The difficulty that some of these young people have been through and how they persevere—it's simply inspiring," says Leslie.

Leslie became chairwoman of the building committee and then started the Friends of the American University of Afghanistan. Besides getting funds for the building, the group began raising money to defray students' costs, especially for women. Not only are college costs an unreachable luxury for many Afghans, even well-off families balk at paying for a daughter to attend school.

The Department of Defense gave a grant that made possible the construction of a sixty-thousand-square-foot building on the new campus dedicated to women's economic empowerment—in effect, a business school for women. The building and its marble façade are a stunning statement about the importance of women's education.

Then came housing for professors, a women's dormitory, another dorm, a technology building, a cafeteria . . . all in addition to the original buildings across the street.

The U.S. funds are well spent. Empowering a more balanced system is a great way to help build a democracy where once a terrorist regime held the land and people hostage. It has to be the best sort of defense—shining more light through darkness.

"We're still dependent on USAID and the State Department," says Leslie, but the Friends of the American University of Afghanistan are making inroads raising private money, knowing that eventually that funding source may dry up. It's a challenge.

"Americans don't hear the good stories about Afghanistan," admits Leslie, and that hurts fund-raising. "They don't hear about the progress that is being made. But we continue to have strong supporters."

From its name to its mission, the university is a target for any radical wishing to destroy the country's progress. Unfortunately, that proved all too true in August 2016, when the campus was attacked by a small band of terrorists.

Some seven hundred students were on campus around 7:00 p.m. that night attending evening sessions when a truck drove up against the wall of the campus. After it exploded with a thundering flash, two gunmen ran onto the grounds and began shooting everyone in sight. The gunmen holed up in a building as guards, police, and the Afghan army responded. Students trapped in the buildings barricaded doors with whatever furniture they could find, waiting for salvation.

Rampaging through the building, one of the terrorists came upon a girl with polio and a leg brace on the floor of a classroom. He shot her in her good leg, leaving her to bleed out. Five hours later, as the battle continued to rage, he returned and shot her again.

Dozens of others were shot; yet others were injured trying to escape. Two freshmen on their second day of class were killed, including a musician who had performed at the Kennedy Center. A professor who had studied at Stanford, and was loved by his students, was killed after successfully evacuating his kids from his class. He died as he lived—a hero for his students who trusted him. All told, eight students were killed, and more than fifty others were injured. Two professors, three security officers, and three Afghan policemen were also killed.

For six and a half hours, the two men held off the authorities, trapping about two hundred students in the process. The assault ended only after elite units from the Afghan army, the U.S., and Norway were able to fight their way in and kill the assailants. While the Taliban was suspected of being behind the attack, no group claimed responsibility.

Leslie wasn't there during the attacks, but she went afterward. Security improvements were immediately put in place, including the hiring of a private security force, ordinarily something not allowed under Afghan law. T-walls—large, modular concrete barriers that offer some protection against attacks—were installed.

Fourteen thousand of them, in fact, each about eighteen feet high.

There are also guard towers and other security posts and improvements.

"There were moments when we didn't think we would open again," says Leslie. "The trauma was beyond belief."

Funding, consoling families, the wounded—it was an enormous undertaking. But most of the incredibly courageous students insisted that the school reopen. It did, in March 2017.

Enrollment was actually higher after the attack. Students were defiant, some declaring that they were willing to die to get an education. Their actions proved it.

"They are sacrificing to get an education," says Leslie, who calls the day the university reopened one of the best of her life. "That's why we do what we do."

Social media is accelerating change, not just at the school but throughout Afghanistan. People accept progress and differences more readily. Women are more likely to be accepted as full members of society.

Leslie notes a "mushroom" effect—students at the university influence their families, their villages, and their tribes, encouraging education and attitudes that accept other Afghans who are not of their tribe or particular branch of Islam. Students encourage family members to apply; friends and other acquaintances follow.

I **had** the privilege of meeting Onaba Payab during one of the organization's fund-raising event in 2018. This quiet, unassuming young woman has extraordinary strength. She was the first female valedictorian of the university—a triumph over the tragedy of the terrorist attacks. Among the dead were very close friends and a professor who had inspired her to take chances. Onaba may not have anticipated all that she has faced since attending school, but her brave pursuit holds much promise not just for her but for her country. I listened in awe as she expertly moderated a talk between Laura Bush and Michelle Obama; she set a perfect, understated tone that some of our media people would do well to emulate.

She's respectful of her heritage and yet is finding her own way—surely the way progress is made.

Leslie's husband passed away unexpectedly a few years ago. After that, her two adult sons got together and "grounded" her, telling her she could not go back to Afghanistan. "We can't afford to lose you, too."

She listened to them . . . for a while. After a few months, they had to concede—their mom was too energetic and independent to be tied down. She travels now with their blessing, or at least without overt objection.

Support for the school crosses lines of gender, religion, and politics. First Ladies Laura Bush and Michelle Obama joined forces recently to help raise money at a gala—you can't beat bipartisanship for a good cause.

As for Leslie, she has many more things she wants to accomplish, both with the school and her professional life. And she has a bucket list.

Near the top is skydiving in eight countries.

She'd done two when we started working on this book. I haven't checked back, but I'm sure she's done the rest by now. Pioneer women in the nineteenth century harnessed themselves to plows to turn up the fields; nowadays, they hitch themselves to parachutes and turn up wherever they're needed and least expected.

TEN

CKFF

My Motto and Goal

Do More

The foundation of the American Spirit is the idea that community and independence are important. To build that community, we need to help others. We help others find their own independence so they can truly be free and ideally go out and help their neighbor. Sometimes in big ways: building a college for them. Sometimes in small ways: holding a door for someone. Whether saving a life or smiling when it's least expected, there's a ripple effect that helps make our communities a better place.

That's all very well and good, Taya, you're thinking. But what have you done? What tangible thing are you doing besides cheerleading the rest of us?

Fair questions.

Even before *American Sniper* was published, Chris and I had discussed different ways of using whatever money we got—we weren't expecting much—to help others, specifically the families of the two men who had died while serving with him in Iraq.

Events overtook those plans. You can read some of the details in *American Wife*; suffice it to say that it's harder to give away money than you or at least I would have thought. Some didn't want it, and some thought whatever we could give wasn't enough. In any event, Chris was murdered before we could work out the mechanisms. That and other complications presented me with a need to do what Chris and I had already decided—find a way to help more families; find a way to give a hand up to those who were in the action or transitioning out of it and who needed the help the most.

We didn't know how we would do it, but the idea of setting up some sort of foundation or nonprofit had been planted in our discussions. Chris's last comment on the subject came about two weeks before he was killed. We sat with a financial planner, and Chris told him, "If something happens to me, then my family is now the family of the fallen and every penny goes to them." I balked at what he was saying, insisting nothing would happen to him, urging that we stay on the course we had started. The seed, after all, had already started to grow roots in my heart.

As I recovered from the shock of his death and thought about different ways to carry out the wishes we'd had, I wanted to do something that wasn't being done already. I knew from my own experience of loving the marriage we had achieved and the many, many times it was threatened by a life of service that this was the need being unmet: supporting the marriages of those who serve. I knew from our life together and the lives of our friends, that military and first-responder marriages were similarly under attack, and the high divorce rates solidified the need.

While I knew Chris would have liked the idea of a permanent organization to help others, I also knew that establishing a foundation to do it was way beyond what I alone was capable of, especially in the midst of legal battles, grief, and finishing the projects Chris had been working on.

Then, like a miracle, helpers started appearing. The first was my brother-in-law Stewart, my sister's husband, who along with my sister and the rest of my family was a rock in the midst of the swirling chaos that was my life at the time. He not only recognized that I had the opportunity to do something positive, but he was full of gentle encouragement and advice to help me get going.

Everywhere I went, I seemed to run into people with expertise in the different areas of nonprofits and their intricacies. I truly believe a higher power was putting people in my way to help—but of course, God works on earth through people, and I was lucky to find a collection of talented and selfless helpers.

We officially started the Chris Kyle Frog Foundation in 2014 and have managed to grow since.

Today, we have ten full-timers, with some outside contractors to fill in the gaps. And volunteers—Stewart especially. (As the head of the foundation, I am also an unpaid volunteer.) My payment is knowing that families who could have been broken are living out the life Chris and I worked hard for in our own family. We learned and achieved so much in our marriage, against all odds. This is a way of saying the dream doesn't die; it just plays out differently with different characters, different families.

At CKFF, we also acknowledge that the landscape is ever-changing; we try to change and adapt with it. We're diving into job connections for transitioning service members, as well as addressing mental health issues in a holistic approach to marriage and family wellness. As I'm writing this, we have a number of programs based on things I know worked with Chris and me, as well as for our friends. They're a combination of things we learned and things I wish we would have known so much earlier in our marriage.

Date Night Out is just what it sounds like—paid-for dates centered around simple activities. The premise came from a friend who told me during some of our difficult times, "The time you want a date the least is the time you need it the most."

This proved to be so true. There are a thousand reasons why it may seem impossible or difficult to take a few hours off, but a simple date night out reminds couples that their marriage comes first. The little bit of effort can make all the difference for couples who are hanging on by a thread.

We make the plans, sometimes organizing a group event and sometimes doing an individual experience for just the couple. The goal is always the same: remind them how good time together can be. Shared, joyful experiences are an essential component in healthy marriages.

The group experience also lets couples meet others and share those "me too!" stories, discovering they are not alone when it comes to dealing with the unique challenges of service life.

Our Revitalization Retreats are a little longer and

more intense. These are, well, usually weekends, where a couple spends time reacquainting themselves with why they married in the first place. We facilitate the weekends in different ways, catering to individual needs. We take care of everything from child care to selfie sticks, depending on the couple's personalities and needs. We also do two to five coaching sessions before the weekend. This coaching alone has been credited with saving more than a few marriages before they even left for the retreat. And we pay the expenses for what in some cases may be the first vacation or even honeymoon they ever had. Our goal is to alleviate all the stress, including financial and planning, providing opportunities for these couples to connect.

Corie Weathers runs our programs and does most of the sessions. She wrote the book *Sacred Spaces*, which is amazing. I wish wish wish her book was around when Chris was deploying. She is amazing.

Our Empowered Spouses Retreats represent a dream come true for me. The spouses in a service marriage are very often beyond depleted. They are constantly on; the non-service spouse generally carries the majority of the load at home for both spouses. While one is saving the world, the other one is saving the family. One is with a team; the other is often isolated. Our Empowered Spouses Retreat takes spouses to a remote area where they have no cell phones or internet (aside from emergency communications). That's a real leap of faith and a hard adjustment for many of the women, who are used to being the family member always in contact with everyone else.

During the retreat, the women do things they may never have had a chance to do back home—things like skeet shooting, archery, hiking, yoga, or fly-fishing. We also encourage them to take time for self-care, helping them understand that the family will not only survive but thrive when Mama takes care of herself.

There are group coaching sessions starting early in the morning and going until after dinner. The women bond quickly, forming friendships much like kids at summer camp who take that intense emotional bonding into lifelong friendships. There's a lot of informal sharing about different challenges military and first-responder spouses face in marriage. Currently, we're doing two of these a year and hope to expand each year, depending on funding.

Presently, we're concentrating on women, though we hope to branch out to a men's program. I look at it like triage—right now the women seem to be the ones who, when helped, flip the dynamic and put the family on a whole different trajectory.

If you look at our programs as a progression—and

we encourage people to do that—then Mastering Your Marriage is the pinnacle. Working with the Baylor University Diana R. Garland School of Social Work, the program combines retreats with some intensive but nonintrusive counseling aimed at giving couples the tools to thrive in their marriages. Service marriages are unique, and so is our curriculum, as it directly addresses the specific strains such marriages face that are different from those faced by the civilian community.

It's a six-month program. Baylor is developing curriculum with us that we hope to eventually share with outside counselors and others so we can form a network of verified counselors who understand the issues. I have heard so often from couples from the Vietnam War era who sought help only to find the counselor unable to help with their specific issues. When that happens, divorce typically follows. With night shifts, long deployments, and duty stations in different states, this often means the kids lose out on life with one of their parents.

As I often say, our military and first responders see the worst of human nature day in and day out. It takes a toll on the individual, and their families. There can be no healing if they don't have a safe place to come back to. CKFF tries to give families the tools to find that safe place.

The events and programs have an impact far beyond the few days they last. Listening to the comments couples make after the retreats fills my heart with hope for not only them and their families, but our country as a whole. Couples talk about how they've improved the way they communicate, learned to build support systems, and found the freedom to grow while still being connected.

It's not easy, or always pretty. Some compare the early going to ripping a Band-Aid off and seeing open, oozing wounds. But hopefully that leads to healing.

For Levi and Danielle, the retreat changed the way they see their marriage. "It restored the traits that have faded from the years of war and deployments," said Levi afterward. "I feel renewed in ways not thought possible and have a new outlook on the way I need to be in order for our relationship to grow stronger. . . . Everyone always thanks veterans and first responders for their service but your foundation is the real hero. You give so selflessly and we couldn't do what we do without the support of so many great people."

"I remember Taya telling me to always remember I'm worthy at the empowered spouses retreat," said Kathy, "but it was at the couple's retreat that both of us felt worthy. Thank you for helping each of us see that in the other, reminding us just how important feeling worthy is in our marriage. Feeling worthy is a powerful thing that we rarely feel in our marriage . . . and this weekend we felt it and knew why we need to make changes to feel it regularly together and individually."

"The revitalization retreat reminded us of how important it is to give back to others," said Juan and Courtney. "Throughout our trip we constantly talked about how incredible it was that this foundation was supporting us in such a meaningful way. . . . We're forever grateful to be a part of the CKFF family."

Often, people think service people and first responders have a tight community, which offers support not only in crisis but day to day.

Sometimes that's true. However, for many—and especially the non-service spouse—their typical experience is emotional isolation. Often they are afraid to share details about their relationships, or life in general: say the wrong thing, and maybe you've put your spouse's career in jeopardy.

We've seen results. One young couple pulled back from divorce after one of our retreats; a recent graduate of the Mastering Your Marriage program related a tale about Christmas being unexpectedly pleasant this year.

"Unexpectedly"?

Yes.

The verdict actually came from the couple's teenage kids, who revealed that for the first time in their lives, there had not been one blowup. For years, the tensions in the house, at a boil under normal circumstances, reached an explosive level every holiday season.

Actually, the kids were slightly disappointed—they traditionally bet on when the blowup would occur, and no one had collected that year.

For the record: we get our money the way other organizations do—donations, grants, and fund-raisers. We strive to keep our overhead low, aiming at putting 80 percent directly into the programs.

You can find more information about donating or applying for a program on our website, www.chriskyle frogfoundation.org.

I remember Chris and I talking about the value of family and how, while service is so important, there really is no substitute for family. Families are a source of great joy. Greater joy, as Chris was surprised to find, than anything he had in the military.

Work stress can get in the way of that. And there are few stresses as severe as those that come from military or law enforcement careers.

I want the foundation to help service members and first responders experience that joy, even while serving others. I want to help them cope with the special strains that come from their service, small and big—the stress of moving or being alone for extended times, the strain of not knowing if the fleeting kiss after breakfast will be the last one you'll ever have.

We want people to serve for twenty or thirty years, if that's their career path. We don't want them to just survive; we want them to thrive while doing it. I can only imagine how much easier our life would have been if we had been involved in programs like Chris Kyle Frog Foundation. We were hungry for information with nowhere to turn.

The military has a job—to fight. They were never intended to be the provider for all facets of life. There is a saying, harsh but true in many ways: "If the service wanted you to have a wife, we would have issued you one." And no matter how family friendly they try to be, they are still an organization run by more bureaucracy than anything you will find in the private sector.

If life is a battle, love is worth fighting for. CKFF is here to help. The impact goes beyond the couple; it changes the world for this generation and the next. The children in these marriages don't just stop betting on who ruins Christmas; they see the value of working through impossible odds and letting love win. They learn tools to peacefully work through strains others don't have. They see how just when the chips are down, love wins.

I saw this with my own parents and their friends who have all been married about fifty years now. It changed me, and it will change these kids and the world. Love ripples throughout the community, just like the American Spirit.

And that's why I do what I do and why I believe I should always try to do just a little more, whether it's with the foundation, the kids, or everyday life. One more smile, one more time rolling up your sleeves for someone else—it will ripple out and have its own effect on the world.

What about you? What will you do today to help make the world a better place and keep the American Spirit alive?

People think about their legacy. They think about the mark they will leave on the world. Oftentimes they think there are grand plans, careers, or buildings they need to leave to show they lived. But I have seen in my own life, and those of others, that sometimes the biggest marks we leave on the world start with one small action, one step in faith, one opportunity to show up.

You never know if your sandwich on the windowsill might lead to a homeless shelter in the next generation.

Each of these people in each of these stories braved rough terrain. They were inspired by a spirit of independence and freedom to make a difference and traveled unknown territory to do so.

Each time you wonder if the American Spirit is lost, I hope you remember these stories and channel your own pioneer spirit. When you hear the politicians and the fearmongers tell you all is lost, I hope you reject that notion. When you see the flag and wonder if it has any meaning anymore, I hope you see more than an archaic symbol flying in the wind. I hope you see as I do the real stories, the real lives—yours and mine—alive and well in the red, the white, and the blue.

Acknowledgments

We wish to thank everyone mentioned or quoted in the book for their time and kindness in speaking with us, but most of all for their incredible efforts making their communities and our world a better place. You are all truly wonderful.

Countless staffers and assistants helped fill in the blanks when we were writing about the organizations, and we appreciate those efforts as well. In the end, there were many stories that we might have included if we'd had more time and space. Thank you to everyone who shared ideas and suggestions.

This book took us over a year to write, and we were helped by many along the way, especially our editor at William Morrow, Peter Hubbard. Also at William Morrow and its parent, HarperCollins, we have been blessed with the friendship as well as the assistance of Sharyn Rosenblum, the best publicist in the business. In editorial, Nick Amphlett helped keep everything on track. Thanks also to copyeditor Andrea Monagle, production editor Andrea Molitor, managing editor Nyamekye Waliyaya, and designer Bonni Leon-Berman.

Finally, to you our readers—we hope some of these stories will inspire you to do what you can to help others. It doesn't have to be a huge gesture; living right, helping your neighbors, befriending someone in need, simply listening—that is where the ripple of kindness starts. If you can be one person's light on any given day, you will have made a contribution.

We don't always know the good we do, or the effects we have. But the American Spirit is present in each one of us, waiting to be expressed and shared.

THE NEW LUXURY IN READING

We hope you enjoyed reading
our new, comfortable print size and found it
an experience you would like to repeat.

Well – you're in luck!

HarperLuxe offers the finest in fiction and
nonfiction books in this same larger print size and
paperback format. Light and easy to read, HarperLuxe
paperbacks are for book lovers who want to see
what they are reading without the strain.

For a full listing of titles and
new releases to come, please visit our website:

www.HarperLuxe.com